PRAISE FOR

WHITE WALLS

"More than a marvelous coming-of-age tale of one woman's journey toward motherhood, *White Walls* is a delightful, delicious, and daring account of how, seemingly trapped forever within the wild absurdities of a mad family, she learns how a frightened and loving daughter can become a loving and happy wife and mother. This is a gorgeously textured, beautifully crafted book that touches the heart, tenderly, with laughter and with wonder, even as it reminds us of the strange, unyielding, often magical force of family in our lives."

—Jay Neugeboren, author of *Imagining Robert* and *Transforming Madness*

"Sharp, quick, funny, but the kind of funny that sometimes has you feeling kicked in the stomach and teary with the delight of recognition. For the girl who leaves Montreal for Harvard, a room with white walls was a dream of order after the panicked hoarding of her mother, the daughter of a Holocaust survivor. But hang on for memoir as romantic comedy—part Nora Ephron, part Woody Allen—and the hilarious resilience of a heroine who ends up in Manhattan with a husband, two daughters, and, yes, white walls, starting the world anew."   —Honor Moore, author of *Th   Daughter*

"In this terrific and powerful book about hoarder   d children, Judy Batalion tells a laugh-out-lou   ther and daughter—and shows how profou   y events before we were born, how trauma mo   ow responsibility can be the most meaningful p   ie who has ever been a parent, or had one, needs to read   eautiful book."

—Dara Horn,   *A Guide for the Perplexed*

continued . . .

"This book is honest, difficult, and perfect. Batalion's sharp wit and hard-earned wisdom provide the reader with hope that we can all somehow find it in ourselves to embrace the inevitable chaos and change that come with living an imperfect life."

—Nicole Knepper, LCPC, author of *Moms Who Drink and Swear*

"*White Walls* is an unforgettable trip into a truly original mind—from Montreal to London to Manhattan, from childhood to adulthood, and from worrying about parents to worrying about children, with many strange, uncomfortable, and beautiful points in between. You won't read another memoir quite like this one."   —Matti Friedman, author of *The Aleppo Codex*

"Clear-eyed and compassionate, Judy Batalion's *White Walls* is a sharply funny, evocative, and moving memoir chronicling her voyage from daughter to mother as she finds her place in the world amidst the shifting currents of history, religion, time, and place. The wisdom of how to move forward while caring for the past emanates from every page. Batalion brings a palpable warmth to difficult subjects that will leave her readers inspired to contemplate the construction of their own stories and how transformation is possible."

—Ruth Andrew Ellenson, winner of the National Jewish Book Award
for *The Modern Jewish Girl's Guide to Guilt*

"This relatable multigenerational tale of stuff and survival moved me equally to tears and to laughter. It is funny, wise, and real."

—Jessie Sholl, author of *Dirty Secret: A Daughter Comes Clean
About Her Mother's Compulsive Hoarding*

WHITE WALLS

A MEMOIR ABOUT
MOTHERHOOD, DAUGHTERHOOD,
AND THE MESS IN BETWEEN

Judy Batalion

 NEW AMERICAN LIBRARY

NEW AMERICAN LIBRARY
Published by New American Library,
an imprint of Penguin Random House LLC
375 Hudson Street, New York, New York 10014

This book is an original publication of New American Library.

First Printing, January 2016

For more information about Penguin Random House, visit penguin.com.

LIBRARY OF CONGRESS CATALOGING-IN-PUBLICATION DATA:
Names: Batalion, Judy.
Title: White walls: a memoir about motherhood, daughterhood, and the mess in between/Judy
Batalion.
Description: New York, New York : New American Library, 2016.
Identifiers: LCCN 2015032314 I ISBN 9780451473110 (paperback)
Subjects: LCSH: Batalion, Judith. I Batalion, Judith—Family. I Jewish women—New York
(State)—New York—Biography. I Children of Holocaust survivors—New York (State)—New
York—Biography. I Mothers and daughters. I Healing. I Compulsive hoarding. I Dysfunctional
families. I Montreal (Quebec)—Biography. I New York (NY)—Biography. I BISAC:
BIOGRAPHY & AUTOBIOGRAPHY/Personal Memoirs. I FAMILY & RELATIONSHIPS /
Parenting/ Motherhood.
Classification: LCC F128.9.J5 B38 2016 I DDC 306.874/3—dc23
LC record available at https://protect-us.mimecast.com/s/oX1gB6CLEgzaHo

Printed in the United States of America
10 9 8 7 6 5 4 3 2

Designed by Tiffany Estreicher

Penguin
Random
House

DISCLAIMER

Names, dates, and identifying characteristics of certain people and events portrayed in this book have been obscured for literary cohesion, to protect privacy, and to make myself seem younger and thinner.

For my mother,
who taught me to tell stories and
find truth in make-believe

You can never go home again,
but the truth is you can never leave home,
so it's all right.

—MAYA ANGELOU

· PROLOGUE ·

VOYAGEUR
New York City, 2010

"It's time," my father's voice creaks through the phone. My father has called me exactly three times since I left home, in 1996, and never at eight thirty in the morning.

"Her threats are serious. She's really planning it," he says. "The details."

He doesn't make any of his usual jokes: *she is plotting her plot for when she plotzes.* Or: *she's ready for her seventy-two virgins.* That's how I know it really is time.

I feel my esophagus battering through me like a pendulum. "I'm coming."

I dial my brother. "Eli, book us in at court for tomorrow morning," I say, as if I'm referring to a mani-pedi, and not requesting an injunction against the woman who bore me.

I hear my blood pump, quick, staccato; imagine hers gushing through her thick veins. Imagine it stop. *She just likes the attention,* I remind myself, attempt to console myself. Eight hours from New York to Montreal. I can make it. I must.

I look out of my all-window apartment at the new high rises and old water towers, at the buzzing Mondrian grid of Manhattan streets. I see their arrangement: parallels and perpendiculars, squares, equal angles. They are numbered in order, so no one ever gets lost. Someone is looking out for you. I live on the eighteenth floor, reminding me of *chai*. The Hebrew for one and eight, the symbol for luck. The word for life. I am on top of things here on my mountain—I can see the moat, protect myself.

"What's going on?" Jon, suited up for work, comes into the living room, which is sparse, airy, barely furnished. The exact opposite of both of our mothers' homes.

"I'm going to get the court order," I say. "Finally."

"Finally," he repeats, knowing that I've been trying to do this, waiting for my dad's support for years. I smell his Irish Spring. *Like the Irish are so known for cleanliness,* he jokes in his British accent. To me, it's the scent of savior. "Call me."

"If you're lucky." I grab his hand. He squeezes back. I memorize the pressure of his knuckles on my skin, think how our bodies' link is entirely different from the bonds that hold together DNA.

I am wired. It's actually happening. I have only twenty-five minutes to catch the bus. Within ten, I am packed and in a taxi headed to Port Authority station.

I call Mom as we stop and start in the traffic around Times Square. "What's going on?" My stomach is clenched.

"I can't go on. They're coming to get me," she says. She is terrified of *them*. "There's no point. Even God is telling me to kill myself."

"Well, God's made a lot of mistakes," I say, but *God*? When has she ever once mentioned God? I try to breathe, feel the pulse in my eyes. Eight hours is a long time. "I'm coming," I say, as we pass a billboard for yet another *Shrek*. "Don't kill yourself." It's very simple: just don't kill yourself. The concept of her nonexistence short-circuits my neurons. The area behind my forehead goes numb. "I'll be there soon," I add as the cab jerks to a halt. The need to check in with her became worse over the past few years. Sometimes she doesn't call back for hours. Usually, she's just on Valium, or engaged in her fantasies, or deeply ensconced in *Masterpiece Theatre*. Thanks, PBS, for your riveting programming that has aged me ten years.

I hop on the bus, clutching a southwestern tuna wrap from Au Bon Pain. The difference in my two lives has never been more apparent. Within a quarter of an hour I go from an aerial condo to Greyhound. Sashimi to sandwich. My chosen family to my birth one, and accordingly, I revert.

I find an empty seat. I know this route well. "Voyageur" is the Canadian branch of Greyhound. Meaning "traveler," its rolling French connotes wild adventure, Jules Verneish explorations, singalong expeditions across the Yukon's blazing horizon, instead of the reality: the alcoholic luggage schlepper, the characters who travel back and forth with plastic bags instead of suitcases, and the racist customs officials who interrogate them. Seeing my Canadian passport, their main question is: did you buy anything? Well, I always want to answer, considering I've been away for fifteen years, I *have* done a touch of light shopping.

I text my friend Melissa, who I'm supposed to meet for lunch later that day, a mini celebration for my thirty-third birthday. "Heading to Montreal," I explain. "Just a little impromptu vacay." *To prevent my mother from hanging herself with her vast collection of pencil cases.*

I check in with Mom. Still alive.

I e-mail my brother: "you're on call when I lose reception in the Adirondacks." I'm thankful he's on the ground, can pacify her with his soft voice, his slow gestures, until I get there. He soothes her more than I do. She likes him better.

Then, I take out a pen and the forms that have been sitting in my drawer. I need to fill in the blanks, and to do it perfectly. For years, I've tried to find ways to get my mother into treatment, secretly speaking to social workers, doctors, therapists, driven by the image of her cured: smiling, laughing like she used to, maybe even leaving her house, coming to mine. I've done more research for this project than for my PhD. Then again, my mother is much more complicated than Representations of Domestic Space in Contemporary Art. *You won't have a good chance at court unless your father participates,* they all warned. *He's the one who lives with her.* Enables her, they meant.

Only now, staring at the legal questionnaire and the "patient's history," I'm not sure where to begin. How to narrate the tale of my mother falling apart? The brain that turned in on itself over decades, in little unremarkable steps, like the ascent of the Nazis, I think, and wonder if I should start with the Holocaust. My grandmother's escape from Warsaw to Siberian work camps, my mother's wartime birth in Kirgizia, in transit, her formative years in ravaged Poland, DP camps, born into the fresh smell of a murdered family, a refugee before she knew what home was. Eventually coming to Canada, but never really settling, never committing to a house, a stable structure. The way a few extra piles of books turned into domestic mayhem, mounds of old paper towels, thousands of videocassettes, stale Danishes that formed a barricade across her kitchen, a fortress to protect from the next world war that was always just around the corner, especially in suburban Canada. The slow stewings of a victim complex. The disputes, the real estate battles, tens of thousands spent on lawyers, not to mention the rooms filled with spy devices used to record every meeting, the gradual disjoining from friends, cousins, siblings, her own name. The stacks of "research" to help her track down "the people who are after her," who—she claims—break into the house, leave her cryptic messages, mess up her papers. The house bolted stiff with locks and alarms, loudly ticking clocks in every room. Cameras. Laptops. Binders. The pill vials. The story of how a person becomes a shadow.

I read the next question on the form. "Is she a danger to herself or to others?" *They mean life danger,* the social worker had explained.

"Yes," I write.

In "family history," I write that her mother suffered from the same thing. The exact same thing.

We reach Albany's bus station, our pit stop, the midpoint. Transitional space. Not here, not there, but a halfway house. The cafeteria hosts middle-aged women in miniskirts, and might just double as a brothel. Over the years, I've pushed myself into constant motion, moved countries, climates, crossed borders, waded in endless hinterlands. An expert at layovers. In the rancid bathroom, the metal door is shiny but offers no reflection, as if my short body, brown hair, plastic-framed glasses are not really there.

I buy the one remaining bottle of sparkling water—my insides, at least, feel sharp, bubbly. A few months ago, my mother said: you were the normal one born into an abnormal family. I'd felt both vindicated and angry at that truth. Then again, a nerdy, workaholic, insomniac, recovering academic, former stand-up comic—I wondered how many people would call me the normal one. But chez Batalion, I am the metaphor for normal, the simile for the sane.

Please don't kill yourself. Please.

This time, I'm going to get it right. I'm coming home to save you. I'm coming.

Back on the bus, my cell rings. Mom, still alive. "Where are you?" she barks. "Where?" Definitely still alive. And kicking.

"Four hours away," I answer and spill fizzy water on my thighs. I sigh: they will be wet for that whole time.

"What good is that?" she wails. "I need you here. I have so many problems, Judy. No one ever does anything for me. It's like I have no family."

I bite my tongue until the pain feels good, salty. "I'll be there soon," I say. I don't want to lose her. But blotting my damp lap with napkins, I also think: I am so fucking tired of being the mother.

4 WEEKS: INCONCEIVABLE CONCEPTION
New York City, 2011

I was sitting on an examining table at my local clinic when the Israeli doctor threw open the door and pitched a small object right at me. It hit my arm.

"Photograph this!" he yelled.

"Ouch," I muttered. I reached over to the other side of the table where the white plastic object landed and picked it up. It was small, and square, and had two lines on it. Thin, parallel lines, was the first thought that ran through my mind, their ends never meeting.

The second thought was: Wait. What?

Wait. Fuck.

"What is this?" I asked, my voice shaky.

"Text the photo to your husband!" he commanded. "You're having a baby!" A passing-by nurse squealed. I felt my eyes pop. My cheeks deflate. My cilia stand on guard.

"But I'm here for my *infertility* blood work," I tried to clarify. This made no sense. Based on a history of abdominal surgeries for colitis, an internal palimpsest of scar tissue, and a family history of early-onset menopause, doctors told me it would take at least two years for me to get pregnant—a time period that I secretly thought of as my safety net. While I liked the concept of one day toasting my union with Jon by going forth and multiplying, my mind shut off at the thought of even burping a baby, let alone raising a child. *Let's at least see what's wrong with you,* Jon had urged. He was *ready.* So at thirty-three, with a forty-year-old husband suffering from his "biological cock," and the fear that I was on my last eggs, I had reluctantly stopped the pill just to begin the medical process—which I'd assumed would be very, very long. Especially when I started reading about pregnancy: all those years of birth control, and yet, there was approximately one second per month when you could actually conceive.

"Well, you won't need that progesterone flush today!" the doctor said, patting me—gently, this time—on the back. "Mazel tov! Aren't you thrilled? You are thrilled. YOU ARE THRILLED. Text your husband!"

He left the room, which was now spinning. A whirlwind of scales and swabs taunted me. I felt nauseous, and knew it wasn't the estrogen. I managed to fumble for my iPhone, my fingers trembling as they glazed over numbers. Jon answered right away.

"I'm pregnant," I said, the words like squares in my hole of a mouth. My insides felt like white noise. Alive and cackling but inaudible at the same time.

"Hold on," Jon said.

"You're putting me on hold?!"

"I meant, to my colleague on the other line," Jon said. "Sheesh, hormones already . . ."

"Aren't you shocked?"

"No. You went off the pill three weeks ago."

My damn reasonable husband.

"It's early days, we shouldn't get too excited," I blurted out.

"I'm not too excited," Jon replied defensively, but I could hear the shimmer in his voice, his British accent hitting unusual crescendos. "Come home right away," he almost sang, tenor tingling.

Doctor Crazy pranced back into the room, his lips stretching across his tanned visage. "We'll need a whole new set of blood tests now!"

"I'm shocked," I declared, to him, to myself. A hard bolus, like a freshly blown metallic balloon, appeared at the center of my throat. *What have I done?*

"Life happens," he said.

Quite literally, I thought.

My sweaty thumb and pointer finger gripped the edges of the white square, trying to squeeze the two lines into one—a no, a negative, a singular slit of nothingness.

They didn't budge.

OUTSIDE, TRAFFIC WENT on as usual. The noon sun still shone. The February wind thumped my cheeks. I stopped to buy a frozen feta cheese bureka. I needed a moment to stall the rest of my life, a calm before the seismic, entropic storm like Wile E. Coyote running in midair before noticing that his feet touched no ground. How could the most incredible news I would ever receive have come to me at the bacteria-infested local clinic that Jon and I referred to as "the petri dish"? I meandered on the wide sidewalks, weaving from building to street, taking swaying steps, feeling my feet slip within my ballet flats and sensed a new state set in, a mood crystallizing in my cells: not despair, but not thrill. More of a weight, a heavy, unsettling blankness. Fear.

My mind flitted to the legend about the foundation of Chelm, the folkloric town of Jewish fools. An angel had been passing over Ukraine with a slew of half-baked babies destined for mothers across the globe, when it tripped and dropped them all in this random spot. Rootless, homeless, these were the lost baby spirits that set up the Slavic city of the idiots. I gulped hard. This could not be a mistake.

But why couldn't I find the feeling of *wanting* this that I knew must have been somewhere inside me?

I stepped more quickly, zigzagging along the pavement, cutting off workmen on lunch breaks, women carrying matcha lattes. I was having a *baby*. *I* was having a baby. Nebbishy, infertile me. A baby had taken up tenancy in my uterus. My arid uterus.

Minutes later I walked into our new apartment, my perfect space, my decorative and emotional pièce-de-résistance. This abode, our Chelsea loft with enormous windows and open plans, marked the culmination of years of work; it was the manifestation that I had solved my life. I insisted we get all white counters, white sofas, white carpets. Who really needed coffee tables? "Less is too much" was my mantra when it came to space. I would live in a gallery if I could. I'd spent a decade working as a design curator, becoming a Doctor of Domesticity, for just that reason. Finally, I'd met a partner who uncannily understood, who'd helped me to make my own clean rooms. We had moved into our pale palace just four weeks earlier. Now I realized that was the same week that my egg was cooked.

Jon was waiting in the kitchen, smiling with his eyes.

"I'm pregnant," I repeated. "Two years took three days."

"Super sperm." He came over and gave me a firm hug, squeezing my sides.

"Better not cuddle too hard," I joked, breaking free of his grasp. I needed air. "Let me warm up this bureka."

"I'll do it," Jon offered. I sat down at the kitchen table as he flitted around the pallid counters, unwrapping, turning knobs, cutting, his moves graceful like a Romanian gymnast. I was trying to count months in my head, but kept messing up the numbers.

"I guess we're due in October? November?"

Jon didn't reply. He was generally gregarious; I knew his silence meant elation. An extrovert par excellence, it was in moments of true happiness that he turned inward.

"Hello, Jon?"

"Yes."

"Nothing," I said. *How can you feel so secure?* I wanted to scream. *So sure? It's not like* your *family's so normal. Who knows what meshuggener, messy offspring our shared acids will sprout!* But I kept my cool. I couldn't disturb his euphoria. I smiled.

He cut open the bureka, showing the cheese filling nestled inside.

I forced myself to swallow three enormous bites in a row, their edges smashing against my trachea, blocking me from uttering the high-pitched sound that had been brewing near my tonsils.

THAT NIGHT, I pulled even more blankets over me than my usual three.

"Good night, mum o' my child." Jon gave me a head massage.

For hours, I stared at the white ceiling above me, making sure it stayed far up. Do not collapse, I told my walls, do not.

"Jon," I finally said, nudging him and adjusting my voice to be louder than his snoring, which he did like a wildebeest with bronchitis. "Jon! Where will we put it?"

"Huh?"

"Where will the baby go?"

"I don't know," he mumbled from his pillow. "I guess the office."

Oh God. My office.

I might have a PhD in the history and theory of physical space, but I did not know how to make room for a baby.

I stared at the ceiling, listening to his nasal expulsions. The TV fuzz feeling set in again, tingling through my eyes, nose, spine. Then it dawned on me: pregnant women weren't supposed to eat unpasteurized feta cheese. I was screwing up already.

I got out of bed and sat in my white tiled shower until morning.

How could I, who came from such a pathologically messy home, with no blueprint for normalcy, make one? How the hell was I supposed to become *a mother*?

1ST TRIMESTER:

The Basement

•══════•

· ONE ·

BERMUDA SHORTS TRIANGLE
Montreal, 1986

All I wanted to do was go home.

To be picked up from school by a mom who played doubles at the Hampstead tennis club, stuffed into OshKosh winter couture, and escorted into a luxury-car-pool that would whisk me westward to the airy suburbs with shiny built-ins and lemon-lime scents. To do my homework, watch *Video Hits*, and eat SpaghettiOs and thinly sliced carrots before being bathed in bubbles and tucked into my pink trundle bed that hosted matching throw pillows with embroidered Judys.

Instead, I clutched my red-and-blue coat, procured from the basement of a Lubavitch woman who served as an underground wholesale importer of factory seconds. Thank God I'd found one that looked vaguely Esprit, and that my mother had not been forcing me to wear one of the fifteen fake Howard the Duck T-shirts that she'd sourced at the same time. I made my way to the back of the lobby to wait for Bubbie, my mom's mom, to pick up me and my brother, Eli. Mondays through Wednesdays she took me to Yiddish drama, dance, or judo. (Despite my being barely four feet tall and the only girl in the class, my father's philosophy: you must learn how to fall!) Thursdays and Fridays we went to her and Zaidy's house. A few years earlier they had moved with us to a duplex in the suburbs, but averse to the local quietness, quickly headed back east, in the direction they'd always run, making my father—who had bought a house just to fit them—vow he'd never talk to them again, despite their babysitting services.

In the recesses of the foyer, I did not make eye contact with a single fourth grade classmate, but put my coat on slowly, sleeve by sleeve, conscious of directing my every movement, negotiating the position of each of my limbs, convincing myself that if I couldn't see anyone, they couldn't see me either. Being short helped me to shrink out of sight. Eli, playing kick the can with an empty cardboard juice box, was stuffed into a puffy snowsuit and wire-rimmed glasses with enormous lenses that made him look sixty instead of six.

Bubbie was usually late, which was fine with me, for when she did arrive she did so palpably. I saw her approach the glass door, flinging plastic bags full of briskets and at least one of her myriad old leather purses stashed with money and mysterious papers. She cackled with glee when she spotted me. Her back was hunched; the handkerchief wrapped around her head, bright green. Even her name—Zelda— was the epitome of conspicuousness.

I'd made my way to Eli before she even touched the knob.

"Judaleh!" she called, her eyes lighting up.

"We're coming, Bubbie," I said, pushing my brother out into the dusk. Even if my classmates had noticed Bubbie, I absolutely did not want them to notice me, leaving school by foot and eastward, toward my grandmother's cramped house with the original gray carpets from 1957.

Outside, icicles hung from traffic lights. It was too cold to talk, even for Bubbie. This was also fine with me and I walked silently, slightly ahead of her and Eli. I buried my face into my scarf, pretending to myself that we were walking to a doctor's appointment, or tennis lessons, or our cream-colored Jaguar that just happened to be parked far away.

But once I'd climbed through enough piles of snow and seas of slosh, once we were far enough in the east, deep in the area of 1960s low-rise apartment buildings, Vietnamese corner stores, and street names like "Côte-des-Neiges" and "Lavoie" instead of the upper crusty "Westmount" and "The Boulevard," I forced myself to look up. There were neither classmates nor their mothers here. Anyone who could see me was also in the east—we were all the same. Breathing easier, I stepped right into pace with my bubbie and simultaneously slipped into a different genre of fantasy, a historical one. Now, I was foraging through a Siberian work camp, or sneaking across bridges over the frozen Vistula, or running through the blustery Polish countryside, or something else that Bubbie might have done during the war.

"You are Hitler!" Bubbie screamed at a grocer, waking me from my inner world and directing me into a fruit store. "*And* SS," she said, gesturing to the Sri Lankan assistant schlepping wet boxes across the slushy floor. She was not the kind of Holocaust survivor who suppressed her memories or pretended it never happened. On a regular basis, I heard how she escaped Warsaw by swimming across a river. And in a truck filled with oranges. And at a convent. And thanks to a Nazi, who, of all things, turned the other way. Her best friend was a Polish woman who had helped save Jews; her other best friend had recently been accused by a livid man at the local shopping center of being in the Warsaw Judenrat. Forty years later, these were still topics of gossip here, in this Yiddish outpost of a Polish shtetl in the middle of French Quebec in an ex-Anglo colony.

"Nazi," she muttered. "Turned my sister into soap!" I was used to my bubbie's public explosions, especially in this stretch of fruit stores, one of which she was convinced was owned by Hitler's cousin who charged double for his apples.

Eli and I waited at least an hour while she haggled with grocers. "For the best eekelech, *for you*," she said, flailing a cucumber in my face. I knew she had medication to help her craziness—when she took it. As Dad always said, it was the paranoids who fled and survived, giving rise to paranoid children.

Finally, when she was pleased that she'd selected the best roughage at the best price ever offered in the universe, she stuffed her new wares into her cocoon of bags, amazing me that she could fit more inside. I pulled up my backpack, made sure Eli's was on tight, and we headed back out, again me pretending that it was 1939, and we'd just stocked up to save our lives.

TWENTY MINUTES LATER, we arrived at Bubbie and Zaidy's house on Campden Place, the bottom flat of a duplex on a pedestrianized street, its center filled with trees instead of cars. A quiet pocket of the city, unnoticed by passersby. I'd lived on the upstairs floor from ages one to six; back then, our home was cluttered but in a free-spirited, hippie sort of way. My parents hosted drinks nights where they served Breton crackers and peach schnapps on their teak tables, Mom's raucous laughter trickling through the walls, reaching me as I dozed off in my bed. My early birthday parties, overstuffed with guests, offered buffets of bagels amid the seventies crochet. On weekends, Mom taught me to illustrate puns in little homemade booklets as we sat on shag rugs, listening to folk music and her spirited Socialist-Zionist records. Now, my bubbie's house hosted faux French regency sofas covered in plastic, golden lamps, and a smattering of photographs and Judaica from Poland, though I was never sure how they'd carried large framed photos and crystal vases when they escaped east to Russian work camps where they ate horse meat, and then after the war when they walked back to Poland via Kirgizia, where my mother was born.

My favorite photos were of Bubbie and Zaidy when they were in their twenties, with their dashing slicked-back Warsaw dos and Bubbie's striking high cheekbones, like a model for *Vogue* (Vodjz?). My other favorite photo was my parents' wedding portrait, which hung in a thick gold frame in the living room, showing my mom as a slender beauty with long dark hair and an innocent smile that graced her cherubic cheeks, my dad as a dashing man in fashionably gigantic 1972 eyewear. No pictures of my parents' wedding hung in my house. Each time I was here, I took a few minutes to stare at this evidence and imagine what it must have been like when they were young, happy. I wondered what it would take for Mom to look so elegant again.

As Eli and I disrobed, my zaidy, now with only scattered white wisps of hair crowning his barely five-foot-tall body, emerged from his basement hideaway—his makeshift workshop where he busily fixed pipes with masking tape and smoked cigarettes. His twinkling gray eyes peeking out from under swollen eyelids, Zaidy giddily played with us as Bubbie got down to the business of cooking. Everything was done by hand. Orange juice was squeezed by hand. Bees were killed by hand. Floors were scrubbed by hand, though I'd noticed lately they were starting to smell acidic, like stale urine. Zaidy, Eli, and I played a game where we ran from wall to wall trying to catch one another—Bubbie joining for some rounds—and then I cleared us a picnic place on the floor of the dining/TV room, which hosted heaps of leather bags and clothes draped on golden chairs. There, my grandmother spread out newspapers for our five-course dinner—cut up vegetables drenched in oil; chicken soup; meatballs with no sauce and spinach latkes; apple compote and Neapolitan ice cream; a petit four of Kit Kats—which was served over the next few hours, until Dad came to pick us up.

When *Three's Company* came on, Bubbie sat on a chair, cackling loudly at her major crush, John Ritter. "They should put this on for cancer patients, for victims of war. I don't even think about my mother dying in gas chambers when I watch Jack!" she cooed, munching on toast with cottage cheese and jam. "We used to swim in the Vistula, all my sisters," she whispered, as if letting me in on a secret from her old world—*the* old world—even though I'd heard these stories a thousand times. "The Zionist groups swam. That's how I saved myself. I swam." I remembered a photo my mom had shown me of Bubbie walking on the banks of the river. She was wearing a long dress, her long legs taking long strides, next to a man in a suit who did not look like my zaidy. At all. "Who's that?" I'd asked.

"Oh, I think her boyfriend," Mom had answered from the couch, as if my grandmother having a boyfriend—a life before Zaidy, a life before the war—was nothing. Her having had a romantic, carefree existence felt more foreign to me than the daily stories of partisan violence on the Russian front. *There was a drop of normalcy somewhere in my lineage?* I hadn't asked any more questions. I hadn't known how. I just packaged up this bit of knowledge, storing it for later.

After the meatball course, my grandmother slowed down her service, and as usual, came in to show me her victories of the day. "How much you think I pay for this?" she asked, holding out a mint green sweater with gold lamé weave.

"Ten dollars," I played along.

"Less!" my grandmother cried in delight, our reverse bargaining session beginning.

"Five dollars."

"Less!"

"One dollar."

"Twenty-five cents!" She applauded herself. She had taken me with her a couple of times to the bazaars where she trawled through long tables piled high with shiny clothes, and then fought it out penny for penny with the sellers, always emerging triumphant.

I had no idea why she kept shopping, considering that opening her closet resulted in a mudslide of dresses. Purses were piled high on the living room couches. A full room in the basement was unlivable, the pool table buried under a mound of skirts. Yet, it didn't bother me that much. I didn't live here, and the stuff wasn't for me. *These* piles wouldn't drown me, pull me under. *Please don't let my house become this bad,* I begged inwardly, but I already sensed the slopes were slippery like the wintery ground outside.

Finally, after all the desserts were brought out and scattered across the floor, I started to check the clock. At a commercial break during *A Different World*, I went back to the living room with my parents' almost-fictional wedding photo, and practiced my moves as I sang Tina Turner and danced in front of the full-length mirror, checking every few minutes to see if Dad was out back and if he'd honked. If we made it to his car quickly, there'd be no time for him to think about how mad he was at Bubbie for moving and there was a better chance he'd put on CKMF radio so I might catch Falco's "Rock Me Amadeus." When I noted his Pontiac station wagon outside, the headlights spotlighting the snow that sprayed in all directions, I ordered, "Eli, let's go!" I made sure he put on all his layers and that we both had our schoolbags before hugging Bubbie and Zaidy so tightly I thought I'd break their osteoporotic bones. "I love you, Judaleh," Bubbie said, nuzzling her smooth chin with its maze of thin wrinkles into my hair for an extra-long second. The warmth diffused across my scalp.

"Gotta go, Bubbie." I pushed off. From the corner of my eye I saw displayed on her kitchen table the crumpled piece of paper that was a photocopy of my picture that had appeared in the *Canadian Jewish News* for winning a Jewish studies award. The paper was worn from her clutching it, from toting it around to her friends in the park, showing off how far she'd come from the world of the Judenrat, showing off *me*.

THE CAR RIDE home transpired as usual. Dad was quiet, seemingly intent on listening to his talk radio, so I didn't ask for the station change. Though known to his friends as a joker, and popular on the wedding/funeral/Christmas party speaker circuit, he was reserved when he was hungry. His day before coming to get us was always long: after working at the government-run hospital, taking his sauna and attending his weekly medical lecture, he stopped on Carlton Avenue, at his parents' house that was now inhabited by his older brother Moishe, a chain-smoking used-carpet salesman bachelor who slept on the sofa in front of blaring ESPN snooker matches. Dad still had a bedroom there; it was "his room" and he visited every day to "check up on the house," but he never ate food at Carlton. As he drove, he complained about the insane number of stop signs on the way west, the route being the hypotenuse of the triangle of my family's three houses. Carlton-Campden-Kildare. None of these Anglo streets were remotely posh, but the trifecta sounded like an upper-class family, or a pharmaceutical company, like the names on the polyp-shaped stationery that Dad brought home.

Our house, a 1960s white brick rectangle, was tucked into the bend of a cul-de-sac. As we pulled into our driveway, I felt a wave of discomfort in my lower abdomen. Behind "Mount Kildare," as Dad had named the hill of snow that the snow blower dumped on our front lawn every winter, allowing us to toboggan right outside our door, I could see that the living room lights were on. Did that mean that Mom was up or asleep? I secretly hoped it was the latter. By now, it was bone-chillingly cold out, not just hitting my face but invading the stitches of my clothes, and I braced myself for leaving the car, for the one minute in which I had to open the garage door and wait for Dad to let us in. I also braced myself for the entry.

Fortunately, the house was warm. Then I noticed—*all* the lights were on. As were the radios. And the television.

"Hi, Mom," I called, knowing that whatever awaited me I might as well find out right away. "Hi, Mom," I said louder this time, also knowing that if she was up, she'd be slow to forgive me if I didn't say hello first.

As I removed my layers of damp, cool clothes, which I draped over the rail to the basement stairs since there was no room in the closet, I heard Mom stir. "Hello," she said. Her voice was thin and wavering, as if she'd been roused from a deep slumber.

I inhaled, exhaled, and walked into the den. "Hi, Mom." I found her lying on piles of pillows and under several blankets on the couch. The coffee table was covered in papers; I prayed my latest report card—which still needed signing—was somewhere in there, hiding along with her. Even my success vanished in the domestic chaos. Next to the sofa stood a tower of newspapers and free magazines— "your mother's cocaine," my dad called them. I'd long been used to Mom's stacks of records that overcrowded the wood shelving, but lately the bohemian aesthetic had been deepening. Now books—

many severely overdue at the local library—piled up on the floor between the furniture too. Not to mention the clutter in her bedroom, the files and clothes that were slowly spreading across her bed, making it hard for me to reach her when I had a nightmare.

My father slept in a cleared-out area in the basement.

I thought of Bubbie's sartorial stashes and my heart plunged. It was too late. Mom's mess was metastasizing, taking over our family space.

"Hi, Mom," I said, for a fourth time.

"Hi, Judy," she said groggily. "I'm just taking a nap. Just a second, I'll get up."

She turned the other way, to face the inside of the couch. Her gray formless knit sweater peeked out from the blankets; she did not wear Roots aerobic gear like the other moms.

I carefully stepped over piles of family albums. Mom had taken thousands of photos of me as a baby, and I normally loved looking at them, proof that she had noticed me, that I was a main character in her life. But now, they too seemed in the way. I found the remote under last week's *The Suburban*, and flipped channels, looking for *Yes, Prime Minister*, my mom's version of *Three's Company*, with Nigel Hawthorne as her John Ritter. If she would only laugh, I knew, she'd wake up and want to talk, maybe even have a snack with me as Dad ate his dinner.

I couldn't find anything good, except for a repeat of *Video Hits*. "Mom," I said, pointing at the "Land of Confusion" video. She loved the Royal Family, she loved caricature. "Look at the puppets." I did a parody dance of the parody dance, writhing like Nancy Reagan.

"Judy," she said. "Just give me a minute."

I reminded myself that she woke up at five a.m. to go to work at a military school outside Montreal where she developed English curricula for French Canadian soldiers. "Sorry," I said, and went into the kitchen.

My dad was eating dinner from behind a Berlin wall of sauerkraut and tuna cans. He ate only cold foods at home. The rest of the kitchen was similarly fortressed: stacks of Russian whole wheat loaves, half-used tissues tucked into Kleenex boxes, an army of Sweet'N Low packets amassed from coffee shops across town.

At my mom's place at the table sat the phone and a leaning tower of coupons. I cleared coffee-stained paper towels and gestured at the clippings. Dad rolled his eyes. "Nature abhors a vacuum," he said. "And a vacuum cleaner."

I laughed loudly, relieved that he knew something was askew in our house, which was just when my mother came in.

"What's funny?" she asked, serious. I froze. She was right. We had been laughing at her.

My father didn't answer.

"Nothing," I said, and looked away. "We were just talking about the kitchen."

"Well," she said, her eyes darkening, darting quickly around the room. As if a switch in her brain had been flicked, her hand movement suddenly became jerky, her breathing, heavy and staccato. "Why don't you ask your precious father, your best friend, to take care of all the shopping?" she mocked me, and slammed the phone as she moved it to the counter. Then she tore open the fridge, threw juice onto the counter, and poured herself a pink plastic cup full. I tried to remember her better moods, the time she took me and Eli downtown to see *The NeverEnding Story* and we sang the *Pirates of Penzance*'s "My Eyes Are Fully Open" to the rhythm of our steps as we walked from the metro to the theater. "So it really doesn't matter, matter, matter, matter . . ."

"It wasn't about shopping," I mumbled now under my breath. My pulse quickened, and I swiftly left the room. *And my father does take care of it,* I wanted to add. She was forcefully, frantically stacking plastic cups at the opposite end of the kitchen, behind the cluttered counter, as if making herself yet another shield to protect herself from me.

"It's getting late," she shouted after me. "Get ready for bed."

"I have to finish my homework," I mumbled. Of course it was

late. I was brought home at only nine thirty. *What, now you're a disciplinarian?* I wanted to yell.

I went to my room, closed the door, and sprawled out on the small area of carpet cramped between the four chests of drawers, trying to ignore the little crumbs nestled between the bobbles of wool. I quickly did my reading, my Hebrew, and my math, before putting away my clothes. My closet was so jam-packed—acrylic-blend hoodies with metal zippers, Ocean Pacific–style Bermuda shorts—that I had to get up on a folding chair to slot my shirt in. I checked up on my perfume sample collection that I had placed neatly—each little clear vial getting its own space—on the top of my wooden bureau, pretending it was a makeup table and I was a movie star. Then I put my books in my schoolbag, and put it on top of the secretary desk, which my mother had loved for its rounded closing top, but which seemed to me like just too much furniture.

At least she'd let me trade my double bed for Eli's single one, which I'd pushed lengthwise along one wall so it would take up less room, even if it meant I had nothing against which to rest my head. Pretending it was my pink trundle, I crawled in and tucked myself into the layers of unmade blankets, hugging them, as if they were throw pillows.

Then, like most nights, I had a sneezing fit from the dust that accumulated on the side of the night table.

· TWO ·

FUN HOUSE MIRROR
Montreal, 1988

When Mom slept, the house could breathe. The walls exhaled, the roof slumped. I climbed into my mom's chair at the kitchen table. It was still warm from the hours she'd spent sitting on it, on the phone to her friends, talking about their problems, winding her fingers around the phone's coiled cord and then pulling it apart, like stretching out a strand of DNA. I marveled at the doodles she drew in pencil across the increasingly large pile of stained paper towels that covered the table. I traced my hand along her marks, following as the lead pooled in the pores of the Bounty, reminding myself that she'd been an artist, a published poet who'd trailed Leonard Cohen around Greece. I followed these incredible drawings, drawings that would never get seen if I didn't see them, drawings of women's faces, always in profile with dark eyes, high cheekbones and sharp features, draped in cowl necks, staring into the distance, alone and haunted.

"WHAT *IS* THIS?" I raised my voice the next morning. I couldn't believe what lined my credenza. A row—a full row—of ceramic piglets. One in overalls, one in a pink party dress playing violin, one skipping rope.

The worst part was, they weren't even cute cartoon piglets with frizzy pigtails doing step aerobics. They were old-school toys, textured so that the ceramic was grooved, accentuating their black porcine locks, making them seem country-house goyish, particularly unkosher.

"For your collection," Mom said, smiling, her yellowing teeth showing above her thin dry lips. Her large frame overflowed in my doorway. She even hoarded calories.

"My collection?" I said aloud, rolling my eyes. I'd just used wet toilet paper to wipe my dusty mattress. Where had she gotten these pig trinkets? How much more would be coming? What was the point in my cleaning up if there was always more stuff? Two full dining room sets plus an extra buffet were now stacked in the living room. The other day, Mom had brought home an entire discount Disney wardrobe, which I had to stuff into my drawers, pushing my special Roots T-shirts into corners, creasing them.

"You mentioned you liked pigs." Her slit eyes twinkled in hope. Above her chins, her face was red and soft like a baby's. She had dozens of albums of me, but never let anyone photograph her. She couldn't bear to look at herself, she explained. "You said there was a pig you liked."

It was true. I'd mentioned a pig. *A pig candle. One* pig candle. I liked candles, not pigs. Besides, that pig was cuddly, like my sassy hero Miss Piggy. And, that was months ago.

I turned to stare out my window. It was afternoon, wintery dark. Over the Christmas holidays, we tobogganed with our neighbors on the mound outside our door. For two weeks, our house was a happy nucleus. But now the black crusty snow just looked like another pile that kept me hidden, that made the world hard to reach.

Mom waited for my reaction. I knew she'd had only one doll as a child, which was why I'd been showered with Barbies—a hundred of them—not to mention three fully furnished dollhouses. Pigs were the last thing I needed. I needed nothing more than to NOT add to the mess, the feeling of drowning, that I'd never be able to get what I wanted because what my mother wanted was already there and I had to use that up first. The feeling that I could never want anything.

"It's a waste of money," I said quietly, lowering my eyes. How could she go on about early-bird specials and liquidation sales, my steep tuition, and then, *pigs*? If our lives were mapped on a budget, they wouldn't add up.

"Don't be silly," she answered, still on the threshold, an in-between presence. The center of everything, yet already becoming a shadow. "They were only a few cents each."

I looked in the mirror above the bureau. "Your vanity," Mom called it. My reflection made no sense: I was angular and round, sharp and hazy. Olive skin and red cheeks, thin visage atop rounded tummy, young eyes with old bags, my features looked like they were pasted onto my face by accident, a collage with no outline, set against a backdrop of tattered window blinds and piles of worn towels. I squinted so that my image merged with my room and my contour dissipated, as if I was a character on a TV with bad reception, streaks emanating from my head every time I moved, like my brains were leaking out. Why would anyone *like* me? Nothing matched. Nothing was contained. I was eleven. Prime. Odd. Awkward. Parallel lines that never met.

I squinted and squinted until all I made out was a blur of eyelash and darkness, until the whole image of me swirled and sank into the glass and I saw nothing.

"Forget it," my mother snapped, then stomped down the hall. I closed the door, bracing myself for whatever yelling and slamming would come next by getting down to my math homework, plotting graphs that were logical and clear.

From my desk, I stared at the pigs, sitting like lonely rejects, out of place. Now I felt bad for them. Instead of throwing them away or into her room, I integrated them into my candle collection, standing them at the back like the royal family on a chessboard, wishing they hadn't messed up my system, trying to make some room in which I could grow.

. . .

THE NEXT WEEK, I bought my first bra by myself. At the local mall. I went early in the morning. I'd locked the door to the fitting room into which I'd dashed with every small-sized lingerielike item that I could rip off the shelves while no one was looking. The saleslady kept asking if everything was all right. *Yes,* I'd answered, chipper. I stared in the mirror. I was alone. I had no clue. I did not know what I was even looking at. There were no clasps, no wires. *Was* this even a training bra? How could I be sure I needed one?

Two weeks later, on a Friday after school, I was at Lila's house getting ready for Daniel Fishbein's party. How I'd managed to be included was a triumph and a mystery.

In Lila's bedroom, I pulled out from a plastic bag the clothes I had packed the night before after hours of careful selection. A blue polka-dot skirt, beige overalls, a pink-and-green sweater, a white T-shirt with a collar. Only now, laid on her bed against the backdrop of pillow shams and duvets (oh how I still craved pillows in the shape of candies, embroidered with flowing cursive JUDYS) my options seemed appalling.

Getting dressed was impossible. I could barely marshal my limbs. My tongue was dry, my ears rang. Lila effortlessly slipped on her gray Mexx sweater dress and was looking in her mirror, her head cocked to the side. "Belt or no belt?" she asked.

"Belt," I said, because it was easier to eke out one word than two.

I was out of my depth, and my panic was building, even in this house, with its sweet grape drinks, working VCRs, and a white coiffed dog named Kibbles.

And then, salvation. Lila's mom. She had short brown hair and a Filofax. She waterskied. "I love that blue-and-white skirt," she said, from the door. *She did?* "Why don't you put it on and come to my room? I'll do your bangs."

I giddily, quickly, slipped it on along with my collared shirt and pranced across the hall to her bedroom. One wall was entirely made of mirror. Next to it stood a little table lined with makeup and perfume bottles that sparkled. She led me there and I faced away from the mirror, following when she told me to close my eyes as she sprayed, blew and teased with a comb, not seeming to worry about whether my mop harbored lice. My bra strap dug into my side.

"Can I ask you something?" I said, my voice trembling.

"Of course."

I paused. "Do I pull my socks up, or roll them down?"

She glanced at the white pair I was clutching in my moist palm. "Roll them down."

Then she put away her hair dryer as I dressed my feet, noting how soft and thick her rug was. I imagined what it might be like to run in here in the middle of the night. No tripping over boxes. Possible.

"Look at yourself in the mirror," Lila's mom said, smiling.

I turned around. I looked like an Israeli flag going to play tennis with Mötley Crüe.

But, I saw *something*.

I saw a collar that stood tall, socks folded neatly around my ankles, polka-dots with even white spaces in between. I saw a dark complexion, big brown eyes that perched over a large nose and thick rosy lips, all of which fit together, on the same face, even if just for an instant.

LESS THAN AN hour later, as if I'd been passed along an escalator of maturation, passed between mothers, I was being escorted by Mrs. Fishbein—her hands on my back, warm like the orange of her cashmere sweater—to the family's basement.

I'd been so busy worrying about getting ready I hadn't had the chance to panic about the actual party, about spinning bottles and minutes in closets. But upon disembarking the final step, I realized— terror. We were the first girls to arrive. It was one thing to spend my days joking around with these boys in class, another to see them in Mrs. Fishbein's *house* (she also was a substitute math teacher), in serious beige pants and tucked-in shirts.

Especially Gregory. I'd forgotten to panic about Gregory. Smart, lofty (for a Jew) and funny, he was my dream date, my math buddy who sat behind me for eight hours a day. Even though we spent a good percent of our lives in conversation, our romance existed only in my mind, comfortably nestled in my synapses.

The boys huddled on one side of the snack table and noble, noble Lila (who was, no shock, more advanced than me—she talked to guys on the phone) stood with me at the other as Daniel came over. Ran his fingers through his hair. Some kids just had it.

I did not. I felt sick. Mom's physical affection was reserved for tears and tragedy: I did not know how to touch.

But, as Lila and Daniel began to chat about ski camp, I knew I needed to figure it out fast. I looked down at my socks, thinking of Lila's mom's encouragement. I had to succeed at parties, at people, at life outside Kildare. I had to keep myself afloat.

Thankfully, the others soon arrived and a gloriously ordered social began. Daniel—or probably his mathematical mother—had ensured an even number of boys and girls; for each song we all danced in two long parallel lines. During the pause between tracks there was a moment of shuffling panic, but it always worked out since *no one* wanted to be left out. (I hadn't counted on others being insecure too.) Like a team of chess pawns, we each swayed side to side, playing our parts in the geometry of prepuberty, me relaxing into "Pour Some Sugar on Me" and INXS and the system.

Until Daniel announced that we'd be switching gears. The beats stopped. My insides raced. People gathered in small groups and I didn't know where to go so I found my old friend, the bathroom. My social victories felt so fragile, but as I desperately rerolled my socks, I reminded myself that I *had* been invited, that I was not a fraud, that I was doing well and could survive another hour, that I could spin a bottle and kiss kiss kiss! I examined my lips, and though they seemed adequately unchapped, I delayed opening the door, no idea where I'd head from here.

Fortunately, as soon as I crossed the threshold, I was approached— by Gregory. My heart flapped. He was so tall, I wanted him to fold himself over me like origami, swallowing me whole. "Judy, can I talk to you?"

I froze, felt hot and cold, sweet and sour. This was actually happening, my dream come true! This was exactly how it had worked in my mind—he would pull me aside and ask me out. I knew I had it in me somewhere. I thought of the time in first grade when I walked into the advanced math class even though they hadn't called my name, assuming *they'd* made the mistake. Despite everything, I had a sense that I could get things I wanted.

Now I nodded, completely unable to speak, and followed him to a corner of the basement, my legs on a moving walkway. Then he stopped and turned, and in order not to smash right into him I forced my legs to halt too.

"Judy," he said. How could this person who saw my back and side every single day, who heard me laugh, sing, read, calculate exponential growth, who I heard chuckle and recite poems and divide fractions, now seem like a stranger, a landscape of uncharted humanity?

"Yes."

"There's something I need to ask you."

It all became a sitcom, a bigger-than-me moment colored with a pink border. I had never been so happy. "Yes."

"Will you go out with Stu?"

"Ye—What?"

"Stu really likes you, and he wanted me to ask you out for him."

Stu? *Stu?* I'd barely noted that Stu was at the party. He was nerdy, with enormous glasses, huge eyes, extreme dental work. A laugh like a rooster. Stu liked me? Stu?

"OK," I said, my mouth working without me, not sure what was happening or how life could just take you and throw you here and there like a Skee-Ball, bouncing off the wrong ring.

"She said yes!" Gregory called triumphantly across the room.

There was a murmur of "yes" that spread like mess around the room. Yes yes yes. I'd said yes. What had I done?

"Time for a special dance," Daniel announced from his ghetto blaster, swapping mix tapes for a slow tune before ushering me into the middle of the room, where Stu was waiting. Stu was my counterpart, it hit me. Awkward, nerdy, also a bit unclear why he'd been invited. I half smiled and did as Lila had told me. Hands on shoulders. Side to side. Everyone else formed a large circle around us and swayed to Belinda Carlisle as my and Stu's romance was anointed. Gregory's smile couldn't have been bigger.

They say in heaven love comes first.

And Judy is going out with Stu.

Who was I supposed to discuss this with? Where could I seek advice? I'd never seen Mom and Dad kiss, not even once. I thought of the boxes from our 1983 move, still sitting full in the basement, unpacked histories forming walls between them, between all of us, a family joke, a heavyweight suggestion of Mom's ambivalence: I am planted here and yet, not settled.

"How was the party?" Dad asked when I got home. He was nestled in his corner of the den, behind the newspaper, like always.

"Great," I lied, then tucked myself into my cramped dusty room, repeating over and over my new identity as a girlfriend, repeating it so I would believe it.

But Monday was a disaster. As soon as we sat down in class, Stu looked my way and grinned, his braces glistening in the fluorescent light. I smiled like I'd had a stroke, half my lip shaking, then looked away. At recess, Stu thankfully ignored me, but lunch was inevitable. As I tried to hide the tuna-and-cottage-cheese-stuffed-between-slabs-of-old-challah sandwich that Mom had cobbled together before leaving for work at six a.m., Stu sat down next to me. "How was your weekend?" he asked.

I closed my lunch bag.

"Good," I said. My mouth was a desert. Was this how you were supposed to talk to a boyfriend? What else? *Cumberlands drugstore had a great special on liquid soap. Mom got four dozen bottles.* Amid the giggles, I could feel Gregory, Lila, everyone, staring, assessing. I'd wanted a boyfriend to make me seem normal, but it didn't. I was used to oblique attention, to being seen over hedges; the fact that people were noticing me felt too much to bear.

"I got your number," he said. "I'll call you tonight."

When the phone rang that evening at eight p.m., slightly too loud, too lingering, I knew it was him. He was a man of few surprises, except for picking me in the first place. "Judy," Dad called from the den. "Phone for you."

It's my boyfriend, I told myself. My *boyfriend*.

But I had nothing to talk about, nothing prepared. Would I be expected to kiss him? How would I move my body? His braces? My tongue? It all seemed so dangerous, so complicated. Everything about me was wrong, out of place. I ran to the den. "Tell him I'm not here," I whispered. "Please."

Dad looked at me, knowingly. "Sorry. She's not here right now," he said into the beige receiver, complicit in my hiding.

I retreated to my room, and nestled in my unmade bed among the palimpsest of budget blankets. The headboard was dusty, and the pink edge of my Holly Hobbie comforter—the one with the girl whose hood was so large it hid her face—was frayed. I felt like the bed. The mess was me. The ugly reflected off me and back to me, an endless pattern.

AFTER A WEEK, I heard a rumor at recess. "Stu dumped Judy," it went. "He said it wasn't a *real* going out."

They were right. It was not real. I was not real. I was just a blurry reflection of the person I should have been.

I was rejected, dumped, ditched. And elated. No more pressure. No more having to worry how I would ever bring him home.

· THREE ·

7 WEEKS: I'M LATE
New York City, 2011

I sprinted to Sixth Avenue, running late. For three weeks, I'd existed in a closeted daze, harboring this secret life in my belly, Googling Web sites that went on about orifice development and lanugo hair, alternately fascinated and horrified (I was hirsute enough, I joked to Jon, I'd have to book this kid's eyebrow waxes in the womb). But none of it felt real. Sure, my unusually fierce daily cramps had me checking continuously for miscarriage (as the books said to) and I napped more than I had since my own babyhood, but it was all so temporary, fragile, an idea. Until now. My first ob-gyn appointment was due to take place in an hour. And, it was all the way uptown, blocks from any subway.

Ideal location for an emergency hospital, I mused, stepping into the street, despite the fact that I was now negotiating traffic for two. I waved my arm in the hope of attracting a yellow cab. *I'm late* resonated through my mind and I let out a cackle. The one line I hadn't had the chance to utter.

No taxis stopped. Their lights were off. I looked at my phone, watched a minute go by. Then three. Then six. I waved more frantically.

I can't be late, I thought, now conjuring images of my mother, her den stuffed with asynchronous clocks, the colons flashing between the numbers, here and not here. As if the abundance of watches helped her keep track of time. I, on the other hand, was a scheduler par excellence. Being prompt was my ultimate sign of social awareness, of respect for the other. I revered the base-twelve contract around which the entire world functioned. I was the to-do woman who had to-done it. Deadlines were deaths I craved. I was urgently early, forced to walk around the block when I arrived to gigs or meetings so that I wouldn't appear overly eager, underly artistic. I did not stay for eleventh hours; I lived by clean spaces, and numbers. A calendar girl.

If there's one thing I learnt from all this, I'd said to Jon the other night, *it's that the pill really works. Or,* he'd answered, *we were* beshert, *meant to procreate.* Damn romantic.

I peered into the horizon for the light of availability. "Shit."

I hated being late. *Last to the party. Left behind. Like the world is going on without me.* I kicked the curb. This pregnancy was not part of my narrative, not how I planned for it to happen. Not here, not now.

I could feel my world, my ways, slipping from me already.

Then an open cab turned the corner. I ripped open the door. Finally.

Settled inside, I watched as minutes passed on the television screen, my hand on my soon-to-be-examined belly. I'd read that babies loved reggae. Its beats per minute were the same as the average maternal heart. In the womb, they became accustomed not only to the sound of their mother's voice, but to her internal mechanisms. Stomach gurgling, gas, the rhythms of her organs. What beat had I heard, did I grow to? What tempo formed my blueprint for marking time?

My mother was a fetus in 1945, I thought, conceived in the Siberian work camp to which my grandparents fled from Warsaw in 'thirty-nine. During her stay in Bubbie's uterus, she was taken from Siberia all the way down through Russia, on horse, by foot, crossing various Stans, finally landing in Kirgizia, where she made her way out. She'd been conceived into the tempo of a heart stalled, terrorized, waiting to see if parents and siblings were still alive, waiting to see if her parents themselves would get out alive. She'd been formed in the cadence of hiding, running, survival.

The taxi sped.

What pulse had been passed on to me, ticking away? What bpm would I pass on?

ON TIME
Montreal, 1989

"Is everyone ready?" I called from my room.

One of my eyes was focused on the mirror as I checked out my creation—an all-white *Working Girl* power suit from Jacob Jr. with shoulder pads, a pleated skirt, and a blue-and-white polka-dot shirt that sported a medieval jester's six-inch collar, all of which molded my twelve-year-old shapeless physique into the strong, sharp contour—of a square. I'd had my hair done the day before; I'd gone with Samantha Horowitz and her mother, Fran, to the salon in the Cavendish Mall. Samantha got a flowing perm, but I knew Dad would freak out (*no piercings, tattoos, or perms—NOTHING PERMANENT*) so I just said "tease me" and lord. Sylvain the Quebecois Indian hairdresser who bore an incredibly suspect resemblance to Vanilli (including both leather pants and mane) had split my fringe in two, making half my hairs stand on guard, while the other half were plastered down my forehead. Then he'd blow-dried my long frizzy tresses straight, his arms sinewy as he drew out the strands, humming at how alluring I appeared. *Girl . . . you know it's true.* Of course, sleeping on it all night had not tamed the look, shall we say, and now several areas of the do were fully erect. Worse, the bottom of my hair turned outward like a seventies artsy fling. I used two brushes and all my strength to try to curl these tasteless waves under, power-woman straight. Overall, the look had the sexual appeal of smoked trout.

"Everyone? Anyone?"

My other eye was on the clock. June 12, 1989, nine forty-eight a.m. In seventy-two minutes, I'd become a woman!

I brushed harder. Damn rebellious hair ends. "Hello?"

No answer, except for the sound of morbid trumpet calls and a voice so deep it was as if the speaker had awoken from his own death. *It's Jewish hour,* emanated from one of the many radios that were always on in the house, crowding even the air with sound waves. *Today: a new story from the gas chambers.* "Hello?"

I ran down the slippery hall (particularly so due to my fishwife beige stockings) to the den, where Dad lounged hidden behind his papers. I smelled rare minty aftershave and saw his shoes sticking out from beyond the newsprint. He was ready, as always. Eli, on the other hand, was wearing a shirt and navy blazer, but no pants. "Eli!"

"I have two hundred and twelve lines," he said from behind his Game Boy.

"Wow." That *was* pretty good. We were both obsessed with Tetris. I spent my days trying, in my imagination, to make the shapes around me fit neatly together—which this house's piles of expired *TV Guides* and bargain basement towels did not. At school, I'd dropped out of drama, choir, and the annual reading competition to become a scientist, like Dad. I was a math nerd, drawn to balanced equations, ordered graphs, patterns that plotted neatly along the x-time-axis.

"It's getting fast," Eli said, his thumbs punching with force.

The more blocks that dropped, the more time that passed, the faster it all became, heading toward frenzy. I understood. Nintendo was one of our sibling ways of interacting along with a slew of imaginary characters—the Ukrainian Robot, Tony the Tiger, the jailer of Nottingham—that had peopled our make-believe games and our real conversations. "When you're done, please put on your pants, Captain Crunch," I pleaded and left for the kitchen, where I assumed I'd find Mom among the piles. "Mom." I took a deep breath. Gentle, abrupt, I was always saying the wrong thing. "Mom, I—"

She wasn't there.

"Mom?" My heart skipped, but excited for the day, I had hope. Her absence could be a good sign! Perhaps she was ready, slipping on her shoes, grabbing her coat, spraying on the final touches of her Charlie or Jean Naté or even Dior Poison that Dad had bought her as a special gift last summer (the name was so apt, Dad *hadn't* even made jokes about it), beaming, proud. Normal. Her present to me.

I hopped to her room. "Mom!" But as I opened her broken blue folding door, the one that was missing several hinges so it actually lunged toward me when I moved it (a relic of the former home owners, 1960s divas whose bold taste we never erased but instead covered over with layers of mess) I glimpsed Mom's backside, her beige tights pulled over extra-large underwear, the rolls on her sides. She was sitting at her desk, in front of a complex of boxes filled with colorful fastening supplies: paper clips, pins, sewing kits. "Mom."

"Shut the door, Judy. I'm getting dressed."

"We have an hour," I said. "Until my actual bat mitzvah."

"I know." She didn't turn around. "Now go."

Behind her loomed her king-size bed, the real Mount Kildare, stacked with clothes, blankets, and papers that now covered its entire surface except for a small edge where Mom slept. I wanted to hang out with her in the evenings and watch *Thirtysomething*, pretending I understood it and laughing along with her chuckles, but there was no room. A broken door wasn't the same as an open door.

I tucked my worry into myself, and decided to go practice my speech. This wasn't *really* a bat mitzvah, just a group *simcha*; the girls—all nine of whom I would be celebrating my personal coming of age with—would not read from the Torah. Though my Montreal Jewish community was obsessed with Club Med and teppanyaki dining, and though my school taught experimental Hebrew poetry instead of prayer, the synagogues were strictly orthodox, and there was no such thing as a bat mitzvah in Jewish tradition. Instead of reading from the Bible or leading prayers, we girls gave speeches about Jewish themes we'd studied. This was fine with me. School— with its clear systems, tests, grades—was my forte; my solidity.

For my speech, I'd picked my favorite holiday. "Passover is the celebration of freedom. It commemorates spring. It is a time of fresh starts. A holiday symbolized by the egg, itself representing the circle. Life. Cyclical life." Then there was the fact that Passover was the quintessential holiday of order. Obsessive order. The word *seder* means order; the whole evening begins with a chronologically determined to-do list and ends with a repetitive chant about goats. Ten plagues, ten commandments, four glasses of wine, three forefathers, two tablets.

The one meal of the year that my family ate at home, together, at the same time.

"Mom?" Forty-five minutes. No answer. The rush to flee Egypt. *Why is this night different from all other nights?* But, of course, it wasn't.

THE WOMEN IN my family kept stuff, not time. Neither Mom nor Bubbie arrived at any destination less than extremely tardy, be it after-school pickup, or a play where I had to squeeze between legs to get to my seat for a show that had started without me. When I was five or six, every Saturday we used to go shopping and it would take hours for Mom to get ready, while Dad, Eli, and I engaged in the elaborate gymnastics of peeling on and off coats, circling in the rusted blue faux-wood-paneled Pontiac station wagon with the engine running, the heat blowing into the backseat from the one working vent at the front, the freezing and boiling air mixing, causing the windows to fog up like a dream scene as Dad silently grew angrier and we waited for Mom to come trundling out of the house, dredging heavy bags on each arm. Then there would be stops: the bakery, the library where she had to negotiate fees for her overdue books, and finally, Bonimart—the discount store with a psychedelic orange-and-yellow globe in its "B"—the crowning glory atop the Decarie Square, a mall that was an architectural mess, not a square at all but a conglomerate of crevices and levels, arriving at four fifty to a store that closed at five o'clock.

We had to climb several escalators to reach the apex of Decarie, which always seemed to be perpetually on its last legs, dying since the day it was built (even the name sounded like decay). Mom planted herself on a step, Dad carried Eli, then two years old, and I would lose my mind, alternately staring at the mock marble walls with gray splodges that looked like ash, and my black Casio watch, wishing for the numbers to freeze, running up the moving walkway that never moved fast enough. Did she not see the time? What if we were locked in, forgotten?

Mom would finally arrive and start her full-on shopping mission, examining circulars, picking up products, while my heart beat, my colon bloated. She was in no rush, took her time price-shopping for the best toothpaste deals, while the metal grate at the front of the store began to descend, clinking with each inch. I was on watch, noticing every movement, aware of each announcement on the loud-speaker: *"Chers clients, nous fermerons nos portes dans cinq minutes."* The voice may have been chipper but the message was militaris-tic: customers, you have five minutes left. We would be stuck here forever, trapped. I would cry, tears streaming down my ashen face, begging for us to go. None of this bothered my mother, and even my father could not understand my panic. *Who's gonna lock us in?* he tried to calm me. *They don't WANT us here all night.*

But no rationale helped, and eventually I refused to enter. While they shopped, I waited on the threshold of the store, looking up at the gate's metal teeth, making sure that I was on the other side of the boundary. I would not be swallowed up by Bonimart! I felt safer being alone outside the store than inside with my parents, with my mother, even though, as I reminded myself now, she never did get locked in.

"ELI, PANTS!" I called, and went to his room to lay them out on his bed next to his *MAD* magazines, risking Mom's anger. *You're not his mother,* she accused me when I tried to care for him. She was right. Even then, I knew my efforts were as much an attempt for me to take control of my world as they were to help him. I felt guilty for being bossy, selfish, needy, but also angry. *Do you think I want to be his mother?*

My heart pranced out triple lutzes. I needed distraction. Forty-five minutes until womanhood, until somehow, I prayed, I would magically be transformed into a specimen of grace and self-composure, with hair that turned inward and bangs that never clumped together due to increasing forehead sweat.

Why did it have to be this way? This delay made no sense, especially since I knew Mom wanted me to have the bat mitzvah. I thought of the enormous birthday parties she threw for Eli and me when we were younger, the house overrun with cakes and party sandwiches. How long would it be before she returned to that state, the star storyteller who entranced the kids, my cousins all wanting to sit in her lap as she spun tales about fallen heroes, a chatty host with piquant laughter, the extra dining room sets coming into their own? When would she finally be less tired again?

Mom wanted this celebration, I consoled myself. She'd participated, gone to all the meetings in the living rooms of the other mothers (families who went to Benihana and sang "hands up, baby, hands up" while mine went for early-bird specials that included unlimited trips to the knish bar, and "hands up" reminded them of the Gestapo). Each of the other girls, most of whom I had anxiety just conversing with, let alone blossoming into my full womanly expression with, had invited ten family members to the service and luncheon, whereas my mother, the least wealthy but most caught up in abstract notions of family, had fought vehemently to secure us eighty tickets—every third cousin, each hairy-eared uncle, the entire transplanted shtetl of Radzymin would be in attendance.

They'd all be there. Waiting. Thirty-eight minutes. "Mom! We have to leave."

"It doesn't take a half hour to get there."

"But there's parking, and red lights, and . . ."

"I need to do the place cards." *Now?* "You're the one stalling me, Judy." *Me?*

Sweat was trickling, my armpits dampening, tights chafing. I tried to rehike my shoulder pads and straighten the power angles of my suit. Then I remembered! I splayed my hands out in front of me, stretching each finger to its maximum: my first manicure, electric pink French, selected by Fran Horowitz. My nails were shiny, neat with a perfect sliver of white crowning their rounded tops. Samantha had also had a pedicure, but I declined. (*Ay, who's gonna see your toes?* Dad's voice echoed in my mind.) Dad had taken me shopping, let me buy the full-priced white flats with the blue polka-dot bows that matched my shirt, a detail I was sure would command attention and awe. I ran to my room and took them out of their box, smelling their fresh leather. With my flawless fingers, I slipped them on—they fit perfectly. Then—my final anointment accessory—a shpritz of Exclamation eau de toilette. I smelled like orange-crush-scented baby powder. I was completely ready.

I scurried back to Mom's room, her door knocking on me, her boundaries flailing in every direction. Lately, I'd been using this door as our messenger. I'd wait for Mom to be asleep, then tape a note on it, reminding her to please find and initial both my and Eli's report cards in the morning before she went to work. Written communication was easier, safer than telling her in person, which risked unleashing her moods, no matter how softly I tried to put it. I knew she got upset because she knew it was her fault—how could it be mine?—but still.

"Relax, Judy. I'm almost ready."

Years after Bonimart, on the first day of second grade, a woman knocked on my classroom door and asked me to grab my bag and come with her. I'd turned red. Had Zaidy died? I shook as I gathered my items and stepped out in front of twenty-five staring students, only to be taken to the library where Eli was reading a book. Apparently, my parents had been late in paying tuition—again—and we were not allowed to stay in our classrooms. From then on, I spent each August anxiously leaving notes, pleading with Mom and Dad to pay for the upcoming year, which would never happen until the last minute.

Then again, I'm not sure what I expected from parents who couldn't decide on my name for three months, each petitioning for the labels of their own relatives who'd died horrific deaths in murder-camps and blood-soaked countrysides, my title flipping between Cheryl, Celia, and Rebecca until a compromise was struck: Judith (means Jewish girl—neutral) followed by a series of middle names from each side commemorating various atrocities. Three months! Why would I expect anything different?

BUT THEN I saw her. In a slip. Still sitting at her desk, writing, her hefty frame resting too comfortably on her brown cushioned swivel seat. Not. Going. Anywhere.

I expected something different because this was my bat mitzvah. I felt the door swing behind me, connections unhinged, wild breeze on my back. *Not a store, or a puppet show. My bat mitzvah.* A night different from all other nights. A chill ran along my damp skin. A slick of papers slid off one of the dozens of folders on her bed.

"Mom." No answer. "Mom?" *What are you thinking? Why are you doing this to me? Where are you?*

"DAD." I RAN to the den. "We have to go."

"Don't look at me," he grumbled, hidden behind the papers. He was ensconced in the room, planted in his chair, yet seemed detached from it all, like a realist figure set in a cartoon painting. I knew this lateness wasn't his fault. She was the artist, he was the scientist. She was a hippie, he was what hippies rebelled against. He was always on time, early even, but forever being coupled with latecomers. *Jack was always late,* he used to tell the story of his best friend with whom he'd traveled the world. *The plane would be taking off—TAKING OFF—and Jack would run up to the gate, dragging his suitcase. It was a compulsion, a need to squeeze out every second and use it twice, to trick the clock and conquer time. We once climbed Mount Sinai. Jack insisted on finding the exact spot where God talked to Moses. Then he dumped orange peels right there. On the spot where God handed Moses the ten commandments! And, of course, we missed the guided climb down.* Dad laughed. He never laughed at Mom's lateness. But he also never left without her.

"We need to be there in twenty-eight minutes," I said.

"I'm ready," Dad said. *I know.* I rolled my eyes.

I couldn't take it any longer. If we didn't leave in *one minute* I didn't see how it could happen. I'd have to walk across the sanctuary by myself, my bangs clammy, my family's dysfunction glowing neon. I held back tears. My insides burned, my stomach coiling in on itself. "Mom!" I screamed.

"For God's sake, Judy," she yelled back. "I'm coming."

But when I reached her threshold, she was still in her slip, at her desk.

"How could you?" was all I said, before sprinting down the hallway, into the vestibule, and right out the front door.

I DIDN'T REALLY RUN.

In my fantasies, of course, I fled. I dreamt of galloping across intersections, speeding through the city. I imagined racing down highways in European cars, jet-setting to the Florida Keys, surrounded by a different family. But that day, I did not run, because the synagogue was far, and I wasn't sure how to get there, and also, I didn't *want* to take the bus alone to my bat mitzvah. I wanted to go to my bat mitzvah with my mother.

"Ay, let's go," Dad called in the direction of Mom's room. Even his forfeiture had its limits. Always, there would come one moment when he would suddenly realize how odd it was, how wronged he felt. Anger was tucked inside him like toy streamers buried in a box, building pressure. Then the lid would fly open and the strands would spiral out and attack everything, hissing like snakes. "Let's get the fuck out of here."

"Don't hound me," she yelled. "Fuck you."

I cringed, relieved that my father was taking action, yet bracing myself for more yelling. I checked on Eli, who was OK, folded into his Game Boy. Pants on.

The method worked, and Mom emerged bedecked in Poison, pearls, and a purple dress. On top of her head, I saw, was a doily, the fragile, intricate covering that indicated a woman's married state, loosely fastened with a bobby pin to her hair, which was thinning, while her body was thickening. Mom knew I was guarding her and we didn't speak. She slowly made her way down the front stairs to the new Pontiac, tan, with bucket seats and electric windows. We all clicked our seat belts and the engine started and I looked at the digital green clock flashing, and my heart pounded and I knew there was a chance that Dad would drive crazy fast and drop me off before he parked and that I would make it by a hair of a fraction of an instant, and then Mom said, "I told Bubbie we'd pick her up."

THAT'S WHEN I zoned out. It was too late. The math was impossible. Strapped in my brown seat belt, trapped in this Pontiac, I surrendered to the clock, squeezed my cue cards and squinted my lids until the green numbers became blurry, nonsensical. I closed my eyes and retreated inward, exiting time, to a fantasy world of kitchens neat and white like the crescent of my French manicure, imagining the moments between every second inflating, imagining myself softly slipping into the Mississippis, time melting around my limbs, warm and wet, washing over the discord between my mother's world and the social contract that I now saw was quickly growing too great, too confusing.

DAD SPED, AND as we pulled up to the synagogue with Bubbie in tow, and I saw the stairs littered in loitering, overdressed relatives who did not look like they'd been anxiously waiting for the final crazy bat mitzvah girl, I was once again able to breathe. The almost-summer sun was sharp, each guest's shadow crisp and dark against the jagged architecture. The treelined street looked particularly green, itching with verdancy.

"So she's here," a great-uncle said as I loped to the lobby. "Fashionably late," teased another, ruffling my now disastrous hair with his tobacco-reeking palms.

When I got inside, it was chaos. People were everywhere, in the hall, in the reception room putting out place cards. I tried not to notice that a large percentage of the attendees comprised my disgruntled Yiddish relations who were drenched in anxiety and knock-off Drakkar Noir, high from endless discussions about their bowel movements.

"You see"—my mother came up behind me—"I told you you didn't need to worry."

"I have to go," I said.

I found my teacher and joined the group's formation. I only hoped my father was back from parking the car as the organ music began and we all proceeded down the central aisle of the sanctuary. I then sat down on the stage, finally able to be nervous about what I really should have been nervous about all along.

"PASSOVER . . . THE CYCLE . . . the egg." Each of my words rang out through speakers altered—rich and textured—as if whole symphonies were braided together in my syllables. I heard my own sounds, wanted to squeeze them in my fists. *The Angel of Death, the sacrifice.* I spoke these solid words to a sea of smiles, bobbing heads, to kippahs and dye jobs. And, to my shock, I loved it. One-on-one I would have choked, but up there I was the confident center of attention. I controlled time. My voice, my tempo, even my silences, marked the passing of tenses, focused everyone's experience and shifted their states. Each second felt stretched out like caramel, like I could lick every side of it.

"On Passover we celebrate the fall of the Egyptian empire. Which never really surprised me. What kind of regime puts the Jews in charge of manual labor?" A burst of guffaws and applause. *I could live right here, forever.* In my cadence, I heard my dad, his shtick, his humor mantra: *it's all in the timing.*

It was Dad who'd helped me reenter Bonimart, pushing me, each week, to take one additional step into the store. (His twelve-step program, he joked.) He'd hold my hand as my turquoise faux-Reebok lifted off the linoleum, and while my leg dangled in the air, he'd point out that I hadn't been crushed or trapped. *You're fine!* Then I'd plant my toes down and feel the hard ground beneath me, holding me up.

"Thank you," I said to the audience, my speech complete. I glanced up at the applauding crowd, but unlike a movie scene, I did not lock eyes with a widely smiling, wildly nodding, crying-tears-of-joy parent. Into the anonymous blur, however, I held my gaze firm. For a moment, I sensed—albeit hazily—a future, the possibility of being alone in the world, and surviving.

· FOUR ·

9 WEEKS: KARMA
New York City, 2011

"Let your arms lie at your sides," the prenatal yoga teacher instructed. "No, *lie*, Judy." She stood over my fair-trade hemp-infused Guatemalan-commune-woven mat. "Allow your legs to just be on the bolster." She leaned over to correct my knees that apparently were having trouble existing. "Belong within your breath." She moved my neck. "No clenching, dear."

I was a longtime yoga obsessive who'd powered through the rest of the class, but shavasana, the end pose of resting on pillows, I couldn't do. "No clenching." "Stop moving." "Relax!"

"I'm try—"

"Sh!"

Even though I was still closeted with friends, I'd come to this downtown studio hoping to connect to my pregnancy through the physical. But the exercises made no sense on my nine-week body. My little lump was nothing compared to these women who had stomachs to the sky, kvetching about sciatica, practice contractions, breech babies. They held sacred knowledge, knew whole worlds I didn't know, here, in my measly first trimester pudge. I folded my hands over my torso with its "Puy lentil"–sized baby as the books called it, or something equally ridiculous compared to their "Swiss chards." (And by the way, barf. I barely had morning sickness yet the last thing I wanted to eat was legumes. *Your baby is the size of a pizza slice; congrats! You've reached the camembert wheel!* Now *that* would make sense.)

"Arms by your side, Judy." "Stop moving." "Relax!"

Finally, my forehead was anointed with paraben-free oil and we were released. As I rolled up the mat, the guru approached and I looked down, knowing I was in for it. "Are you a dancer?" she asked.

"Oh." She'd noticed my perfect warriors! "I've done some dance. A lot of yoga."

"I could tell," she said, and I smiled, proudly. Then she continued, "You have exactly the kind of body that falls apart. By the third trimester, your stomach muscles will protrude right through your skin."

"Huh?"

By now she was rearranging my rib cage, shaking her head. "I can already feel the abdominal cracks."

My poor abdomen.

I was twelve when my colitis hit, just a few miles from this very studio. It had been our first family trip to New York and I'd stood out on the Statue of Liberty's crown, gazing in awe at the dazzling metropolis, imagining the exhilarating life that awaited me outside Kildare, when suddenly the magical feeling of freedom and potential was swapped for nausea.

Dad became the coach of my colitis, for three years schlepping me across Montreal to every doctor he knew, following my blood test results as if they were stocks. Layers of my colon disintegrated like snakes shedding their skins. We debated the cause: Was it autoimmune, my self-conscious body attacking itself? Or was it, as the old theory went, a stress response, channeling my amorphous dread and anxiety into a physical organ? Finally, a soft-spoken surgeon with deep blue eyes promised me salvation by removing my entire colon—which Dad thought was barbaric and insane. I begged for that surgery like most teenagers angled for a late curfew.

It was that dashing surgeon (or "henchman" to use Dad's term) who had told me earlier that day that I had to have a cesarean; even Dad agreed. Unlike most of my friends, I didn't mind. I was drawn to the idea of a planned, ordered delivery. I didn't want to make a mess of my insides. I didn't want pain. I fainted putting in contact lenses; the idea of labor terrified me. "Oh," was all I could muster as the guru felt up my back.

"You should do all my classes," she said. "Also, I run a doula service. Come to my seminar, I'll find you someone for your birth."

"Actually, I'm having a C-section," I blurted.

"A C-section?" She looked aghast. "Why?"

"Medical reasons," I said, but it came out sounding like a question.

"Well, I guess that's OK. But remember to refuse the Demerol!" she proclaimed. "Women *in Europe* don't take painkillers."

"OK," I said meekly, though I wanted painkillers just thinking about it. Even Jon did. Then I looked around at all the warrior mamas collecting their fairly traded maternity coats, probably preparing for their pool births and placenta brunches, stocking up on diapers made of recycled sweaters. Bubbie had delivered Mom on the refugee run, in a makeshift hospital inhabited only by a cleaner who was mopping the floor. When I was a newborn, Bubbie locked my babysitter in the bathroom so she could do everything herself. "Bubbie's strength made me feel strong," Mom had told me many times.

I grabbed my jacket, dizzy and flushed. I'd thought I was strong for executing cat-cows and demi-planks, but was now wondering if I wasn't the weakest one here. Perhaps I *should* refuse the drugs, insist on a natural birth, fight. Perhaps I was chickening out, doing everything wrong wrong wrong.

How would I remember to find myself in this whole new world, one of infinite all-important decisions? There were no right answers, no scientific codes for raising kids. The "results" of parenting would appear decades later, and even then, it wouldn't be clear whether showing a child too much *Sesame Street* is what led to their tendency to date self-effacing commitment-phobes. Would I ever be strong enough to just go with my gut?

TELL KAUFFMAN
Montreal, 1991–92

"Man alive, it's *cold*," my father said. His breath emanated from his mouth like a smoking chimney, white wisps curling up from his plaid woolen scarf—an accessory reserved only for the most pungent days of Canadian winter and which clashed in every way with his puffy purple ski jacket, black Russian hat, and rubber overshoes that formed cocoons for his brown Wallabees, the same type he'd been wearing since the 1960s. Dad was committed to his footwear. Whenever he saw this shoe in stores, he bought at least two pairs. *Stock up on things you like,* he said. *They'll be discontinued.* "Wowee, cold," he now insisted. But he was not complaining. The chillier, the better—not for his nose, which ran on its own accord, clear fluids dripping from one oversize nostril as if it was a broken kitchen sink—but for his pride.

"Minus seventeen today," I said from beneath layers of wool and Thinsulate.

"Minus thirty-eight with the windchill, don't forget," he added, gleefully.

We were on our weekly workout walk in the wealthy neighborhood of Westmount, climbing up Mount Royal, the mountain that formed the center of our city, the apex upon which French Quebec was crowned, the height from which you could see New York state, Vermont, the North. Dad was born in Montreal, making him—despite his wrinkled brow, balding head, unabashedly Jewish nose, droopy ears, and Yiddish mother tongue—all Canadian. His parents had come over from Poland in the 1920s after anti-Semitic attacks, after my grandmother whipped out a butcher knife and threatened to commit suicide right in the immigration official's office if he didn't grant them a visa *tout de suite*. Dad's parents arrived to the shores of Halifax with seven dollars, and his father, Zaide Abe, religious and scholarly, worked around the clock fixing sewing machines, through the Depression, even on Shabbat, until he was able to start his own sweater business. We didn't know anything more about Zaide Abe's family. As a teenager, he'd run away from his small town and drunk father for Warsaw. Then he and his wife left for Canada and within twenty years, every other Batalion had been killed.

Zaide Abe had died of lung cancer two years earlier. The black hole of our history had been pulling on Dad, and he'd become obsessed with the rare name Batalion, which was particularly unJewish. He'd written to genealogists and historians, trying to make sense of our roots. "Batalion is Polish slang for undomesticated animal," was our only concrete answer. *Zaide made it up*, he guessed, *at immigration. They said what's your name? He said, eh—Batalion. Who knows?* Dad said.

You never asked? I never asked.

The air was heavy, solid with cold, its electrons too frigid to keep circulating. Gum hardened and tasted mintier. Though it was just three p.m., the blinds on all the houses were drawn, as if the homes too were wrapped up. The odd car passed us by, and Dad imagined what the passengers might be saying about us: "What *meshuggeners*! Who walks outside on a day like today?" Eli was at a friend's house, as on most Sundays. This trek was mine and Dad's insanity. Needless to say, we were the sole pedestrians.

The sidewalks were caked with snow. As we walked, I could feel my cold feet slip within my boots, my boots slip on the ice. Simply stepping involved resistance.

"Can you believe I'm *shvitzing*!" my father huffed with delight.

"Me too," I said, noting dampness in my armpits and inner thighs under the three layers of pants and sweaters. I feared the amorphous, ectopic moistness. Sweat was suspect—it could transition to ice at any second, your body's regulating system turning against itself.

"This is the best route for this weather," said Dad, the urban orienteer. He'd mapped out four different itineraries for our Sunday walks, which we took religiously. Each one started near Carlton, and all ended downtown. The routes, like our family's houses, had names: Westmount, Outremont, Côte-des-Neiges, and the Hospital. It was like the joke Dad endlessly told, about the family who numbered each gag, so to garner a laugh they only had to call out its digits. (Forty-two! attempted a guest, but no one guffawed. *It's the way you tell them. . . .*)

As for this quest, it manifested Dad's philosophy. His competitiveness, unusual for a bald, chubby, five foot six at the height of his height Jewish doctor named Hyman Simon, was not about excelling at school, but battling the elements, defying the physical, controlling decay. He'd dedicated his life to prolonging life so much that he developed a long career as a geriatrics doctor just so he could always seem young compared to his patients. The trick to Dad's extreme-living game was that it had to be done naturally. No pills or potions. The point was winning by suffering. Tylenols were distributed to me only if my fever was above a hundred and four (and that's Celsius). The body was a temple that had to be glorified through exertion and self-control.

We reached the top of our climb, and stopped in front of a mini-mansion for a mini-moment to acknowledge the expensive houses and the vista: the whole city—its majestically rusted green-and-gold buildings and the 1950s low-rise apartment blocks—all covered in white powder. Snow was an equalizer, a foundation that evened out the urban skin, covering messes, balancing sides.

"Beautiful," my father said, proud of his city, or perhaps, soothed by covers.

Côte Saint-Luc, our suburb, was far away and I couldn't make out our house, where my mother sat and seethed. I wondered if she was still having the tantrum that had begun as we left, her latest hysterical accusations that we were going off without her, leaving her, leaving her out. Our invitations. Her "you don't really mean it, you just like Dad better." My biting of my tongue (*I wonder why*). I pushed aside the thought that I was indeed leaving her, somehow stealing Dad, guilty as charged. The irony made my insides clench. I thought of how, when I was young, I crawled into Dad's sofa bed, carefully maneuvering around the metal grates of the foldout mattress—Mom's queen-size bed, of course, had no room. Her piles pushed me away, pushed the rest of us into small spaces together, resulting in bonds that then made her angry. I wanted to spend time with her, at least a her that wasn't yelling at me, so her accusations felt doubly unfair.

I imagined I saw smoke rising from our roof, not from a chimney but Mom's psyche. If Mom embodied home, then Dad was the streets. An escape route. A chance at normalcy. I'd spent whole days imagining what my life would look like if Dad had had a different wife, someone skinny, with straight brown hair, clothes she bought downtown, who cooked Shabbat meals and vacationed in Boca Raton. That world was *almost* possible, just off by a few angles, off by a chance meeting at a party in 1967. He was a doctor, ten years older. Mom was the pretty poet, the patient.

My toes began to burn, and I wiggled them in my boot.

Going down the mountain was harder than up. Dad found us a trajectory with less ice and slope, and still we had to step sideways, our legs crossing awkwardly as we faced the houses instead of the road. We didn't talk as much as usual. It was harder to discuss punch lines and histology—Dad's favorite topics—in these conditions. *You are not like the girls I knew growing up,* Dad had told me a few months earlier on one of these promenades. We'd been analyzing the difference between polyps and cysts. *Fourteen-year-old girls just wanted to talk about lipstick.*

Ha, I'd laughed. *How silly.*

I'd been proud that he was proud, but also upset, because I wanted to talk about lipstick, but didn't know anything about it. But I did know about unusual growths. I took advanced math and biology. I studied my colitis, and together, we reviewed theories of auto-immunity, heavily analyzed my many doctors' analyses, and debated the benefits of medical versus surgical intervention (*no intervention!*

was Dad's preference, of course). I could never complain; *I hurt more than you do,* Dad would reply, and his crinkled brow and sad eyes showed me he did, suffering over his inability to fix what was wrong.

At the bottom of the hill, we hit Sherbrooke, the longest street in Montreal, which stretched right across the island, spanning the French and English sections, relentless fighting factions. Each wanted independence and sovereignty, each wanted its own traditions to rule, neither acknowledging that heritage and language are arbitrary accidents of birth. This dispute, the core of our nation.

Inside a Dépanneur, tears ran from the crevices of Dad's eyes and then, like pucks on a Plinko board, spread along the deep wrinkles in his cheeks. For a minute, his glasses fogged up completely, and I felt like I was alone.

I got herbal tea. Dad got nothing. No coffee, no water. These would subtract from his solo conquering of physical existence.

"Il fait froid dehors," I said to the cashier, who was herself bundled in sweaters and scarves. I could smell her cigarette habit from across the counter. She grumbled.

"Central casting," Dad said as we walked out, using our code for when a character plays to their caricature.

"From another movie," I replied, our code for when someone is angry from a previous context.

Dad laughed, which was his highest accolade. His only accolade. He was proud, I knew, that I lined up metaphors.

We walked along Sherbrooke, all the way downtown. I thought of how by this time of day, Mom was probably also trudging through kippers of snow, a massive cloud in her full-length duvet coat, bulbous hat, and puffy boots, making her way to visit Bubbie and Zaidy at one of their nursing homes. She was likely schlepping totes and wheeled luggage filled with potato knishes, seven-layer cake, and Klezmer CDs—the many bags that were starting to travel with her outside the house. Bubbie had developed dementia, Zaidy had had a stroke; their former characters and immigrant lives were hidden under unruly facial hair and bloated eyelids. Their faces disfigured without their dentures, like deflating balloons. Though Mom used to fight constantly with Bubbie, forcing her to the psychiatric ward for shots for her paranoid rants about people stealing her houses, she was now obsessed with comforting her; it was her raison d'être. *They're survivors,* she said. *They deserve it.* Each day, Mom spent hours with her parents as they moved between rehab centers, bringing them snacks and Yiddish entertainment as if she was a roving nomadic convalescent home. She organized events and hired a round-the-clock roster of caregivers for them and their houses, including Hutchison, their first home in this country. Meanwhile, every evening after Carlton, Dad visited his mother at a different old-age home. Eli and I spent weekends waiting in the car, bouncing between these hospitals and all the homes—they too seemed like dilapidating patients who needed looking in on.

It was nearly dark now, and Dad and I strolled quickly, until we arrived at our current Sunday night restaurant of choice. Originally discovered by Mom through coupon cutting, La Poissonerie was a small seafood bistro with low lighting, aquaria, fishing nets, and a salty beach smell. Inside, we took off numerous layers, and the maître d' smiled, as people often did when they saw us together, father and daughter. A fifty-five-year-old man and a fourteen-year-old girl who shared an almost identical countenance. Later in life, this became a slight slight for me (*thanks for letting me know that I look like a seventy-two-year-old man*), but back then, I was pleased. I had an anchor. I came from *something*, concretely, the Batalions, My Father's Side, even if the generations of running had left soft gaps.

My father ordered for us, as he always did. No one in our house cooked; we had a long family history of restauranting, even a happy one. Years earlier, after shopping at Bonimart, we'd head to Pumperniks, a kosher-style Chinese diner with copious early-bird specials and an all-you-can-eat salad bar. We were friendly with the waitstaff and regulars, sharing with them the colored pencils and paper Mom stashed in her purse. One of the waitresses—blond, tall, not ours—smoked in the bathroom. She left her ongoing cigarette in a crevice on the side of the mirror. Each week I checked for it, fascinated by how something so illicit could be going on right there in the cracks, in my small reach, as if signaling a secret warp zone to a different universe. Afterward, friends would sleep over. There were dress-up fashion shows, Care Bear weddings, trips to the video store. On one particular weekend when my mother's friends from Toronto stayed over, Dad made jokes about Canadian taxation ("GST, PST. Feh. To me it's all *BST*") and I heard them howling over strawberry cheesecake, even from my room, Mom convulsing in fits of delight.

Tonight, Dad ordered us the same meal—the salmon. His with French fries, mine with a baked potato. Dad, the conservative and Conservative, was the world's most unlikely vegetarian. He claimed his diet was due to his high cholesterol, but I knew it was due to his empathy for the cows. He was a secret softie. He loved telling the story of how he drove a taxi to put himself through medical school. The cab was owned by a Mr. Kauffman, who never maintained it, causing endless problems for the drivers. One day, the next shift's driver, Mendl Eisner, was bringing Dad home when the car stalled in the middle of one of Montreal's busiest intersections. Eisner had had enough. He did not scream, or yell, but opened the door, stepped out of the car, and called back to my dad, "Tell Kauffman to go to hell," before disappearing forever into the traffic. This story delighted my father—sure, the guy had left him stranded in the middle of the road, but he adored that Eisner had simply walked off. Poof. Ta-da. No ties at all. We used "Tell Kauffman" as code when we wished we could just run away.

At the table, warm over hot white rolls and butter, we launched into a heated conversation about Raynaud's syndrome, a circulation problem in which one's fingers and toes become cold and numb with stress. My hands and feet were always icy, and Dad wondered if I might be suffering from this capillary shutdown. I liked the idea of numbness. I liked the idea that my circulation was saving itself for more important things. I liked the idea that Dad was diagnosing me. I showed him my fingers. I kicked my boots to the side of the table, gesturing toward them while talking about how my feet's vessels had withdrawn, gone on strike. Halted any feeling. This disease seemed like great restraint, one that would make him proud.

The meal arrived, and as always, Dad was in awe. "Such perfect portions," he said. Usually, he was not one to go for normal amounts of food (what bargain would that be?), but here, he said, it made sense. It left him feeling "just right" full. It was the perfect meal to walk home after.

I liked it too because it was contained. I counted the calories quickly in my head, subtracted what I assumed I'd lost on the walk, and took off a few more for the cold, my usual equations. The math of comfort. I was petite, but still, I'd begun to crave control anywhere I could get it.

When the bill came, Dad was pleasantly surprised. "Your mother knows how to find the bargains," he said as he signed. Then he looked down, silent, and so did I.

Sunday night. The end of the reprieve.

How I dreaded going home.

Sometimes, we brought Mom a hot meal.

"Should we get Mom a salmon too?" I asked, a yes or no question. But really what I wanted, what I needed, was for him to say *something*. For him to acknowledge that her yelling was inappropriate, or stressful, or just, her yelling. To say: things are not right. To say, I'm sorry for how it is.

Dad looked me in the eyes, for the one split second he could. Here was our moment, the way the walk should end, the journey that moves, the conclusion that connects the dots. The new arc.

"Not if you want to walk back," was all he said, zipping up his ski jacket. Putting his hat on. Layers of down. Thick rubber soles.

The truth about my father was: he did not have a different wife.

"OK, let's walk," I said, because I had to.

"You're crazy," he cackled, with pride.

"I know."

And then we walked home. A full circle.

"I'm NOT A fucking truck!" I screamed, my lungs now burning as much as my gut. *I'm alive, breathing, sensitive, real.*

Mom was on the phone, sitting at her desk—now even her organizing containers had proliferated, hundreds of filled little boxes sprouting in all directions. A wild fractal of school supplies for an entire district.

Dad stood on the threshold.

"I'm having the surgery and that's it," I yelled, dizzy, the objects around me swirling into one another. I was shocked at my outburst, that there was even room for my strong emotions. "Asshole." I gestured to the doctor, my new pediatric gastroenterologist, who was on the other end of the line. Did he not know how long it took me to convince Mom and Dad to let me have surgery? Did he not know how many times we canceled the procedure, Dad hoping my latest colitis flare-up would resolve on its own, and that today was the last chance for months? Did he not know that my stomach hurt every hour of every day, that I hemorrhaged repeatedly? That I lived in and out of hospital rooms? That my whole life revolved around my organ that was attacking me? How I was a fifteen-year-old with the social life of a senior citizen? Did he not see how there needed to be a cure, at least a promise of escape, healing, renewal? An answer.

How could he be suggesting, now, at the eleventh hour, a new drug trial? And one that would keep me at the hospital for two months. There were PSATs to be taken! I was not putting any more of my life on hold, on the toilet.

"You don't understand the stakes," Dad yelled back. "This is major surgery. A million things could go wrong. This could affect you forever."

"A million things are wrong," I shouted back. "I might not have a forever."

My body was hot, took over my mind. I could do this. I ran to my room and grabbed the suitcase I'd packed the night before when I'd felt good enough to get off the sofa bed in the den, where I slept so I could watch TV when I was in pain. I'd played "I'm Every Woman" as I packed and danced to Whitney Houston's guttural sonic gestures promising me a feminine future. *It's all in me!* I grabbed that luggage, then headed for my front door, bumping against piles of coats and pushing aside the mass of dusty shoes in the vestibule, growing like moss along the dirtying walls. I dragged the rolling bag—one of a dozen, Mom's new obsession, stashed in the basement—right outside, into the cool March air. "If you won't take me," I screeched, "I'll take the bus."

This time I did it. I used real steps and ran. I had no idea how I was going to get to the Royal Victoria hospital on top of the mountain, but I didn't care. I'd find a taxi, I'd hitchhike. My heart sprinted, my legs soared; this was more physical activity than I'd done in weeks. Some kids may have rebelled by doing drugs, having sex, joining cults; I revolted by having major surgery. I knew what was right, even though it drove me crazy that I had to make all the decisions, that my parents never *did* anything, never took chances. Even Dad, who taught me to step forward, stalled and stalled.

Now he pulled up to the curb in the station wagon. "If this is what you really want," he said from his open window.

"Yes!" I cried, wanting it as much as anyone had ever wanted large-scale organ removal.

On the way to the hospital, Dad broke the silence and stopped at a diner. "Tuna melt?" he asked as he got out of the car. I smiled. I'd been on an all-white, no-fiber diet for months. "Sometimes, you have to live a little."

ONCE I WAS checked in (checked in, like it was a hotel—then again, perhaps this was my body helping me escape my home?), filled up on fries, resting in my robe, the nurse told me she needed to mark me with a speck of tattoo to guide the surgeon in his cuts. She smiled sweetly as she prepped a long syringe, liquid splashing from its menacing spout, and I laughed, picturing what Dad always said about people with tattoos (the DMS says it: *insane!*). I imagined the cursive result: "my other stomach is a BMW." Here at last was my appropriate teenage act-out. Plus I'd be getting a morphine pump—heroin anyone? Then, I screamed. That one tiny dot was horrifically painful, sending sharp spasms across my whole front. *Insane*, I thought, as I stared at the blue period punctuating my middle. *But worth it.*

· FIVE ·

10 WEEKS: GETTING METAPHYSICAL
New York City, 2011

"Surprise!" Jon said, leading me outside by the arm. I was the one who usually planned elaborate birthday adventures, but this year, for my thirty-fourth—a number so thick, substantial, so midthirties where I still didn't feel I belonged, at the point where I woke up in the morning thinking "Oh God, not *me* again"—Jon had warned me he'd been doing some planning.

Downstairs he ushered me outside to the cool, cloudy April day and pointed to a Ford Escalade. "You got me a minivan?" I shrieked, horrified. "I'm not even in the second trimester."

"No, idiot," Jon said. "I rented a car. I'm taking you out on a special surprise food day—a tour of artisanal Brooklyn!"

"Oh," I let out, genuinely surprised. "Amazing." Though I didn't like to admit it, I was as much a foodie as the next hipster, analyzing meals for weeks, drooling over cuisines from small African countries (even when I didn't eat half of it), studying menus like literary texts, relishing unusual juxtaposed flavors—fish and fruit! Fries served in mini washing machines caused frissons. I had no idea how to even turn on a food processor—hell, I couldn't work a toaster—but was guilty of watching *Chopped* marathons. A culinary Sunday, a chance to ingest with abandon, planned by a husband who otherwise never planned anything, should have been my dietary dream come true.

But, as my arm brushed my voluptuous side, my heart (and hips) felt heavy. In the past weeks, I'd gained twelve pounds. Twelve! A dozen pounds was half my entire recommended gain. Every single book said that the normal first trimester weight increase was between *negative* one and two pounds. Not to mention, I boasted the facial complexion of a bar mitzvah *bocher*. The worst part was, nobody knew why. I appeared to be undergoing a radical transformation into a pubescent boy, and could not explain to my friends who stared quizzically at my double-layered torso what was transpiring. I imagined their reaction at learning my condition. *Huh? You?* In my circles, being thirty-four and knocked up was akin to being a teenage mom. It would be like when I introduced Jon to friends as "my husband" and their expression said *your what?*

Now I turned to him, squeezed his hand. "How perfect," I said, trying to stay positive.

"Also, it's an SUV, not a minivan," Jon muttered as he helped me up into the passenger seat.

At our first stop—Smorgasburg, an outdoor food flea by the water—I giddily went along with his plans, stuffing my face with artisanal cannoli, state-of-the-art pigs in the blanket, super chef schnitzel bits and other carbs that were not forbidden for the fetus. "Should we try the spare rib–infused scallion pancakes or Bolivian soda?" I muttered among my munching. The cool maritime wind blew a few strands of pan-seared locally-raised brussels sprout shavings into my coat collar.

"How is that even a choice?" Jon asked. "Both!"

"I meant, which one *first*. . . ." But he'd already sprinted off to fetch our treats.

I sat down on a bench facing the East River, feeling its dewy moistness on my nose. Though I tried to focus on that sense along with the zingy smell and tangy sensations of limeade munchkins, I couldn't help repeatedly patting the extra stomach that now rested above my old one, and hiking up my (new, large) underwear to cover my masses, blend it all together, to make it feel like one.

When Jon returned, calories in both hands, I tried to transcend my appetite with rhetoric. "What do you think fuels our obsession with food? Why has hunger become the art of our time? Are we so screen-based, so visually overstimulated, that we seek experimentation in the realms of taste, touch, smell?"

"Or, because it's delicious," Jon said, gently bringing the soda bottle to my lips as if I was a child. "Happy birthday." I felt the liquid drool coolly down my esophagus, even though I knew from X-rays that it actually dropped down, heavy, in an instant.

On our forty-minute riverside drive out to Coney Island for the original slice (authentic trumps artisanal), I stared at the waves, cresting and falling, recalling car rides with Jon in Montenegro, Poland, Israel, how together we jetted along the highways of the world. And before that, my solo journeys in trains and buses, through France and Austria, England and South Africa. Now there were fewer options, I knew, feeling little palpitations. I had to forgo saunas, sushi, sun, even Sudafed. I couldn't use zit cream, down the Diet Coke, or purchase plane tickets with liberty. The coping mechanisms I'd relied on for decades—the ways I'd learnt to navigate my fears and flaws, to make peace and structure in this world—were crumbling.

"That was a great fennel quinoa crumble," I said.

"Actually, it was kind of disgusting."

"Yeah."

The pièce-de-résistance that evening was a shmancy dinner at a restaurant on a boat moored on the shores of Dumbo. Jon and I sat at the white tablecloth, drinking sparkling juice, its sweetness coating my front teeth. "God I'm old," I said.

Everything I'd spent years trying to contain was leaking, bursting at its seams. The stretching of my skin, of my fundamental boundaries, this mimicry of my mother, itched in discomfort. I stuffed my face with hot caraway rolls, trying to dissociate myself from the body hidden under my empire-waist dress, from my physical being that was distending and distorting, marked with blotches, pocks, and streaks that might never subside.

I stared out to the limitless water and imagined unanchoring the whole ship, floating off to sea, away, afar, forever.

THE PUZZLE PIECE
Montreal, 1993

The doorbell—a shrill reminder of the outside world, coming in.

I couldn't do it. I had to do it. How could I do it? Do it. "Coming!"

I jetted to the vestibule, brushing off my sleeves. While other sixteen-year-old girls might have spent the two hours prior to hosting a Saturday night get-together dabbling with eyeliner and Nair, I spent mine engaged in mad housekeeping, scrambling to throw cheap suitcases and endless magazines into the cold storage room and shut doors leading to the wrong spaces, like the room with *still* unpacked boxes from our 1983 move.

When I'd found out that I'd have the house to myself that evening—Mom and Dad each visiting their respective parents—I'd casually suggested to Lisa over the phone that "people" (i.e., the group of girls and guys she hung out with every weekend, and I, sometimes) come over here. "We can watch videos," I'd said. "We have hundreds." I did not mention that they were the result of Mom's obsessive recording of movies shown on TV (free films!), leading her to buy additional VCRs so several movies could be captured at once—but never watched. Despite the mess, I wanted to host, pushed by dreamy fantasies—that Josh or David or Ian might grab my hand, ask to see my room, pull me close, kiss me tightly, not caring about where I came from or how little experience I had.

"We also have banana cake," I added like a pert saleswoman, not mentioning that though my mother didn't cook, she'd lately gone baking-berserk, making half-a-dozen loaves at a time; hot tins constantly perched precariously over the kitchen counter's uneven surfaces permanently saturating the air with the scent of burned sugar. Sometimes, I ended up standing at the counter, eating an entire cake, chewing to silence my anxiety, unable to stop, unable to discern a normal amount among all the excess.

I held in my post-op stomach, which in its new formation, had been gloriously cured. I was wearing Mom's 1960s loose-fitting pink blouse stamped with cartoon vegetables that I'd dug out of my closet, imagining I wore her pretty young self who'd had fiery love-not-war romances. "Hi," I said as a sudden thrall of bodies heaved their way into our tiny anteroom with its blue-glass chandelier, silver wallpaper painted with wall-length brown trees, and mock-marble linoleum. (I wasn't sure which was worse—the mess that covered everything or the hideous diva decor that underlay it.) My guests, *my guests*, were so tall, with hot pizza breath, their substantial weight a new sensation for this creaking floor, bringing whips of cold in with them. "Come in," I said quickly, neck craned, my voice choked by closeness. Goose bumps spread from my arms to my ears. "No cover charge tonight."

I led everyone directly downstairs along my carefully choreographed pathway that delivered the fewest vistas of domestic pathology. Though the playroom hosted piles of books and mismatched furniture, not to mention bright green-and-yellow stained glass windows (thanks again, divas) this traditionally children's space, I figured, had an excuse for being messy. I didn't mention it also served as Dad's bedroom. I frantically kept tabs on everyone's gazes as they made themselves comfortable on the dozens of pillows I'd scattered on the floor—how did people make themselves at home so easily?—and no one seemed to notice anything awry. Their warm solidity planted on my floor made me want to dive from the staircase right in between their torsos, melt into them forever.

"Holy shit," Josh said, pointing at a full wall of videocassettes. "This is amazing."

I was reminded of my younger years, when friends came over to play with my overpopulation of Barbies or to host weddings among my ludicrous congregation of Cabbage Patch Kids, delighted by being surrounded by this fun fantasyland. They never saw the underside: the boxes of children's clothes, board games, and puzzles, all bought on sale, growing into mountains in the closet and leaving no room for my and Eli's clothes.

"We have hundreds of movies," I said, grabbing the binder where Mom had begun, but never finished, to classify them alphabetically and by tape number. Shaking, I handed it to Josh, who smiled, looking right at me. I could smell his deodorant. A gentle, foreign mélange of mint and beef. My heart flittered.

The guys scoured the wall, closely reading the titles that Mom had written in meticulous, tiny script on each tape as if with this organizational act she'd find an answer to the kaleidoscopically confusing world she herself created. The three girls chatted in a corner. No one seemed horrifically shocked. *No one knew.*

I breathed in relief, but still felt uneasy, unsure where to place myself. The soft piles of banana cake! I escaped to the kitchen, shutting the door behind me, particularly aware of the divas' shiny golden-pink wallpaper and mismatched chandeliers, not to mention the mountains of Tupperware that bulged out of the unclosable cupboard and the fridge with its green-tinged cottage cheese, limp rotting bananas (being cryogenically preserved en masse for the making of said loaves) and expired Kodak film. I grabbed a cake and one of dozens of two-liter bottles of Diet Coke before heading back downstairs, promising myself that I wouldn't eat anything tonight, that I would be pretty and graceful; that using my same talent for cleaning up, I would slide myself right in the middle of the gaggle of guys, making my body open, accessible, alive.

But by the time I returned to the basement, it had been decided that we'd be watching Pink Floyd's *The Wall* and everyone was already settled on cushions. I saw Lisa grab Josh's hand, and they both laughed. I sighed and bid farewell to my fantasies.

"For all your loaf needs," I said instead. I set the cake down and walked over to a mound of blankets on the side of the room, tucking myself into it, understanding for the first time how these alienating piles could be useful, could offer me protection, a hiding place. Then

I watched cartoon figures hammer down The Wall and thought, "People" are in my house, and they are OK, and I am OK.

THE NEXT MORNING, the fight began because Mom couldn't find the papers that I'd moved into the kitchen. "Cleaning isn't your job," she said.

I know, I wanted to say. *It's yours.* But I didn't. I sensed my mother's pain. I didn't know how to help, how to change anything.

At the same time, my annoyance at her annoyance made me snappy. She seemed to think that having stuff gave her some kind of control over her life when it was obviously controlling her. "Here are your useless things," I mumbled, pointing at the papers.

"You"—her voice hardened—"have no idea what's useful. Your father's things—maybe those are useless."

I rolled my eyes, she slammed the door. I did my homework on my carpet, snuggled close to the radiator for warmth, angry that I was angry, that this—and not pancakes and phone calls from or about someone I made out with—was my Sunday morning.

"Judy, sweetie." An hour later, I heard a soft voice approach—the version that did not yell—and my guard was momentarily let down. I looked up to see Mom reenter my room and sit on the edge of my bed, her toes just touching the ground, her balloon body leaning forward, slightly off-kilter. She was one with her surrounds, her own self perched oddly on her oddly perched piles. "I'm sorry I got angry. I didn't mean to. I love you so much."

I love you too, I should have said. "Fine," I said.

"Judy, we really need to talk. We need to discuss our relationship and why we've had such a difficult time communicating with each other for so many years."

Her eyes twinkled gently. In this second, she really meant it; she really wanted to work it out between us. My heart pulled toward her slanted physique, but then it halted. I'd been hearing a lot of this "annoying girlfriend" act lately—let's talk, we need to talk. Every time I responded, I got sucked into Mom's maelstrom, into the mess. We would analyze our every interaction and then I would cry and apologize and we would say how much we loved each other, but nothing ever changed.

I was so sick of that. I didn't want to talk. I didn't want to cry. I didn't want to pretend, to fold into her. I didn't want to not-explain the obvious, to avoid saying that it was all so unfair.

Mom had once told me that a psychiatrist had once told her never to have children. *Ha!* She'd cackled. *What an idiot. All I ever wanted were children.* But I knew she was telling me this because she feared he was right.

"I can't," I now said, and looked down at my homework. "I'm busy."

What was I doing? I knew she didn't mean to hurt me. She was the one who struggled, who was ever busier, more tired, stressed, constantly taking care of her own mother. I glanced up at the bags under her eyes, shelves that stored sadness. Had I wanted to hurt her, to make an imprint on her as she pushed into me?

The capillaries on her cheeks lit up sequentially like a flaming fractal. "Fine," she said, and stomped down the hall, leaving me on my floor feeling strong and horrible, independent and guilty, all at the same time. After that, I stopped inviting people.

WITH SPRING CAME the ability to go outside without being strangled in scarves. To look up if you wanted to, not hit by wind. To not distinguish so brutally between in and out. Freedom.

Olivia and I arrived at Jen's "my-bohemian-parents-are-away" party to find a crowd of people standing around her lawn. I clutched Olivia's arm, both nervous and excited to have been included. I'd known Jen had invited Victor, my locker neighbor, who towered over me by a full foot, enveloping me each morning in his magical Paco Rabanne. Tonight, I'd promised myself, was going to be *it*. I would be coquettish, giggly, fiery. I would make out. Become normal. It was almost the end of the school year: this could be my moment. It had to be!

Olivia and I approached a group of kids from our grade, huddling together around Josh. I tried to make hilarious small talk, told some lame jokes about taking drugs (*I learnt it from you, Dad,* I imitated the commercial, cackling) and the awkward silence revealed that everyone was in fact stoned.

So I went inside, straight to my refuge. I turned the bathroom faucet on to muffle the sound of my fidgeting. I felt like I was in a dressing room between acts, a small reprieve amid the performance. *Men don't make passes at girls who make wisecracks,* ran through my mind.

Or at girls in ridiculous shirts. The orange-tiled mirror revealed my jigsaw jersey—a tight, high-necked chemise with a front that looked like two pieces of a puzzle locked together, one black, one white, connected through a series of protrusions like a fat zipper that ran from my neck to my pubic zone, like the stitches of a cardiac case showing traces of her open heart. Above it dangled my face. I sighed. I was sixteen and looked exactly like Woody Allen—in his later years. *Mirror, mirror on the wall: you suck.* When I'd bought it at Le Château the weekend before it had seemed sexy, Madonna Vogue-slick with its big geometry and bold, defined oppositions. But now, I feared, it made me look curvy like a ruler. Conspicuous among all the jeans and T-shirts, it looked less come-hither and more Pierrot-the-mime.

How could you be sixteen and still never have had a proper boy-friend? Never even kissed a boy? Go forth and smooch!

I turned off the faucet and put my hand on the doorknob, taking a deep breath. I was reminded of my first party three years earlier, that Mötley Crüe night, bespectacled Stu, who looked like an accountant, even at age twelve. *Go, Judy! Pull out your moves!*

I turned sideways, released my leg, pretended to karate kick the wall. The toilet roll holder crashed to the ground.

After attempts to reaffix it, I opened the door, but kept my breath in as I slowly walked downstairs to where the cool kids were hanging out, each step taking ages, hoping this very action would consume most of the time of the party. It didn't. In the basement I immediately saw Victor sitting on the couch. My stomach flipped. In a blue shirt and jeans, he looked fresh, strong, affectionate, perfect. He had a round boyish face, but an older-man sensibility, someone who appreciated a witty line, a bout of repartee. I remembered how two years earlier at a bar mitzvah, he pulled me into his lap, set my torso between his outstretched arms, and for a moment, I'd felt completely enveloped, calm, like the melted cheese inside a sandwich.

I'd jumped off.

Now I walked to the other end of the room and tried to join a conversation that Olivia was taking part in about the sourcing of wine coolers. I pulled down my shirt, ran my fingers through too-frizzy hair, crossed and recrossed my arms. It was going to be a long night. A long life. I looked around at well-lined bookcases, built-ins, and a displayed menorah collection: Jen's parents were marijuana-smoking ex-hippies and even *their* house was clean. I donned neat geometry and was still a mess, an extra puzzle piece that slotted into no picture. And yet. I couldn't help but glance back at Victor, just to catch a glimpse of his green eyes.

But in the midst of my glance, Victor looked back. I froze. He smiled. *Smiled.* His perfect smile. I flushed with heat. Finally, here was my chance, my dream of closeness, possibility. My fantasy.

So I ran.

I jetted upstairs, darted past the sofa, the kitchen, the people smoking cigarettes on the front porch. I ducked behind cars, sprinted my way down the street, through the Côte Saint-Luc underpass, all the way along Guelph Avenue, all the way home. Straight to my mother's kitchen.

I STOOD ON a half-broken chair that I'd leaned against the cupboard door, itself coming off at the rusted hinges, frantically throwing boxes of ancient cereal. They tumbled from top shelf to the floor. The bran flakes, the same consistency as their cardboard box, were already too soft, too broken to crack anymore. My trembling hands worked quickly but carefully, avoiding any wildlife hiding out between containers of prunes. *I hate mice,* I seethed while furiously jetting pancake mix into a trash bag. Streaks of brown dripped down its sides. *I hate liquid, I hate anything insidious, that slips through cracks, has no boundaries, no consideration.* I shook, hot all over, and heaved baking sodas and Kraft Dinners, trying to scrub off the shame, to bust the blocks that stalled me.

Then, I started on the moldering tuna cans. They were stacked on the shelf like a barrack, the same formation as the cans on the kitchen counter, which functioned as a real barrier, the albacore guard (the alba-corps) blocking the sink-to-table path, hijacking family conversations, easing altercations. I threw: *can can can you do the can can can.* The window was open; cans fell to the floor with light thumps, as if they encountered less gravity than usual, softened by the breeze, like fish falling through water. *Can can can.* Clover Leaf—the brand of good luck. There were so many. No wonder tuna was going extinct.

I flung and flung, dismantling, deconstructing. *Victor smiled.* Throwing, tossing, pitching, lobbing, launching. *I had to get rid of the mess. Clean up. Become beautiful.*

I knew I had only an hour before my parents came back from their friends' anniversary party. It was so rare, the nights the two of them had an invitation, went out together, like a couple. They *were* a couple, it reminded them, it reminded me. Mom had had her wiry hair dyed auburn. She'd sprayed on her Poison. It had followed her through the halls like a veil.

Mom might even be in a good mood, I thought, which could help.

I used both arms now, like a wild baseball pitcher, waving, sweat trickling down my sides, another, another, watching as the cans formed neat arcs in midair, pausing for a micromoment at the top point, the apex of the sine curve—an infinitesimal point, yet the most important of all, marking the turnaround.

To be looked at—all I wanted, and yet, I could not handle it.

I was stuck, unable to move, afraid to become. *It wasn't a real going out.* Nothing was changing. Just more and more stuff.

For a second, I stopped and stared at the can in my hand as if it had an answer, as if it could explain to me what it had been doing stashed in my kitchen for decades. Its aluminum was green along its edges, and I wondered which way the rotting worked. Had the mold moved from the tuna to the can, or did it spread from the can to the tuna? Or worse, had it come from me, from us? Were we contaminating our own surrounds?

Then I slung a sack of rice, and it rained like confetti, a wedding across my kitchen.

MOM WALKED IN.

"What the hell is going on here? It's not your kitchen." Her exaggerated sibilant sounds, markers of her foreigner status, her refugee narrative, peppering her otherwise impeccable English, shrill on answering machine recordings, now rang out like shots.

"I'm just trying to help."

"I didn't ask for your help." Her eyes darted like laser beams, examining my treason. Her face jutted side to side to side. She swooped down to my pile on the floor, grabbed handfuls of old chocolate chip packages and flung them to the counter. "What are you doing to me?" she shrieked. "Why are you doing this?"

She made me pick it all out of the garbage, every limp cereal flake. Every grain of insect-infested flour, the dead bugs occasionally alive, crawling up my arm, along the ridges of the too-tight shirt.

She went to her room. Closed the door.

Dad was in the den. He read the newspaper.

His chair faced a cheap credenza that was falling apart, its shelves losing shape from the weight of books, 1970s Judaica, but also Dad's freebies from drug companies: polyp stationery, fuzzy hemoglobin molecules, a squishy plastic spine, bendable, collapsing. Literal skeletons were part of the closet's skeletons. His mess was growing inside her walls of scrap. *Dad?*

Afterward, I sat down at the kitchen table and opened a bag of challah. I brought the entire loaf to my mouth, my teeth sinking into its soft interior, losing themselves in its sea of sweetness. Just one more bite . . . How could I feel so empty with all this stuff? What would satisfy my ancestral cavity? I looked down at my expanding shirt and saw the opposing black and white pieces breaking apart from one another, the whole puzzle exploding. I remembered learning in first-aid class that if you rubbed a person's sternum, you could rouse them into consciousness. I rubbed and rubbed along the zipper pattern until my knuckles were numb.

I looked around my kitchen at the piles of ancient oatmeal and rotting fruit, into the dark hallway lined with laundry baskets overflowing with dirty bargains, racing to infinity. If there was one thing I'd learnt over and over, including that night, it was how to run.

I knew I had to leave.

2ND TRIMESTER:

Living Rooms

•══════•

· SIX ·

20 WEEKS: FLIPPING OUT OF MY MIND
New York City, 2011

"This fetus flipping." The Russian technician sighed as she jabbed the ultrasound camera deeper into my gut. "Flipping here, flipping there, always flipping. How much coffee you have in morning?"

"Only half a cup," I answered.

The truth was: one cup.

The truth was: two cups. And large ones. "Is everything OK? Healthy? Normal?" I motormouthed. "What are its percentiles? Anything I need to know? Deviations from the standard?" Coffee complemented my current hyper mood.

"Fine."

The horrific physical transformation of the first trimester—a new stomach above my old one, breasts like weapons, falling asleep at lunch and waking up in the middle of the night with cramping that terrorized me—curtailed much of my thinking, which seemed a clever evolutionary strategy. That fuzzy and low period was sharply followed by second trimester hormones: the mania. Suddenly, my acne was replaced with youthful glow and the exhaustion, with vigor. Now, at my halfway mark, I was starting to feel like I could actually do this. Be pregnant. Grow a person. Hell, like I could do anything! Plus, now my bump was clearly a fetus tent rather than just pudge, and lately people could not refrain from telling me how wonderfully cute I looked, even catcalling me at subway entrances. I hadn't felt so attractive, so seen, in years. And certainly not as seen as right now, with my fallopians in high res.

To think my mother was the first generation in her peasant family to grow up with photographs of her past, to even know what some of her ancestors looked like, and here I was about to see my baby in utero. "Do you think prenatal imaging has an impact on the maternal-fetal bond?" I chirped on. "Does technology reflect psychology or create it?"

The technician sloshed a glob of freezing-cold gel across my stomach. "You want know gender?"

I nodded. Jon grabbed my hand.

"Is girl."

"Brilliant!" Jon said, squeezing my fingers.

I felt a wash of relief. I understood girls, and they were calmer, and could come with me to the nail salon. Mom had kept my baby clothes, of course—I could dress her in my flammable polyester overalls!

The technician reclined the table, nearly turned me upside down, jabbed me from the other side and gave me a short tour: "Is kidney, is other kidney, is face."

And there, on the screen in front of me was a full-fledged profile, a Victorian silhouette of my genetic matter—cheruby round cheeks and a button nose. A little Aryan. She sucked her thumb.

I wiped a tear that trickled, warm, down to my ear.

"You're going to be a horrible pushover," I semijoked to Jon later as we walked along the quiet Upper East Side street back to the subway. "I'm vomiting just picturing your total lack of discipline."

"What about you?" Jon teased. "You're going to dress her exactly like you. You'll go crazy when she doesn't share your taste. You'll be a totally annoying mom-of-a-girl."

Mom of a girl. My daughter. Daughter. An odd word with its

hidden "gh," mysterious, Celtic, ancient, primitive. Suddenly, my fingers felt clammy and I nearly dropped the printout I'd been clutching. I flashed to the image: she was real, in me, a girl like me but a whole other person. She sucked her thumb. Not its. Hers.

All the pregnancy books I'd read dwelt on fears—the mucus plug, bleeding nipples, the fact that bikini season may have ended, forever. But I was afraid of more: having my life sliced open. My interior was threatened in every sense. It had taken me so long to grow up. I'd only just begun to pursue a writing career. I needed more time on my own to take care of myself and achieve my goals before smothering someone else, before having to worry about *yet another* person.

I stopped and sank to the ground. Other women prayed and suffered for this, I chastised myself; I was living their dream.

"What's wrong?" Jon swooped down beside me. "Are you sick?"

"Don't know," I said and thought: *You cannot run away from being a parent. Ever.*

VERITAS
Cambridge, 1996

Our car pulled up to the sign marked FRESHMAN REGISTRATION PARKING and my stomach swirled. I was here! At Harvard. In America. I was leaving Canada, Montreal, my parents' home. I was leaving home.

"That way, Dad," I instructed from the backseat, but as he turned to see a jam of cars with furniture legs oozing out of their windows, I could hear him huff. Again. *All this money and look what I get.* Even though I was running away—not to be a parking-lot psychic at Phish concerts but to the global center of academic rigor—it was still a rebellion. I'd sensed right away: I was betraying him, betraying them. Leaving the overly full nest, which did not want to be emptied. Almost no one in Montreal went away to college; local university was good, and free. It was Mom who played Moses, convincing

Dad to let me go. I liked to think, on some level, she knew I needed to be freed.

And freed I was! I ignored the malaise in the minivan (which Dad had rented, and whose price I was never to hear the end of) and declared, "I'm getting out."

I hopped from the car and bounded my way to the Yard, the archetypal site of world-class learning with its grand golden-and-maroon Veritas statues and slogans. I was not a tourist or a visitor. I was a *resident*. I bounced my way to the welcome tent to pick up my orientation package. "Batalion," I declared loudly, seeing *my family name* typed in a stylish, intellectual font on an official manila envelope. Inside, I found my new address. Weld Hall. Former home of several political oligarchs. Kildare to Kennedy . . . I nearly fainted with excitement. I grounded myself by looking around: buzzing students, laughing parents, siblings dragging boxes and bins. I recognized no one. New people, brand-new potential. Butterflies inside all of me. Pretty ones, though. I'd make friends here, fit in at last. Belonging, I sensed, would just happen. If *I* could be here now, heading to my dynastic dorm, magic was possible.

I made my way to the parking area and saw my family approaching with bits of luggage and horribly awkward oversize skin-cancer-defying sun hats, but I didn't care. "Let's go see my room!" They trudged along behind me as I followed a map and led this incredible expedition. A few days earlier, I'd taken a subway to Mount Royal, an artsy neighborhood of Montreal, where on a whim I had a hip hairdresser dye bright purple streaks in my hair. I'd never before colored any part of myself, and suddenly, I sported punk. Now I was wearing Mom's green polyester bell-bottoms from the 1970s and a purple tank top. My new New Balance sneakers felt like platform shoes; their air soles made me feel like I was coasting over the earth.

I arrived, family behind, to find Victoria, one of my roommates, standing in the living room. She was thin with long blond hair, but was my exact height and wearing black bell-bottoms and a pink ribbed tank top. "We're twins," she said, laughing. Victoria and I had spoken on the phone the week before. She played guitar, was a painter. Loved Ani DiFranco. So cool. "You and I are sharing a bedroom."

I peeked into our room: a long, rectangular one, newly renovated, with blond-wood furniture, extra high beds, the delicious smell of fresh paint. Victoria, who'd arrived from California, had already unpacked. I eyed her magazine centerfold space: her bookshelf was filled with colorful hardbacks and trinkets. Her pale blue–checkered sheets were tucked in perfectly. Her slightly open drawers bulged with piles of warm sweaters. I wanted to crawl into her bed, into her knack for design.

Dad and Eli helped me with the rest of my luggage—which I now realized was hardly anything compared to the others whose rooms had carpets, fridges, large-scale hair-grooming appliances. "We should check into our guesthouse," Dad said.

"OK." I scribbled *my* phone number on a ripped sheet of packing paper.

"We'll call you when we're ready for dinner," Mom said. I waved as they shuffled out my door.

And there I was, solo, in my new existence, my new incarnation. I thought of Bubbie and how, despite her increasing confusion, she was still so proud of me. *From Chelm to Charvard, my Judaleh,* she'd said. I'd made it.

Victoria, who'd stepped out, now returned with bags from local faux-hippie markets, colorful mugs and overpriced tchotchkes peeking from their tops. She dropped them on her small blue rug, comfortable with her own little mess. "My family's waiting downstairs. We're going out for an early dinner. Want to come?"

"Thanks, but my parents will be back soon." I said, noting the browning New England skyline.

"OK, see you later." In one graceful swoop, she grabbed a sweater and keys (our keys!) and headed out the door (our door!). Our other roommates also hadn't returned from family outings, and so, to the buttery sunset—one I'd never experienced from this particular angle, illuminating my belongings and belonging in this way—I unpacked my minimalist stash. I placed clothes in my closet: they barely took up half the space. My shoes stood at attention, lined neatly under my bed. My gray Mac slotted onto the desk and my science books for my premed classes fit into one small area of my bookshelf, each spine straight. Open, neat, dustless, clutterless.

I breathed.

I sat down and went through the rest of the papers in the orientation envelope, skimming pages about test schedules, student clubs, and the visiting chef series. I heard loud laughter spiking in from the Yard outside, and looked at my small digital clock (a plain white one from Mom's stash). It had been nearly three hours since my parents had left. I assumed there'd be traffic and maybe naps, but it was seriously getting late. Too late for the early-bird specials I was sure Mom had staked out from the car.

I checked that the phone was working. I didn't know the number of the bed-and-breakfast they'd booked, so I called Dad's beeper, but it had been turned off because he was in a different country. I tried my home number, even Uncle Moishe. No answers.

Not knowing what to do, I wandered through our suite, then once again examined Victoria's nest, seeking solace. But, as the day darkened and shadows grew, her interior masterpiece began to taunt me. She'd hung a red-and-yellow Keith Haring print above her desk—how did she know how to do that? Her own charcoal artwork, thick bold marks, stood on an easel.

My side, I saw, did not match, and in the harsh fluorescent light, suddenly seemed eerily empty. The plaid sheets that I'd bought on sale were neat on my bed, my pens lined up in a drawer, each item curated by me, and yet. The look wasn't right. My space didn't seem comforting but unbalanced and awkward. It hit me: belonging didn't *just happen*.

How would I do this? What would we talk about? How did normal living arrangements work?

And where the hell was my family?

My stomach rumbled.

The phone's silence blared. I paced, stopped myself from imagining car accidents and armed robberies, random murders in crazy strangers' homes. I didn't want to miss my parents' call, but couldn't bear to be trapped in the room alone any longer.

Outside, the Yard was dark and filled with families wandering in pride and with purpose. I wished I could step into pace with one of them, saunter into their happy conversation as they headed for Herrell's famous ice cream. Instead, I sprinted, leaving the enclosure, crossing Mass Ave, stopping at a deli where I ordered a tuna wrap. I fumbled for the American change I'd had in my pocket, and then, not knowing what else to do, feeling unhinged to anything at all, ran back to Weld. Victoria was in the lobby.

"How was your dinner?" she asked, as I hid the sandwich behind my back.

"Good, you?" I deflected. "Where did you go?"

I wanted to both rush to our room and to stall so she wouldn't see my side, which was complete and yet had not even begun.

She talked about the upscale hotel restaurant her parents had taken her to, how they'd allowed her to have a glass of wine. I couldn't even locate my tap-water-only clan.

"We just went to a diner, casual," I said, nonchalant as we walked into our bedroom. My family had literally disappeared, as if they'd been delusions, apparitions in my younger mind. No one would see them. No one would know about the Tetris-puzzle of cobwebbed credenzas, the secrets stuffed between tins of baked beans. I could make up any backstory I wanted—any revisionist, minimalist, conventional history. I was a champion at hiding. I realized: I could conceal my whole life.

The other roommates were back. We sat in our living room and talked about where we came from, introducing fragments and versions of ourselves to our new families. *Montreal, music, science.* I half participated, listening for a ring that never came.

Finally, after midnight, I grabbed the portable phone and headed for the farthest corner near the window. On instinct, I dialed Kildare.

My mother answered.

"Where are you?" I hissed, my worry madly flipping to relief and then anger.

"Sorry, honey," Mom said. "The hotel wasn't very nice. Dad said it was easier if we drove home."

Why didn't you tell me? I wanted to shout, but saw my three normal-looking roommates smoking cigarettes and laughing on the futon. Plus, I sensed the answer. *Served me right. I had left. I would be left.*

"OK, great," I said, chipper, so everyone could hear, muffling the sense that I was floating free fall in the universe. I stroked my violet bangs, my new costume, reminding myself that I was in America, land of the free refills, endless opportunity. That this was my chance to create a new life. This was what I wanted, why I came. I pushed all my guilt aside, right up into my dark roots. "Good night."

And so began my search for home.

By SOPHOMORE YEAR, I'd figured out a few things. Victoria and I now had a suite to ourselves, and though we still shared a bedroom, our living room was a quirky nineteenth-century space with slanted ceilings and large sash windows. I'd purchased a set of green glass wine goblets, their long stems and bold color reflecting my dream elegance, my dream body; my matryoshka frog dolls lined up along my bookshelf showing my quirky, cultural side. When people came over I offered them black cigarettes, blue cheese, and white wine, hoping I'd pulled off a veneer of ultrasophistication, suppressing niggling worries that they thought my prized flutes tacky and transparent, that I was a poseur. "Welcome to the Shitz Carlton."

My intense amount of frantic, all-night biochemistry study (getting As at Jewish school in Montreal was less tricky than among the math minds at Harvard) had led to a dramatic decrease in my sight. While at first I'd been appalled to hear I needed glasses—lord, *more* nerdy—when I adorned my face with tiny wire-framed circles, I marveled at my new clarity of vision (each leaf was a masterpiece!) and self-vision. The caramel color leather jacket I'd once bought at a vintage market now fit perfectly. I walked into an elite Cambridge hairdresser and he immediately took a scissor and chopped across my mane: I exited the salon with a bright red gamine cut.

To match my new look, and complement my growing exasperation with science midterms, I'd enrolled in seminars in European intellectual history and the influence of primitivism in post-Victorian experimental novels. I raised my hand fiercely, unable to contain my newfound opinions, completely unaware of intellectual trends.

Until Peter. "I liked it that you unabashedly defended first-wave feminism," he said, sidling up to me as I left the archetypal red-brown humanities building. "It's refreshing that you speak with such passion about nontheoretical gender concerns."

I hadn't particularly noticed Peter, a senior, an urban intellectual with large framed glasses, slow speech, understated confidence. *Everyone* agreed with Peter. Miles out of my league. But now that he'd noticed me, I perked up. "Thanks," I said, not sure what else to say, not sure if he was being serious or sarcastic, flirting or just making chat.

He e-mailed me that night asking if I wanted to have lunch with him.

Peter. It was as if I'd skipped all the high school boyfriend steps and was now being courted by the sovereign crush, the grand prize! For a week, I daydreamed about our initial meeting, how he'd relay his deepest affections for me; I rehearsed all my ideas about nontheoretical gender. And some theoretical ones too.

At that lunch, for which I wore a skirt (I *never* wore skirts—first wave?) I grabbed only a salad, not sure how I'd even fit a confetti strand of carrot beneath my beating chest. But, within minutes, he tactically mentioned that his girlfriend might stop by to say hi. But, in the same breath, he added: "Not that I'm sure she'll be my girlfriend for long." I was crushed that my crush had another crush, but also, filled with hopes and dreams for us in the future, for a life in which I could be loved by this charismatic, hip brainiac who was from a family of notable scholars—the rock stars of Cambridge. His inability to fall madly in love with me *tout de suite* was actually reassuring. I found it nerve-racking enough to be having a meal with him, us sitting opposite each other like two bespectacled weights on an oak balance—I wasn't sure how I'd handle more.

We continued to meet for lunch every week or two, in between which I spent hours analyzing our e-mails, preening myself and fashioning my wardrobe (would Peter find my coat artistic?) just in case we happened to see each other on the street. *Peter*, who analyzed our interaction as we were having it, who was tall and had long curly hair and eyes that drank me in, making me feel like I was floating between worlds, outside time, inside his mind. Like many people at Harvard, he had strong philosophies for every situation, which seemed thought-through in ways I just couldn't—I didn't have strong belief systems, set ways of seeing, honed over years and generations.

"Where are you going?" Victoria asked one Tuesday as I sprayed on perfume.

"Just lunch with someone in my class," I said, shutting the door quickly behind me. I never confessed my crushes, knowing how unlikely it was they'd ever be reciprocated. I tried not to dream directly about what I wanted, fearing I would jinx it from ever happening.

I'd just returned from a Passover trip to Montreal, where I still went for all holidays, a magnet to family guilt, but also, secretly hoping that somehow my refreshed world would change the one I was from. It hadn't. I used to love Passover in part because we'd scrub our kitchen, throw away old bread, and for eight days, use only a small number of clear, glass Pesach dishes; now, the counter was lined with four different sets of kosher crockery, extra blenders, juicers, infusers we'd never open. Even our seder had become more dramatic than usual, Mom exploding at the table when she felt she'd been left out of a blessing, then storming off and shutting herself in her room. Dad, Eli, and I had stared at one another blankly. Eli went to coax her back. She didn't come. We finished the seder to the background sound of a shrill laugh-track emanating from her TV.

Back in Boston, however, I was feeling good, able to put my past in my pocket, excited for a new spring and the touch-up to my hairdo.

I held my stomach in as I brought my tray to the long wooden table in my all-wooden dining hall that always smelled of syrup. Peter was already seated, his perfect portions awaiting him. His still-girlfriend, I'd spied a few weeks earlier at the library, was also perfectly composed, blond and skinny.

He glanced at my tray. "Why are you vegetarian?"

"Animal eth—," I started to say, but his piercing stare, his rigorous academic investigation of me and my values, threw me off. I knew he wouldn't buy it. And he was right. The truth—which Peter's intensity enabled me to admit to myself—was that I was a vegetarian because we were the only kosher family at my grammar school. Instead of eating hot dogs at parties, I'd feigned a dedication to pasta and bean burgers, too embarrassed to add another odd difference to my list. "I, I," I stammered. "I don't know."

He leaned over, his energy field close, pulling me in, away from myself. What else would he uncover about me, for me? I wondered what worlds he might lead me into.

AFTER LUNCH, FULL of pasta and empty of purpose, I headed upstairs to my room where the answering machine flashed. My roommates had gotten used to Mom's messages and I'd gotten used to them being public tender. In fact, I'd turned them into shtick for my dinnertime comic monologues ("Judy—don't sit at the FRONT of the plane." "Judy—NEVER use petroleum-based lip salve"). I made her out to be "Jewish mother gone wild." It was almost true, a version of the real story: she was wild, just not as funny. But this time was different.

Bubbie had died.

Bubbie.

I staggered back to the futon, flailed down, held my head. I'd just seen Bubbie two days earlier at her nursing home. She'd been in bed, weak, her cheeks denting inward, clinging to her jaws. We'd hugged and kissed, she'd cackled loudly when she saw me, so happy I was visiting from Charvard. "Zelda, Zelda," she kept calling me, and I laughed, touched. "Bubbie, that's your name, not mine." I'd held her hands. Her bare fingers, which had killed bees, picked me up from ballet, clutched family photos while she ran from Nazis, were still delicate and curved, her nails oval and soft. And now her fingers were gone. The most solid, conspicuous presence of my life was suddenly the most elusive. I made two fists, felt my own pudgy digits grasp onto nothing but themselves.

Hours later, I was back at Kildare, hugging Mom, Eli on her other side. For the first time in years, the three of us pushed aside papers, sat on the end of her bed.

"I just want to be with my kids," Mom gasped between cries. We held on tight, her body so warm, shaking. *What would Mom do now with all her time? Who would she take care of? Me?* I questioned, but then chastised myself for my selfishness at such a horrible time.

MY LITTLE BROTHER, already sixteen, stood up on the pulpit, delivering a speech that was so eloquent and quirky, moving and humorous, I couldn't believe he'd written it in a day. I wished I'd done the same thing. The crowd of mourners laughed.

Mom grabbed my hand. "It's not funny," she hissed. "Not everything is funny." She was livid, her eyes shooting venom.

I was at first shocked. Didn't she feel proud of her son? But I also understood. She needed to experience this loss in a different way. She'd spent years caring for Bubbie full-time, every single day. Not everything was funny. "It's OK, Mom." I put my arm around her. "Bubbie was a character, she would have loved to be remembered like this."

Mom shot the venom my way. I turned, tried to ignore it.

"That was amazing," I whispered to Eli when he returned to his seat. Then I listened to the rabbi speak about Bubbie's life, how she'd escaped the Nazis, how she worked through Siberia, gave birth to my mother, gave birth to another girl who died in infancy, tried to set up a new life in Poland, Israel, Canada. This was my family story, not unlike many of the others from my Montreal shtetl.

I ran my hand through my short red hair and thought of Peter, of friends at Harvard, people who were not Jewish at all, who did not have families who survived the Holocaust (not everyone had survived the Holocaust! Or perished in it either), people who would never assume a refugee background was a normal backstory. For the first time, I saw my story through their eyes and noticed that it was unique, damaging, so much to deal with. My arm was still around Mom's shoulder and I turned to her, examined her profile, its bumpy contours, her round, reddened cheeks heaving with her breath. There was a specific history to my family, a key to its guts. Mom's childhood was precarious, slippery. Torture and fear were packed into her sharply slitted eyes. I imagined her fugitive life, the chemicals that made up her jagged elemental bonds. I saw how my family had run away, which had saved them, and ruined them.

"So," THE PROFESSOR said, as if slowly sipping in this new information. "Victorian interior design." He repeated my field of study, assessing its worth and interest to him as if I was presenting fine jewels. He sat back in his swivel chair that reclined to touch a bookcase. Everywhere, there was a bookcase, stocked with the latest edition of his five-hundred-page masterpiece on the history of measuring tools. *Riveting,* I'd said, when I walked in, hoping it sounded genuine, desperate for a mentor to take hold of me, guide me onto a track.

"I'm studying the way that scientific color theories influenced design," I explained, each word rehearsed but wobbly as I pitched my thesis idea. "That's why nineteenth-century design is so ugly—to contemporary aesthetic sensibility, that is. Can science affect taste?"

I was new at this humanities spiel. I'd dropped out of premed. Competing with Harvard whiz kids had only gotten harder. The more I studied, the worse I did. A teaching fellow had chased me down hallways, cackling wildly, "You got the worst score of anyone I ever saw!" My entire self-concept—the numbers geek, the A student—imploded. Science no longer offered absolute answers, order plotted along neat graphs. Everything I'd excelled at was slipping from me, electrons leaking from my soul.

Plus, Peter had a new girlfriend. Not blond, not even that skinny. It could have been me, but it wasn't. When I found out, my head spun with incomprehension. I'd been so close; what had I done wrong? Said wrong? I desperately needed to *ace* something.

I wanted to win the thesis prize, to prove to myself, to Mom and Dad, to Peter, that Harvard was the right choice, that I really was an intellectual. I'd transferred to the history of science department and enrolled in courses on the architecture of laboratories, studying how spaces created the knowledge made inside them, and seminars on early twentieth-century color theory. That's when I came across British Victorian interior design: rooms filled with garish primary colors, heavy carpeting, wall hangings, flowers in glasses; chambers drenched in patterns, objects, collections. Trying to live 1990s slick, I became obsessed with 1880s shtick. Why did those Victorians love to collect? How could their tastes be so off, how could they not see the ugliness they were creating around them? "Can chemistry create a language for subjectivity?" I added, to sound particularly theoretical.

Professor Halstead was quiet for a moment, ferociously studying his pen cap. While the rest of the campus was covered in ornate, antique woodwork, my major was housed in the Science Center, a 1970s concrete building that apparently, from the sky, looked like a giant Polaroid camera. I imagined an enormous image of our meeting would slowly ooze out of the basement.

"There was a piece!" he declared. I jumped in my seat.

"A piece?" I repeated.

"Enlightenment!"

"Enlightenment."

"Academic Journal of Popular Culture."

I scribbled vigorously.

"On Shrewsbury!"

"Shrewsbury." Shrewsbury? I had no clue what he was talking about.

I pulled my sweater down, covering my upper thighs. I'd flunked both the biochemistry of proteins, and skinniness. All my latest attempts to diet, to excel, backfired, making me feel less in control and snowballing into more panic for success. I'd taken on too many jobs and classes, working through nights; even my room was a mess of books about extreme Victorian ornamentation. I clambered to crest, but kept getting submerged in the wave. Like Mom, I thought, recalling her latest phone calls, frantic rants about money, her inheritance, Bubbie's houses. Eli had moved to the basement of Kildare, into a room next to Dad's, and his former bedroom was now locked with a key that only Mom held. That sealed room had become a giant office storage closet with dozens of calculators, a hundred binders, a thousand pencils and pens—masses of new school supplies that, I couldn't help but think, I was never allowed to have as a child. Mom was working around the clock—reviewing documents, crunching numbers, her brain buzzing, reminding me of when she used to teach chess at the Y on Sunday mornings, gently coaching minigeniuses among the scents of chlorine and kosher French fries, planning every move.

"I know!" The professor jerked up, slamming his hand on the mahogany desk. "You should write about British asylums. Victorian asylums! The asylum as home. The home as asylum!" He scribbled madly, as if this was his project now.

Then again, the home as asylum—who could write about that better than me?

"British asylums," I mumbled as I jotted words on my page. And then it hit me: Boston wasn't far enough. My family was so complex, I was still too close to them, suffocated even here. To become independent, to fashion a new svelte self, to gain control and calm, to find my true home, I needed to go farther.

· SEVEN ·

22 WEEKS: HEADING SOUTH
Antigua, 2011

"This is a-MAZ-ing," I said as the valet escorted us to our room. The lounge was built over a pond; a splash-shaped aquamarine swimming pool hosted lazy tea-slurping loungers; narrow paths through lush trees connected health, fitness, and spa cabanas. Everything was perched on the edge of a pristinely turquoise bay. "We're so lucky." Jon and I had both been looking forward to this dream vacay for weeks. We'd decided that, for our last chance at travel (ever?) we'd literally splash out, participate in ten days of luxurious, postcard, aquatic silence. Antigua, less touristed than other Caribbean islands, seemed like an idyllic spot for our final patch of calm before the offspring storm.

Travel, in all its hecticness, had always soothed me. When Bubbie dashed with me in my stroller between preschool and dance class, I called her "my airplane"; the clicking of that seat belt has since been my most exhilarating sound. Flying promised somewhere new and exciting, a place where you didn't have to answer e-mails or questions except "chicken or beef?", the ability to read with good light and coffee delivered to your seat, a host of on-demand movies starring Adam Sandler that you'd never pay to see but always kind of wanted to. Flying (emphasis on lying?) meant you were suspended between realities, free from time or currency constraints, eating extra meals, touching strangers. I never had a fear of flying! What scared me was landing, where you had to declare who you are, what you do, where you're coming from.

Even my family holidays had always been a pleasant reprieve. Every summer we'd drive to Vermont, the air sweet and soft like maple syrup on my cheeks. We'd stay in motels and, for a few hours, our unpacked room was neat and sparse, smelling of pine, teasing me with the false hope that life could be otherwise. The sheets were starched white, and I'd fall asleep next to Mom, not even a novel between us, listening to the Eurythmics on my yellow Sony Walkman. *Sweet dreams are made of this.* In college, when I felt lost, I got lost professionally. I had a freelance job writing for a guidebook, literally finding my way. If I launched myself into exile, I could perhaps learn to control the sentiment. I was most at peace when my constant feeling of being foreign was actually true.

But not this time. Unfortunately a different storm had begun earlier that morning at JFK when I was overwhelmed by nausea. Pregnancy, I'd thought: this too shall pass. So far it hadn't. We reached the beach chalet only to realize that I had to climb a flight of stairs to get to our room. "I'm not sure I can do this," I whispered to Jon, scared at how weak I felt—the weakest in my pregnancy so far. He supported me as I slowly made my way up to the water-view suite, trying to focus on the rhythmic sound of ocean waves, the soundtrack I'd so been longing for.

"It'll pass soon," I said, lying down for a nap. But waking twenty minutes later with cramps, I took my temperature. Fever. I knew: this was bad. Colitis strikes again. Over the past weeks, I'd spent days carefully trekking to surgeons in state-of-the-art facilities to find one who was both a world specialist in my irregular abdominal anatomy and available at the exact scheduled time of my C-section so he could assist my OB. Up to now, I'd been completely fine. But, thousands of miles away on a random tropical island, voilà.

I stayed in bed, glimpsing the oceanic horizon and blush sunset above my fresh, fluffy duvet as Jon went to explore. He returned with Gatorades, compliments of the fitness club, and the good news that the hotel manager had arranged for a cab to take me to the local emergency room, just to confirm that this was a simple stomach flu. Jon and I grabbed the drinks and a few gift bananas and made it to the car, which, as I feared, headed back along the same exceptionally winding road from the airport. The driver progressed at approximately one mile per hour; Jon requested slightly more speed. "I don't want to rattle the baby," he kept saying, as I kept nearly vomiting into the lush green night.

The trajectory along this "highway," set along mountainous paths and junglelike verdure, had no cell reception, or at least not for more than several consecutive seconds; Jon found it impossible to reach any doctors—in NY, London, even Canada. "And now, a news report about the large number of deaths due to negligence at the Saint John hospital," blared through the radio speakers. Jon and I both froze and stared at each other. Especially when, less than a minute later, we arrived at that very place. Our driver dropped us off at the emergency room door, and told us he'd wait outside.

We entered the ER and were met by at least a hundred silent stares. Unlike everyone else waiting for a doctor, we were clearly flummoxed tourists. We noted a desk and a man standing behind it—with a machine gun strapped across his back. I nudged Jon. "Is this where we check in?" he meekly asked.

The man nodded. I wrote my name down. There were no seats. Everyone stared.

"I need to go to the bathroom," I whispered and Jon and I inched toward a bathroomy-looking chamber. It was strewn with toilet paper, liquids, even blood.

"No hospitality basket?" I said, and then: "Let's get out of here." We swiftly headed right back out the door we'd come in.

We stepped quickly through the busy parking lot scanning for a car that resembled the white minivan that had brought us, only to find they all did.

"Here!" a man called and waved us over. Was it even our driver? I cramped in pain, or anxiety.

"I've talked to people," he said. Calls were coming in to his various wireless devices that were blessed with suspect amounts of reception. "I have ideas for where to take you," he said, not even asking why we'd walked straight out.

"I have to go to the bathroom," I said, pangs thrashing across my stomach.

He gestured to the front of the hospital, the main entrance. Jon and I went in—it was quiet—and tried to explain to another guard (smaller gun) that we needed help. He shrugged. At least he pointed me to a restroom that less resembled a crime scene.

By the time we were back in the car, the entire country of Antigua knew of my predicament, and the driver's phone was ringing off the hook, if hooks still existed. "I'm taking you to a maternity hospital," he announced, which sounded promising, but the next thing we knew our car was headed along tiny dirt paths, running through gangs of boys loitering on fences, inches away from our windows, staring inside. "Drive faster," Jon reminded the driver when we nearly sheared the side of a meandering cow.

The maternity hospital was a pink bungalow in a field in the middle of more fields. The driver parked on a muddy patch near the gate. I hobbled in and tried to explain to a nurse that I had a stomach flu and a history of abdominal surgery, but as the medical jargon gushed from my trembling lips, I could tell I was addressing the wrong audience. She looked at me kindly and said, "If you're not giving birth right this second, there's nothing we can do. Good night."

"Take us back to the hotel, please," I begged the driver.

"OK," he said. "But just one more place—a drugstore. It's on the way!"

Another twenty-minute drive, this time through nearly pitch-black surrounds, found us at a mall that was closed for the night.

"Seriously. Hotel."

At last, I fell asleep, feverish, on my billion thread-count sheets, praying I'd be better after a rest.

. . .

THE NEXT MORNING, the manager told us he'd arranged for Antigua's hotel doctor to stop by ASAP, which turned out to be three p.m. The physician was certainly friendly, jovially reporting on his other tourist patients who were losing limbs by the minute, explaining that he was having trouble locating his syringes because his three-year-old son enjoyed rummaging through his bag, and continually taking calls while trying to draw blood, finally forcing Jon to threaten that if he didn't focus on my veins Jon would throw his phone into the ocean. The chuckling doctor happily agreed to silence his cell, and spent a long time relaying how there was only one lab on the island and it shut at four p.m. *So stop chatting and start blood letting!* I wanted to cry.

Fortunately, he texted us to say he'd made it with my specimens in time. "I'll be back tonight." At nine p.m., when I still had not eaten and was watching reruns of Anthony Bourdain (which I'd seen for the first time only that morning) he jauntily knocked on the door. "Infection, dehydration," he happily announced. Then asked: "Do you have Internet?"

"Um, yeah," Jon responded, flipping open his laptop.

"Google is great," Doctor Internet, as we would now call him, exclaimed. "I like to check with both British and American associations to see what drugs to give during pregnancy. Also, I'll need to give you IV fluids."

An IV? I prayed he wasn't Googling how to do that.

Finally, Jon made contact with doctors abroad who said fluids wouldn't hurt. But the needle will, I thought, scared by the image of a rusty point niggling through my tired skin, injecting unknown liquids into my inner tubes.

Too bad Dr. I. hadn't brought an IV stand. "Some hotels have suit racks I can use! I'll get a nurse. Be back soon."

At eleven p.m. he arrived with one; the nurse spent an hour standing and holding the IV bag over my head. Together, we watched more Bourdain. After that, I felt a bit more alive. "You look so much better," Jon said, massaging my feet. I tried to find solace in the sleek geometry of the glass coffee table, but it seemed transparent, flimsy.

The next day, I was still unable to swallow a bite. "We have to get out of here," I said. Earlier, Jon, with his stay-put Blitz tendencies, kept saying we should wait for the bug to pass. He'd been winning out over my Holocaustic "flee to Russia" instincts. Now, however, he nodded.

Too bad there were no seats to anywhere in the continental US. Jon got on the phone with AmEx insurance: our options were either a helicopter airlift or being squeezed into business class in two days, at an outrageous surcharge. "Fine," I conceded, praying that I'd stay stable until then.

I did, but the weather didn't. If I'd been kept up before by cramps, I was now woken by howling winds and the sensation that our beautiful beach bungalow was being whipped, that the specially imported wooden walls might topple in on us.

Finally, two mornings later, feeling a bit stronger and able to keep down half a slice of bread, I placed the few items I'd unpacked back into my suitcase, swallowed suspect antibiotics left by Dr. I., and prayed that our tickets would be honored in what was now known as the biggest hurricane of the season.

The makeshift island airport was absolute chaos but at least they allowed me to sit on top of a desk instead of stand in the throngs. The flight even seemed to be leaving on time. Until it didn't. Hours of waiting ensued as rains and winds picked up and, we found out, the tarmac cracked in half, making it impossible to take off.

Finally, late in the evening, we were called to our plane. There was no gate, no bus, no tunnel, and we had to walk in the storm down the runway to the door of the aircraft. I instinctively used both arms to protect my stomach from the rain. *It's not just me anymore.* A decade ago, visiting a beach resort with a husband would have been unimaginable, not to mention the safest kind of travel I'd ever done, bordering on boring. But now, even that was fraught with risks. The fetus was so fragile, I was so fragile, it was all so fragile. I sat down and the large, leathery business class seats taunted me in my soaking clothes. *Luxury means nothing.* I was going to be a parent, for God's sake. I needed to plan cautiously, *be* the doctor, the police, the pilot of my family.

WHITE COUP
Cape Town, 2000

"You're doing well," Nigel said, as I changed lanes, even though this autobahn of a road featured approximately three cars per hour. "Really well."

"Thanks," I said, pressing harder on the gas, wondering if he was complimenting my driving or his teaching. His three years on me sometimes felt like thirty.

We were in South Africa, just outside Cape Town, in my rental white coupe, the arctic air-conditioning blasting across our tanned faces and reminding me of the windstorms that swept through the city, blowing hikers right off Table Mountain.

I was driving on the wrong side of the road.

I quickly glimpsed out the window at the magnificent desert. The sand white like snow, the opposite but almost the same as where I grew up. I was as far away as I could be, the literal end of the world. I'd been travel-writing for a couple of years, taking time off college to traipse across Europe, a proud nomad, my backpack like my shell. When I'd told Mom about this post-graduation gig she'd been delighted, mistakenly assuming I was spending the month in Cape *Cod.* Then she panicked, which only strengthened my resolve.

I stepped on the gas again. Then I quickly glanced the other way at Nigel, whose beaked face stared straight ahead, watching the road. He was always watching the road. Careful. Prepared. When he heard about this travel stint, he took unpaid leave from his London financial analyst job to join me, to protect me in this dangerous, beautiful land. He had ordered a care package of sunscreen and antidiarrheals to be waiting for me at the hostel when I arrived from

Boston. He'd included a note saying how much he loved me, how excited he was to see me in forty-eight hours.

We met when I escaped Harvard to write in Vienna, where I'd fallen in love with the city's design museum, its slick wall hung neatly with historical sofas, colorful like candy. I then paraded with my mere pack through hostels in Slovakia, Hungary, Germany, and the Netherlands before stopping to take a breath for a few months in London, where I sublet a basement room near Hyde Park and got a research job at the Science Museum, my entrée into the world of sleek design and cool space. A roommate introduced me to Nigel, a thin, self-deprecating, aspiring cartoonist who'd grown up working class but studied at Oxford, his background complicated, his identity confused. "Charmed to meet you," he said, his eyes twinkling, his understated allure reminding me of my first crush, Kermit the Frog. I was sitting on our floor, which I hoped made me seem adventurous. Really, I liked being close to the ground with nowhere to fall.

"Charmed ditto."

After a drunken first date, and after I called him (taking control!) we ended up a passionate pair. Far enough from home, I was finally able to forget my history. We fell into each other instantly, sensing our mutual shyness and odd pasts, but never discussing them. Instead, we mocked the art world (but secretly craved its acceptance). Nigel got me and judged nothing. He bought me jewelry and clothes, attracted to my whole body.

Over the next two years, as I travel-wrote in Paris and then returned to Harvard, he quit jobs to join me. He showed up in my rooms, ready to carry my bags, fix my furniture, anything I wanted. At first, I glowed in his attention, happy for help with the things I'd always had to do alone. But slowly, his dedication began to confuse me. He arrived as a surprise the weekend before my thesis was due to feed me, make photocopies, glue images. "Thanks," I kept saying but I'd felt edgy. I'd spent my whole life doing my own homework. I didn't *need* help with that. Then again, he was there when I pushed PRINT, calming my panic attack, telling me it was time to let go.

Despite my moods, we kept coming back together, folding into each other's lives like two ends of a collar.

He was the best. My first true love.

And all I could think was that, if I just moved the steering wheel a tiny bit to the right, the passenger side would gently ram into the mountain and I'd kill him. I began to focus on the minutiae of the plan—all it would take was two inches of movement of my wrist, less than that of my ankle, and a relationship would be trashed, a whole life ended.

"Careful here," he said.

You be careful, I wanted to say.

We were driving through a shantytown, which always sounded to me like a kind of low-alcohol Caribbean drink, a euphemism for the pungent poverty. I'll have a shantytown and a fried plantain salad, thanks. We were on the highway, protected from the criminal potential of the fenced-in town, but what I had to be careful of were the kids who used the highway as a soccer field, kicking balls, as I'd done in my suburban Canadian street hockey days. Only, not on a highway in a country with no laws about speed. Really, no laws at all. I slowed down, scared of hitting someone, amazed at how two cultures lived together, in the same exact space, but used it differently, their lives askew. A playing field for the blacks, a mode of express travel for the whites. All the cars in that country were white, as if to emphasize the difference.

"Turn here," Nigel said, forever the cartographer.

I turned and parked.

We walked together to the wooden-slatted hut from which pylons of smoke and of cackles rose to the sky. Nigel was as short as I was, and at times thinner, an old man and a little boy wrapped into one. He explained to the Afrikaans hostess that we had a reservation for the special eleven-course barbecue. South Africans, I thought, had no problems indulging—that is, white South Africans. I did not know about the others.

I sat down at my place in the shade—we were the smallest table, being just two of us in this group-oriented culture—and let myself take in the surrounds. The ocean in front of me was Matisse blue, the coast empty except for our culinary camp and the chefs (all black) who were barbecuing in the pit in the hot sunlight.

Nigel smiled for both of us. "It's so beautiful. I can't wait to show you the rest of the country."

"Mm," I mumbled, wishing he would get his own guidebook to write.

The first course was ready. Apparently it had just been fished out of the sea moments before. Alive to dead in seconds. Nigel and I waited in the line next to the pit. A server topped my plate. It was some form of tentacle, grilled, simple white zeros. I took it back to the table, where Nigel moved his chair closer to mine.

I let him, but did not reach out to touch him.

Our neighbors, a party of at least ten, were cutting dried fish off the netting décor and popping them into their mouths. They told one another jokes, laughed loudly.

"Eat it like this," Nigel said to me, serious, placing the grilled seafood on his tongue. Eating an almost-alive octopus leg was nothing for an Englishman who grew up in a small town. But it was everything for me, who'd been eating unkosher meat only since Peter. I was still unused to opening my walls to so many new things.

I scrunched the circle into the fork prongs, and without thinking, stuffed it in my mouth quickly, as if I was killing a spider.

THAT NIGHT WE arrived at the small hotel outside Stellenbosch that I had to review.

"The only room available has two single beds," the receptionist said.

"Fine," I said.

"No!" Nigel insisted.

I glared at him. This was my work.

And, I'd been relieved.

"It's just for two nights," I said, sweaty from the long drive.

"I came all the way here to be with you," he hissed. "We're a couple, and are getting a double bed."

The more I ran, the more he chased. The more he chased, the more I ran.

"We'll push them together," I whispered. "It'll be the same."

"Find another room," he told the woman.

Thankfully, her long tie-dyed dress matched her demeanor and she calmly flipped through a binder. "I'll make it work."

Nigel grinned. I felt sick. He'd recently been diagnosed with depression, and I made him happy, he claimed. But was it actually *me* that he desired, or just any filling for his holes? He wanted me too much, and wanted too much from me—to save him, to give him joy, purpose.

Like Mom.

I was beginning to worry that everyone I let in was crazy.

"Let's have a great few days here," I said. "And when we get back to Cape Town, let's spend a few days apart, to reinvigorate things."

"Fine," he said, and downed the water from his bottle.

I breathed.

FREEDOM, I THOUGHT, unpacking in my solo room back at the Cape Town hostel. Once the romance floodgates had been unlocked, my physical confidence upped and my reliance on alcohol cemented, I realized: I didn't want to be locked into "my first." Cape Town was a party and I wanted a part. By that evening, after just minimal flirting during my day's research, the hostel phone was ringing *for me.* House parties, dinners, dates. "Sure, let me check my calendar." I was Woman, see me soar. "Yes, yes, yes." I kissed random boys at clubs and fell into bed with a Swiss banker who then ignored me even though we lived down the hall from each other, and I didn't even mind. In the mirror, I saw firm muscles, dark skin, sultry eyes. I was the anti-me. I drank beers at breakfast, made out with the maintenance man who days later started seeing my friend—Derek. And then, Chris. The pool boy at a local hotel. Sweet, exotic; he invited me to a staff barbecue but was too shy to make eye contact until the others left. We ended up spending the night on his tiny bed, in the basement room below the deck where he lived.

The morning after, he asked for my address at home so he could write me letters. Seriously? Why? Then he kissed me and stressed that we'd used good quality protection. "It's really important here," he said. "AIDS is rampant."

I jolted up, covering myself with his sheet. Of course it was. What the fuck was I doing?

I NEED TO MOVE. My hair was wet, my legs were still damp. The shower hadn't washed away anything. *Go go go.*

I fumbled for my keys. I'd take my white car on one last trip. A deletion journey. All the way south. To the Cape of Good Hope.

What did Nigel even know about me, about my past? Nothing. I'd sent him back to England in pain. The one person who liked me, who'd care for me, I shipped off.

What am I doing?

I stepped on the gas, flashing to a scene from Campden when I was three years old. I was sitting on Bubbie's white toilet, my feet perched on a white child's stool, my book *Pig and the Blue Flag* perched on my thighs, when I heard the neighbors' German accents floating in through the open sash window. For years, they'd been fighting with Bubbie about her tree whose leaves fell onto their part of the yard, and Bubbie called them Hitler, but now they were discussing dinner. "Potatoes, wine, pork," rang out, simple syllables jolting me out of my story, crystal clear as if they were directly intended for the crescent-shaped entrance to my ear. There I was, half naked, exposed, in my most vulnerable position, and confronted by the voice of the enemy, unkosher meat right in Bubbie's bathroom. Warmth crawled up the back of my neck, and I pulled *Pig* over my upper thighs. Then I shot up, leaving wet traces along the inside of my leg, and climbed onto the bath ledge where I peeked at their heads and shopping bags through the window. Suddenly, my sweat turned cool, my world sliced itself open and I understood: I could hear and see them but they could not see me, safe, in Bubbie's toilet. It was not always a two-way street. Relationships were not reciprocal. We didn't know how we impacted the people around us.

I stepped on the gas even harder. South Africa had no traffic rules, no public bus system, no barriers to protect hikers along the mountain. It was the land of private police, a country where you clutched your purse, even in your own house. Fishing nets, but no safety nets. Everyone was responsible for herself. There was no one looking out for me, no one. *Bubbie is gone.* Perhaps how it had always been, but it seemed so obvious here.

I drove alone, like Thelma sans Louise, all the way south, until there was no more land, no more Africa. The farthest tip. Cape Point. I got out. In front of me—ocean.

The sun blazed, but the water was Antarctic. I was alone, but surrounded by penguins, who looked cute, but smelled like vinegar.

The taste of metal lingered in my mouth. I tried to recall if there were any holes around Chris' tongue piercing, any way for our blood to mingle.

I noted two penguins having sex. They squawked wildly. Had I even felt it? I was amassing notches on some bedpost that no one would ever count. My nakedness was just another costume. Overinvolved or underinvolved, walls that were too-thick or too-thin, it made no difference.

I was writing a travel guide, but I had no idea where I was going. I could have done a million smart things; instead, here I was, unable to take responsibility for my actions and how they affected others. Just like my mother, I thought.

I was at the edge of the world, teetering on the brink of the hemisphere. Harvard, Europe, Africa. Dorm, hostel, sublet. I'd been pretending to be adventurous, a confident self-contained unit, when really I was just running away, hiding. I wanted to be unattached but I was totally disconnected, empty.

I had no stuff at all, and still, chaos.

· EIGHT ·

24 WEEKS: FLIPPING OUT OF MY MIND, CONT.
New York City, 2011

The therapist's air conditioner was driving me insane. The appliance—a growth in the window like an ugly tumor jutting out of the building onto the Upper West Side streetscape—was so noisy, I felt like I was in an emotional sweatshop rather than paying premium rate to heal my history. "Pardon?" she screamed over the noise. "Can you repeat that?"

Repeat it? Insights, emotions, utterances are *in the moment*, I wanted to say. *Why don't you know that?*

I took a deep breath and patted my stomach. Stillness. In all this hubbub, no response. Eleven p.m. when I was trying to sleep, my pancreas got the shit banged out of it, but now, nothing.

"I'm pregnant," I said. I'd seen this therapist before when I'd been stuck in hair-pulling ambivalence over what career to pursue. I'd felt plagued by potential but was unsure how to harness it; I'd hoarded dreams of varied professions. "I'm freaked out."

"Pardon?"

For fuck's sake. "I. Am. Pregnant."

Her eyes lit up. Large. Shocked. "I just wanted to make sure I'd heard correctly."

Great. Even she thought I couldn't do it.

"So . . ." she struggled. "How do you feel?"

"I'm freaked out," I repeated, slowly, getting louder as I went.

"Parenthood is frightening," she said. "It means financial responsibility. You won't sleep much. You'll have to balance work and family. Is Jon upset? Men can be jealous of the bond."

Huh? What was she talking about? I mean these were all concerns, but not mine.

Then it dawned on me. "Do you have kids?"

"Um . . ." She struggled. "No. Does that make a difference to you?"

"Um . . ." *Hell yeah!* "I guess so."

"Why does that bother you?"

Well, because you've never been through this totally psycho-insane, life-changing, life-disrupting transformation and risked losing every single thing you've ever worked for. "I guess I wonder if you can understand."

"You think I can't connect to the ambivalent desire to mother the interior mother of another?"

Now I felt the cooled air's particles swim into my cochleas, swirl right down my auditory canal, entering my brain, body, lungs, stuffing up each alveolus, pushing out my precious oxygen. I looked around her consulting room (womb?) and its shag carpets, leather chairs, plaid, and books. I hated it. All of it. I gasped. Why was I even here?

"Time's up," she said. "We'll unpack your mistrust of me next time."

"OK," I said as I got up and walked out, but I doubted there'd be a next time. Right now I needed somebody to guide me, a parental role model. I closed her door, noticing the MSW on her gold label. She wasn't even a PhD. Even *I* was a doctor.

I got into the elevator, chastising myself for being snobbish. Who cared? I didn't work in academia anymore. But I knew what I did care about. That gold label. What would happen to my sense of self if it wasn't based around school and work, which until now had defined my standards of success and growth and even how I organized my time? Who would I be if I was no longer known for my brain—an identity that had saved me? What if my thoughts were drowned out and I lost my ability to focus, to think straight, to pursue my many outstanding goals?

What if I lost my mind?

The air was thick, too thick, I needed to run, but when the elevator doors opened I was confronted by a brown brick wall. "Where are we?" I stammered to a stranger getting in.

"The roof," he said. "You must have pressed R."

R was for *rez-de-chausée*, French for lobby. But I hadn't lived in Quebec in twenty years. "Right."

I took a deep breath, remembering that lungs worked through negative pressure. The organ first became big, reducing its molecular concentration, and then, and thus, air entered. Sometimes we do not mature into dealing with situations, but situations force us to expand into them.

I pressed L.

Intellect hadn't always helped me, I reminded myself, as the elevator jetted all the way down. It had also hindered, taken me along the wrong paths.

THE MUSEUM OF HOME
London, 2001

The double-decker passed my favorite road sign, BEWARE: LOOSE CHIPPINGS, and my second favorite, HUMPS FOR 90 METERS. My growling stomach did its own humping and loose chippings as I mentally rehearsed my lines for my imminent job interview: "I'm particularly interested in the representation of domestic experience because . . ."

Because *everything*. Because I was a schlub from Côte Saint-Jew from a family of crusted chaos, an eternal alien, Lubavitch winter coat and all.

Because here was my chance at reinvention.

Four days after 9/11, while CNN whispered *welcome to the real world* and my post-college-post-travel future seemed murkier than ever, I moved to London—which felt like the exact opposite of my roots. Pristine, sophisticated, subtle, cut-glass. A place of history, gravitas, and extreme alcoholism. The antishtetl. The British had a clear class system, banks were banks for three hundred years (and still used the same technology), people lived minutes from where their great-great-great-grandparents had resided, if not in the very same house. They still had a royal family; "order" was as engrained as the tendency to say "sorry" (for anything and everything—the national anthem).

I'd won a scholarship to pursue graduate study on theories of domesticity and contemporary art at a posh British art institute. I was becoming an official expert of the home and insisted on renting my first adult space. Though I'd flipped with stress over which neighborhood—Was I artsy? Hip? Literary? Which flat *was me?*—I gravitated to a large room with shiny wooden floors, their gleaming slats straight lines. The "flat" (ooh, it even implied magnificent geometry) was in central London, Zone One, in an area called Angel for its intersections' resemblance to the star atop a Christmas tree. I adored my sparsely furnished room with its simple desk, two funky chairs, two wiry candlesticks, and exactly ten abstract art books that I placed along the windowsill, hoping I'd caught Victoria's design savvy. Everything in plain sight, no blaring television. Sure, it was set in a small red building on top of a pub with a wooden staircase that would have been a death trap even for Victorians and my flatmates were hard-house DJs who took Ecstasy in order to get the most out of their McDonald's dinner (I'd spent whole mornings staring at the proximity of their toothbrushes to my own, wondering what those strangers' bristles soaked up), but my "empty nest" was worth every pence.

And indeed, I'd spent every pence of my scholarship on my little slice of sanity. I'd rather dehydrate, I thought, than live in a cramped bedroom, lost among Edwardian row houses and the suburban sprawl that made up much of London's Zones Two and up. My dinners comprised store-brand penne noodles on which I heaped chunks of cheese—the cheapest hot meal I could conceive that involved a minor vestige of protein. Dinner or Diet Coke was a daily decision. For the first time, I wanted *more* pounds.

Which is one factor that brought me here, on this bumpy bus ride to East London, heading to an interview as a research assistant at a museum. And not any museum, but a British museum of home, the alter ego of Bubbie's bazaars and Mom's bizarres, of loud emotions frying up in the crowded kitchen, leaving oniony stenches that followed me around all day. I loved the museum's cool conceptualism, sophisticated internationalism, detached intellectualism. I loved the value placed on each individual object, the scent of flowers and citrus. "Curator" was the least Yiddish word I knew and I wanted in. And, unlike the other art history students in my program, many of whom were from families that *owned* old master paintings, I desperately needed the money. My stomach growled again.

The bus now pulled up in front of the building, a long early Victorian three-winged former nursing home flanking a green field. I got off, repositioning my funky blue plastic glasses on my nose, trying not to worry that my black "trousers"/red "jumper" combo was too casual. That morning, after dabbing blush across my face, hoping I looked like a calculated professional rather than an aging clown, I'd examined my wardrobe to find clothes spotted with tea bruises and pen leaks, my bas-couture collection like a Jackson Pollock. Now I rolled up my sleeves to cover a stray thread. I adjusted my small designer watch, a gift from Nigel, with silvery hands that marauded around its surface, each following its own protocol, reminding me that as we age, each second is a shorter percentage of our existence, that time passes more quickly with each tick. I ran my hands through my boy-short hair, grateful I'd recently dyed it a shocking cadmium.

I knocked at the curatorial office, three sharp staccato motions. I. Am. Here.

The green door was familiar. I'd found this museum on my first trip to London during college and was smitten. It was arranged as a long series of living rooms, with one chronological path you could walk through, as if you were visiting the homes of wealthy people since the Middle Ages. Playing out a version of my childhood fantasies of living in Montreal's suburban west, I imagined myself in a slick, wealthy home in 1725, welcoming guests for our pheasant bleating competition, donning my finest ruff.

"Judith," Charlotte said as she opened the door. "Welcome back."

Indeed, I'd come to this very office (with my intellectual name) to do research for my undergrad thesis on scientific color theory in Victorian interior decoration, which I now clutched in my shvitzy arms. I'd ended up basing my study on the museum's 1880s period room—bright yellow walls, glassed-in kitsch flowers, heaps of *objets*, and wild red-and-green carpets—which was, to contemporary taste, the ugliest. But that's what had attracted me. Why did those Victorians love clutter and the grotesque?

"Thank you, Ms. Williams," I said, conscious of every label. The day before I'd tried to open a bank account and the space for "title," which in the US comprised "Mr., Mrs., or Ms.," included over fifty choices. "Yes, that's Dowager Lady Batalion," I'd wanted to say, picturing myself with a fox daintily draped around my neck.

"Call me Charlotte," she chuckled. She was wearing jeans.

I was directed to the table in the middle of the office, stacked with piles of books, wallpaper samples, and fake Jacobean meat platters. "Do you care for a coffee?"

"Sure," I said right away, immediately regretting it, hearing my North American drawl (shewer) stand out next to her crisp vocalizations. At Harvard they'd told us never to accept drinks at a professional interview. But I was so thirsty. And hungry. And, free coffee. I could feel myself crumbling. "Sorry," I mumbled, just in case.

Charlotte brought several worn mugs of instant to the table and we were soon joined by Margaret, the gesticulating "Keeper of Curatorial Services," and James, her second-in-command who was leaving his post next week.

Now that I'd forced Charlotte to brew, I'd better drink up. I picked up my coffee carefully, not sure if raising my pinkie was over the top, and tried to get it to my lips in an elegant swoop. I'd just made it, when the questioning began.

"Tell us about your interest in Victorian design," Margaret said, her arms steady at attention, her eyes slit accusingly as if she could peer right through my veneer.

I took a deep breath before beginning my rehearsed speech about my unbridled lust for living room research. "I'm interested in the relative experience of aesthetic pleasure. I wrote my thesis on why Victorians used such clashing colors in their drawing rooms. The very word 'drawing,' by the way, implies action and cover—it's a space of hidden contradictions. Objects were kept as a sign of wealth, to associate the home with a museum. There was a reason for the mess!" *There must be a reason I come from a mess too.*

"Interesting," James said flatly, Englishly, which meant I had no idea if he found it interesting. "And what experience do you have doing research?"

This I could do: I'd worked for a photographer who shot abandoned homes and psychoanalysts' consulting rooms; for an art historian who wrote about rococo design. I explained I was enrolled in an MA, leading to a PhD, on domestic representations in art, reading Freud, Bachelard, Kristeva, anyone who contemplated how the body and psyche related to intimate space. Was it more comfortable to live in a room dominated by windows, where inhabitants looked out (classic subject/object) or ones that were designed with "theater box" areas so everyone looked at one another (intersubject/subject)? Was the contemporary home a site of comfort or captivity? Feminist or patriarchal? A signifier of capitalism or the essence of the communal? Was privacy merely a theoretical construct or a concrete ideal? I worked myself into a Sorbonnish frenzy.

"I *love* this museum," I crescendoed. I really did. I had no idea where else I could be employed—this was a rare, perfect match. Most of my Harvard friends lived off their parents, or with them, as they figured out their next steps, but I had no fallback plan. I had to run before I knew what steps I should be taking. *I had to run.* "I'm obsessed with domestic interiors." Finally I paused, making eye contact with all three, ready for approval, a round of applause.

Margaret scratched her head.

Charlotte took a sip of her coffee.

James opened his mouth. To cough.

A sweat bead oozed from my hairline. My brain was my everything. I'd always depended on being organized, doing my homework, following rules, the equations that came easily to me and guided me out of messes. I fondled the pages of my damp thesis. "Here are my main theoretical points:

> "*1. Walls are thick, not mere boundaries and surfaces, but whole worlds unto themselves, with layers of ins and outs.*
> "*2. The home is a site of self, of subjectivity, deeply aligned with the psyche, an externalization of the mind.*
> "*3. Interiors mirror each other—a person creates a room, and a room creates its inhabitants. It is not so much that we hang stuff on our walls, but that our walls press into us, make their marks on our personalities.*
> "*4. The home is a site of relationships, which are formed by and create the space they occur in.*"

I couldn't stop. "I've even studied the design of laboratories, showing how spaces mold scientific ideas. I want nothing more than to study the ways living rooms create and reflect the people inside them."

Nothing.

I put my mug down and grabbed its handle to help me keep my composure. They didn't like me. It was clear: I would never fit in with this institution, with its grounded history, its sense of place. They probably wanted to hire a lord's daughter whose dining experience surpassed fake ramen à la cheddar.

Margaret finally cleared her throat. Then she spoke: "It was nice to meet you."

"Indeed," said James, not missing a beat.

But then. He smiled.

Charlotte grinned too.

Were they being polite? British?

I got up and reached for my coat. Keep it elegant, Judy, I reminded myself.

I swiftly, deftly, swung it from the back of the chair, right onto my arm. I grinned.

Then I attempted to slip in my left arm and instead hit my sleeve across the whole range of coffee cups, sending brown liquid splashing across the table like a mudslide.

"I'm so sorry," I barely stammered out, as each of them jumped back, pulled books with them, then clambered around looking for tissue. There it was: my whole attempt at fitting in, my cool museum career, my ability to eat warm food, flushed down the filter. "So sorry."

"Don't worry, Judith," James said, grabbing some paper towels. "All curators are, at heart, klutzes."

He laughed. Then, Margaret and Charlotte did too. I launched into goofy hysterics.

(I did not yet know that my eccentric ungainliness made the English more comfortable than my showing off about research skills or demonstrating any emotion.)

Charlotte and James bashed hands as they tried to wipe my spill. The coffee streamed into ravines right in front of a midcentury staircase mock-up. I reached for a tissue and the whole box fell to the floor.

"Can you start on Monday?" Margaret asked.

"I can start *anytime*," I answered, skipping to the door. I took a full, deep breath. They had used the word "klutz." And they were klutzes too. Maybe all people obsessed with beauty felt they couldn't do it, be it. Maybe inside they all felt like me.

"When in Rome," I said, chugging my half-pint. I stared at Evan across the pub table, noting his chiseled features, strong arms, dark eyes firmly stuck in their sockets. In the dance class, all I'd noticed was that he was older, sweaty. Then again, I'd been distracted. Though I loved dance, enrolling in Modern as soon as I could afford it, dreaming of pirouetting like a paper towel pulled off its roll, today's class was too hard. My limbs didn't cooperate; I more or less did the running-man across the room. I was hoping no one had noticed I even existed, so when Lucy invited me for a drink afterward, I surprised myself by accepting.

"The English need liquor just to chat," Evan agreed, smiling. "It's an intersubjective conundrum." He was a professor. Sociology. He'd been in London for five years. "So glad you also see it that way," he added in his New York patter.

"The reason Brits have such crazy flavored chips—beef bourguignon, prawn and chives—is because, along with their pints, that's their dinner," I played along. "By the way, that's quite an accent. House of Windsor or Saxe-Coburg?"

He laughed. His dark eyes met mine. He seemed to know exactly what he was looking at. "I'm cooking tonight." He lived a few blocks away. "Couscous. Come."

"OK," I chirped without thinking, shocking myself again. Normally a planner, I preferred to enter social engagements with prepared conversation. That evening, I didn't even worry that I had no change of clothes, or that I'd be dining with people who thought I possessed the physical grace of a wounded hyena. Including the teacher, Honor, who was giggling too loudly, like a teenager, and, I noticed, sporadically touching Evan's arm.

His apartment—the first person I knew who lived alone—was centered on a long, cool hallway ending in a living room covered in rugs and hanging plants. Honor climbed onto a yoga ball, flicked her blond hair, tensed her slender spiderlike limbs, and bounced after Evan to the kitchen. She was a fortysomething divorcée with three kids—could she really be flirting like that? I coughed to cover up my stomach growls.

Evan cooked and I realized how starving I was; that morning I'd found a mouse nonchalantly hanging out in my bag of budget bagels. The smell of garlic, now, flirted its way into the fabric of my blue tank top. Evan came in to pour wine and I could feel him watch me as I examined his sophisticated bookshelf. His stare hit my side like a warm spotlight, nestling into my round hips. I did not look back. Honor's laugh got louder.

He served me first and kept seasoning my sauce with parsley that he'd cultivated in his kitchen. I tried to eat slowly, ladylike. "One day I'll teach you to roast peppers," he whispered. "And maybe even my secret decanting technique." I blushed bright red.

Evan insisted on walking me home. My blood raced. We were trudging up the hill between our flats, his steps confident and vigorous, when I saw Honor hanging from the back of the open bus, waving frantically. *He likes ME,* I wanted to call out, realizing it was true. *I'm young, sexy, intellectual, unencumbered. Fresh.* But was I ready? I flashed to Peter's aloofness, which had made me feel inadequate, to Nigel's overconcern, which had made me feel suffocated, to how I then sped through a delayed adolescence, bouncing between men's beds as I bounced between my own beds, parading between dorms, couches, hostels, cities. Was I ready to not-run?

Evan kissed me in my living room. "Let's do this again," he said before he left.

That night, I marveled at my minimalist room that I was sure would impress him, at the clean order of my new life—school, job, fling: check—when suddenly I noticed my bare wrist. I'd lost my one artsy adornment. What would I do without my timepiece? But then, touching my exposed arm, I realized it felt free, uncuffed. I could live without the watch. I could jump in, let someone care for me.

THAT EVENING OF letting-go quickly developed into a relationship. I spent weekends at Evan's, curled up like a comma in his warm side. He taught me how to make coffee from a cafetière with a twist of lemon (cuts the richness) and the meaning of cotton thread counts. He lectured to me on the philosophy of ceramic dishes, the ways that liquids coated the edges, protecting their surfaces from hidden harsh acids. I nodded nervously, exposed to a secret universe that I'd been denied access to for so long.

"You need a separate area for chopping raw meat," he explained the basics. "It's best to hang pots." His face traced his vigorous thinking; his pupils darted side to side.

"So raw meat and pots each get their own wings," I repeated, drying plates with the circular motion he'd shown me, thinking of Mom's kitchen, the repository for moldy cereal and obsolete telephones which now, alongside aged pastries, stockpiled pens and notebooks, blended over into the den's new collection of cassette tapes that included music copied from CDs she borrowed from the library and recordings of conversations with lawyers.

"It's really quite perplexing that you don't know *anything* about cooking."

"Girl power," I said, flexing my drying-arm's muscles. "I'm a third-wave, microwave kind of feminist." It was easy to play my lack of cuisine cool as part of my urban academic identity, rather than admit that my domestic deficiencies made me feel like less of a woman, not more of a feminist.

A couple of months into our affair, Evan decided he wanted to move somewhere more residential, permanent. I gleefully accompanied him on reconnaissance missions, checking out neighborhoods and garden flats (he insisted on growing his own radishes), happy to be involved in such an important domestic decision. I took this as a sign of Evan's commitment, but also, respect for my taste. We took long walks, examining architectural quirks and stopping at ethnic supermarkets where he showed me the difference between portobello and porcini mushrooms, paprika and cayenne pepper. I felt proud to be beside someone who knew so much, grateful that he was sharing his knowledge, as if it confirmed that I was worth it, that I too, one day, when I understood it, or could afford it, would raise herbs.

MEANWHILE, MY JOB at the British museum of living rooms was also progressing well. The museum's crammed timeline of period rooms reminded me of England, a nation poor in space, rich in time; the opposite of America. I loved walking through these reception areas consecutively, from the somber 1600s with its boxy chairs, through the dreaded Victorian yellow velvet wallpapers, 1960s gloriously crisp-edged Scandinavian-inspired wooden minimalism, and the 1990s loft conversion with blue halogen lights and see-through kettles. I imagined myself in these spaces, passing out cigarettes in our Aesthetic gay salon, or partying like it was 1599 with a flagon of mead. All of this fantasy connected through a straight hall, pristine, white. A clear path.

My role was "researcher" for a special exhibition of paintings of modern living rooms, or rather upper- to upper-middle-class domestic English urban living rooms from 1603 to 2001, to be Britishly precise. I spent full days in that office with its pre–Industrial Revolution conditions (it was wet and windy *inside*) trawling through photo archives and museum Web sites, poring over books of paintings by dead artists with names like Boodles Caldercott, examining the living rooms of Samuel Richardson and Thomas Carlyle (who, in his portrait, seemed to be kicking his cat), my eyes grazing pictures of fireplaces covered in ceramics, austere seventeenth-century tea services, or, more contemporary, an open plan flat with surreal floating fish. The detective work was intense: what was the strict definition of a middle-class, urban living room?

Oh, the fights this aroused. Weekly, I proudly, albeit nervously, presented my findings to my superiors. Sitting around refurbished tables, sipping cappuccinos (which had just hit England), the top echelon of curators engaged in hours of debate. Margaret, whose desk was invisible under a mudslide of papers; Emily, a sassy American who'd adopted a British accent and ran the marketing department; Edith, the octogenarian world-class design specialist who angled for the museum to buy her family's heirlooms; and Neville, the Oxbridge director, who managed to sustain an air of aloof British masculinity despite the fact that he spent his days trading in cutlery—would all go at it. They fought vehemently about whether the hearths were urban ("Was Bexley-on-the-Flume a city or suburb in 1747?") and whether these chambers were indeed living rooms

("But Sickert sometimes painted the nude teenage girls in his studio . . ."). After hours of this, Margaret would pull me aside and ask me to ring the author of an academic tome on Regency wallpapers to make sure that what he wrote in his book was right.

"But he wrote it in his book," I'd say, trying to get out of making yet another shameful call. "That's usually because he thinks it's right."

"Doesn't matter," she'd answer. "Check if he knows more than he dared to expose." Every detail in this paranoid world of academic historical design had to be cross-referenced. Footnotes, hidden citations—there was a system for accuracy.

Especially when it came to "class," the Platonic social blueprint. Separate meetings were called just to assess the echelon of the living rooms. "Is a bohemian starving artist from a family of self-made lawyers but who went to boarding school middle or lower-middle?" I'd thought this categorization would come easily to me, presuming that I was middle class myself (after all, I grew up without limos or government handouts). How wrong I'd been.

"No!" Margaret shrieked, peering at the picture I showed. "The artist titled it 'tea,'" (a working-class term, she explained), "not supper, nor dinner."

"That scene depicts a crass tabloid—clearly upper." She demystified: "Ironically, only aristocrats would read *that*."

"That living room," she said, "shows *new* carpeting, i.e., lower made good."

"Old furnishings," she would whisper cryptically leaning right over my computer. "Tall garden hedges." My North American concepts of class were vague, abstract at best. Here, every word one said, one's clothes, car, reading material and even the state of one's home indicated social rank. Uppers were messy, as they had nothing to prove; fortunately, they had names like Fiona and Gaylord, which set them apart from the lower class, also messy because they also didn't care (no mobility, so why try?). Those in the middle, from upper-lower to lower-middle to middle-middle, appeared tidier to show their status, which they were insecure about. So, the middle-

middles attempted to appear slightly upper, but not too upper because upper upper actually looked lower.

Everything had its codes. And I liked it. I wanted to get my classifications right, to intellectually dazzle with my research expertise, to add to this organized world of domestic historical design bliss. I wanted to be a slick, smart, visual culture vulture, and find the most home-ish representation of home. But in all of it, really, I wanted to answer the question: what is home anyway? My goal was to solve my life.

THE DOYENNE OF DOMESTICITY
London, 2002

"But where would I put my bookshelves?" Evan was scowling, his bushy eyebrows coming together like two mice making love. "I can't fit my stuff in this living room."

"Here!" I pointed to a nook in the hallway, proud of my growing design sense.

Double scowl. "Why would I want books in a breezy hallway?"

Why would you want to live in a damp ground floor flat an hour's bus ride from town with a living room that smelled like stale smoke and a bay window that looked onto a gray road? I wanted to respond. But he was stressed about not having found the perfect apartment. I understood. "The kitchen has counter space," I tried to cheer him. "You can cultivate your own seasonings." He had strong feelings about store-bought seasoning. He rolled his eyes.

"Sorry." If it was my fault, at least I could rectify it. I wanted him to be happy, enjoy himself. That night, I suggested the unusual: that he come to mine. I put on pink velvet pants, my flatmate's Euro-trance CD, and opened a bottle of wine to breathe, just as he'd taught me. I downed two glasses and breathed myself.

Evan looked good, wearing all black, his belt firm around his waist. He sat on one of my black Ikea chairs, his back sinking into the fabric, his knees high. I poured him a glass, and he nodded at the label. Encouraged, I leapt onto his lap, kissed his ear and flung my other leg over him. "Whoa, what are you doing?" He pushed me off. "You're drunk."

"Maybe," I said. "But I'm in a good mood." I winked, pulled up his shirt.

"Seriously, stop," he said. "I thought you were *hosting me* at your apartment."

"Oh!" I jumped off. Why was he all of a sudden not approving of me, my body, my home? I burned up, pulled my shirt down as far as it would go. He didn't know the half of it. "Chocolate?" I offered a specially imported, way-beyond-my-budget bar.

He examined the packaging, chewed thoughtfully. "Peppery," he said, which I thought meant he liked it, but wasn't sure.

I sat down on the other black chair, realizing how its strange geometric slump placed a sitter at an odd angle, folded into themselves, feeling as if they were sinking.

"You should get your own place." He grimaced and gestured to my speaker. Not his acoustic world music. "You don't even have your own toilet, or a living room." His voice sounded like it was receding into a distance. I felt him slipping away, myself teetering on a chasm I wanted to not-see. "You pay too much," he added. "Let's go back to mine."

With that, he unfolded himself and headed out. If letting go didn't work, holding on did. I grabbed a toothbrush, and all my control, and followed.

AND SO, MERE weeks later, I found myself cutting back and forth across London on a real estate mission. I'd been so tied to my Angel identity, it hadn't dawned on me that for a similar amount, I could rent my own space. So far, however, I'd seen only dark, secluded flats, miles from transportation, with Toast-R-Ovens for kitchens.

I sighed and walked up to a Whitechapel address—slightly above my budget, and in a working-class religious Muslim neighborhood. (Few whites, I joked, few chapels.) The cement building was a three-story with bright blue doors and shutters, set on a cul-de-sac off the

main road that hosted a lively Indian street market selling saris, sa-
mosas, and SIM cards. It turned out the property was owned by
friendly lesbian artists who had a pottery shop on the ground floor,
a Victorian kiln out back, and a vintage car they'd refurbished. My
eyes perked up.

We ascended the rickety stairs to the apartment on offer. Sure,
the space was both the size (and consistency) of a shoebox, but it was
a light and airy shoebox with a large window, brand-new carpeting
and blond Ikea furnishings. "You can walk to the museum and the
bus outside goes straight to the British Library." An intellectual
shuttle, plugged into culture and multiculture. The place fit!

"Can I come back tomorrow to show my boyfriend?" I asked,
looking around for things Evan had taught me to seek: storage space,
nonstructural partitions, hidden costs.

The landlord, Liz, raised her eyebrow. She was perhaps right. I
convinced a reluctant Evan to come (he was jealous that I'd found
something in mere days, I reasoned). His beady eyes darted around,
examining burner sizes as he asked about safety. I saw us from Liz's
perspective: insecure girl and difficult daddy figure. His brow fur-
rowed and I couldn't tell if he liked it, but couldn't understand why
he wouldn't.

"I'll take it," I said, hoping I'd done the right thing.

Two weeks later, there I was, hoping it again, sitting next to Dad
as he drove his beige Camry from Trudeau airport to Kildare (via
Carlton, of course). Dad always picked me up from my flights, excited when I returned to his turf, but this time he was frenetic, repeating what I'd deduced from recent desperate phone calls: Mom
was "going bonkers" with Bubbie's estate—two properties that Mom
had been renting out to tenants for decades—spending full days
with accountants, obsessed around the clock.

As he spoke, I focused on the feeling of Evan's keys pressing into
my pocket. Two worlds colliding in my pants. Evan had gone to visit
his family for a full month and had given me extremely rigorous
instructions for maintaining his flat: the exact amount of water to

be fed to each plant, the precise location where the mail should be left. I'd obeyed, nervous but flattered that he'd trusted me with his prized domestos.

We arrived at Kildare and I was overwhelmed by both nostalgia for the fresh Northern air and panic about what might be lurking inside the yellowing bricks. I saw the house was now hidden by overgrown trees and vines, like long hair pulled over a shy face. None of our keys worked. Mom had apparently hired a locksmith to install several bolts on the front door. My stomach tingled as Dad pressed on the rusting doorbell five, six, seven times, nearly pounding it with his fist. "She locks me out of my own house," he hissed. Finally we heard slow footsteps and Mom peeked through the broken plastic blinds. She saw it was me, and I heard latches being unchained. *She's becoming one with the house,* I thought as she opened the door. I lowered my gaze to avoid witnessing her decline.

"Judy!" She hugged me. Her body—larger, grayer, more frantic—smelled sweaty. The house looked horrible. The hallways were clogged arteries. Thick heaps of clothes were draped over railings.

I followed her to the kitchen, passing our front room, *our* drawing room. We'd never used it as a living room—it had always been the repository of furniture—but now it was completely obstructed, an impenetrable block filled with liquidation laundry bins, blankets, striped plastic shopping bags, ancient crates of Diet Coke, factory-second lime green place settings bought in the 1970s. Somewhere still tucked inside had to be our light blue L-shaped sofa which, even as a child, I'd never sat on once. In my friends' houses people weren't allowed to enter living rooms because they were pristine, like museums; mine was the opposite, holy only in its pathology. This room that was meant to host guests, to connect public and private, to forge links, dress up and impress, was utterly inaccessible. Here, there was no room for living.

In the kitchen, I brushed crumbs off the seat before sitting down.

"They're after me," Mom said. "They're going to take the houses, everything."

I assumed that by "they" she meant lawyers and accountants,

people she thought were intent on stealing her modest inheritance. But I didn't understand why.

"They're managing the portfolio." I tried to calm her, but was already tired of repeating the comfort phrases from our phone calls. "I understand you're stressed, but Dad will take care of you. Why are you letting this rule your life? It's not worth it. As Viktor Frankl said, 'Man can only control his own emotions.'"

"What do you know from Viktor Frankl?" Mom rolled bits of paper towel into tiny cylinders all around her place setting. "You don't understand anything. You don't listen when I try to explain."

She was right. I didn't quite listen. I didn't go through all the bank statements with her. I didn't follow the logic. "OK, so explain it to me."

"You don't really care."

"I do." I wasn't sure I did. I just wanted all this to recede.

"It all began in 1998." Her eyes turned inward, her focus on the paper towel bits.

"I know," I sighed. "I know the story." Bubbie died. There was no will. Mom's brother wanted his half. Mom had been managing the properties alone for years. She didn't want to buy him out, but also didn't want to sell. The finances were complicated. Their dispute escalated to the realm of bailiffs and lawyers. But legally, she had no ground. "Do you have any *new* information?" It came out whiny.

"You don't understand me," she shrieked. "You're against me like everyone else."

I sighed, tried not to raise my voice. "Why would people be after you?"

"Because they see I'm naive. I'm an easy target."

"You? You're not easy. Lawyers are aggressive; it's their job."

"Are they? How do you know? Did you speak to someone?"

"No . . . Dad will take care of you."

"You think they won't come after Dad too?" I was starting to smoke at the ears. Every conversation felt like a clogged artery, conclusions already drawn.

"Why do you ask me if you don't listen to my answers?" I looked at crumbs, cottage cheese hardened on a plate. I was making her worse. Mom was beet red, fevered, getting up, shifting notes from one pile to the other. "Just give me a lift to a lawyer," she asked quietly, changing tones.

"Now?" I wanted to take a shower, call a friend.

"Yes, now," she said. "Or take me to the bank."

She didn't drive. She was old. She was my mother. I didn't understand what she was going through; what was wrong with me? Why did I not want to help? Why couldn't I just be nicer? Of course I would take her. I went to change in my old bedroom, where I found at least a half dozen obsolete fax machines covering my desk and bed, an appliance heap that reminded me of photos I'd seen of an electronic-waste village in China. The floor was littered with school supplies and cheap office materials, binders and colored pencils, more ironic attempts at organization. I felt a tear wander down my dry cheek, but wiped it away quickly.

Outside the bank, Mom insisted I come in with her. I didn't even know why we were there.

"For what?" I knew the meeting would result in embarrassing fights. I worried Mom's tape recorder would sit in the middle of the room, shaming me.

"To be a witness. It's important for the case."

A witness? The case? I trudged in; she brought two heavy suitcases with her. "Whatever you do," she whispered, "do not use our real names."

In the manager's office, Mom asked probing questions about investments and mortgage fees. I kept my eyes down on my fluttering stomach, feeling like I was involved in some heist but didn't know what it was, or which side I was on.

I DIDN'T SLEEP well that night—the bed, dust, jet lag, Mom's frantic middle-of-the-night pacing and slamming doors—but I decided to try another tactic in the morning. "Why don't we go out for lunch?" I asked her. A change of context. I still dreamed of a shopping partner, a gallerygoer. I was an adult now, with a boyfriend, and I wanted to be that with her.

She looked at me. "For lunch?"

"Yes," I answered. "I'm here from London for a week. It would be nice to just, well, do something nice."

"I don't have time for lunch," she said, gesturing to her piles. "I have to work."

I shook my head, got my gym clothes together, tucked my feelings into my pocket.

But the day before I was due to fly back she approached me. "I found a Greek place that has a lunch special. Is that good enough for you?"

"Of course!" It wasn't exactly the enthusiastic attitude I'd hoped for, but it was our first lunch date. Mom brought several bags that she refused to leave in the car. I tried to ignore them, perched by her seat, obstacles for the waiters.

"I'll have the Greek salad," I said.

"That's not on the special." She was particularly unchatty.

"I know, but it's the same price."

"But we came here for the special."

I reluctantly ordered the special, which was more food that I didn't want to eat.

Mom fidgeted in her seat. "I have so much work to do," she said, reminding me of what I always said, making me wonder if my own academic work—which was so grounding, so all-important—had always been as overblown.

"What are you reading?" she interjected as she parsed fat off her fish. Literature would bind us.

"Some books for my PhD on feminist art and home," I said quietly, suddenly feeling guilty about my endeavor.

"Huh," she said, feeling for her bags, distracted, anxious. The small talk was shallow, distancing us more than distance. I looked around at other lunching mothers. Designer bags. Manicures. Smiles. I was judging her, I knew, and it was wrong of me—she was so horribly insecure, depressed. But I also felt anger fester all over me: why was she wasting her time and energy with things that were so unimportant?

My stomach was full, but I brought a forkful of fish to my lips.

We ate without speaking.

When we got back to Kildare, I checked my voice mail one final time. Evan had not called all week. I packed for my return to London, not really knowing what I should be calling home, and what, away.

"WHERE'S EVAN?" I actually asked out loud. It was eight fifty-five and the mover—whom he'd found advertised on a college bulletin board—was due to come around nine. This was it, the Saturday of my transition from roommates to solo-hood. I'd managed to pack up all my belongings but couldn't believe how many boxes it had taken. From traveling with a backpack to needing a mover—damn. But this was my stuff, I reminded myself, all stuff I'd acquired and bought with my museum money for good reasons.

"'Bye." Micki, DJ flatmate, waved as she headed out to work.

I forced myself to play it cool, to not-text Evan. Since our trips, he'd been more distant, busy at work, but we'd still been spending weekends together. Certainly, he knew today was the big day. He was supposed to arrive with the special reinforcing tape he couldn't stop talking about. I needed him to help carry my black chairs. I busied myself marking up boxes, as if my new apartment was so massive that they required labels. Finally Evan arrived, unshaven.

"Where's the tape?" I asked.

"Oh."

Fortunately, the mover came supplied, and I sat between their sweaty bodies on the front bench seat as I gave directions to my new home. Christian homilies emanated from the radio, and Evan asked the driver about his Nigerian background as we drove farther and farther east—away from Montreal, I thought.

Evan seemed more excited by our trip to the grocery to buy hummus and salad for lunch, and the various cuts of beetroot, and the fact that I had a little blond-wood Ikea table to eat at, than he did by the fact that I was now a woman with a home.

"I have to meet Honor and her kids this afternoon," he said as he wiped his face.

"Oh." Since when did he hang out with Honor and her kids? "Where are you going?" I asked, instead of: *I thought you'd keep me company on this mega-enormous day of my life.*

"Just taking a walk on the South Bank. Call me if there's anything urgent." He pecked me on the cheek.

I tried not to panic. Maybe he was just giving me space to settle into my new space, I reasoned. I didn't call. But for the rest of the day, I had a bad feeling, even in my new sanctuary.

BACK AT THE museum, I also faced the issue of my historical design colleagues, who, as colleagues do, ended up becoming a version of family in that I didn't select them, and yet, they formed my daily context. At first, England was ignorant bliss for me. People seemed tame and nonthreatening; reticence, self-consciousness, and the kind of fumbling awkwardness that I'd always struggled to hide were de rigueur. My shyness melted away amid the shyness of others, and of course the immense quantities of liquor. I blended in.

Or so I thought. When a colleague balked in horrified shame when I told her I liked her sweater, I began to suspect that I wasn't aware of all the conversational codes that were at work in my new life. When I commented on the severe discomfort that my colleagues appeared to feel when introducing me to others, an expat American explained it was because my foreign lack of class-markers was confusing. Never mind living rooms, they did not know how to place *me*. I was well-educated (upper-middle) but asked questions about people's work and lives (lower) and sometimes even complimented their clothing (off-the-charts, very suspect behavior).

I was appalled. I *wanted* to be placed. I observed and interpreted, carrying out my own social study to try to make sense of these rules. I deduced where my officemates were placed. Helen was from the North, which meant she was working class, while Charlotte was

Manchester society and lived in an Art Deco split-level, which meant middle-middle. I finally realized I'd been acting outside the beams of the class-markers that I should have been exhibiting and buckled down to become properly middle. I tried to read the right newspapers, say extra sorries, and leave people alone. I never complimented, made eye contact, or showed emotion. Stiff upper-middle-class lip *über alles*. For my lunch, I became middlingly modest, also bringing sandwiches on white bread in recycled aluminum foil. (With crusts—to cut them off was too upper.) I took off my scarf and braved the office's gales (upper-middle?). I never again asked for Post-it notes (expensive! wasteful! . . . American!). English über-self-consciousness spread through me like a contagion: I was now a decoding machine, constantly translating North American impressions into this aged, nuanced English language, crystallized over centuries, unlike "American" which was direct, catering to immigrants.

Eventually, I was promoted to curator and searched like a sleuth, virtual magnifying glass in hand, taking lunches "al desko," desperate to find the most fitting living rooms imaginable. But I was particularly excited (though didn't dare show it, Englishly) when I came across an interior image by R. B. Kitaj, a painter whose personal story—a perpetual stranger, a self-declared "wandering Jew" who had moved from America to England—was so compelling. An Ohio native, Kitaj studied and settled in England, making collage-like work influenced by British figurative style. Further research proved that the image depicted his Holocaust-surviving relative's living room in West London. He was my champion: a Jewish foreigner whose genes were stamped with refugeeism, but who'd made a home in the British art world. So much so, he could even create its representations. It was a jagged scene, the furniture on different planes, the walls broken, the hard wooden chair its only standing staple. The living room scene was cluttered but flat, skewered with thick black lines, as if a frame held together the largely dark red chaos.

It was called *Desk Murder*.

"Look at this," I said to Margaret, not mentioning its title. "A foreigner's take on home." Then I naively added, "A moving, passionate work, not just about furniture, but showing ambiguities, the home as a site of suffering, loneliness, malaise."

She examined it, then pointed at the abstractly depicted sofa. "Is that middle class?"

"I don't know exactly; it's a nonrepresentational rendition," I tried.

"Call him and find out," she ordered.

I just imagined it. "Hi, Mr. Kitaj. I'm very moved by your expression of sheer heartbreaking loss alluding to your family's time in Dachau, but I just wanted to confirm that their couch was bought at the John Lewis department store."

"OK," I said, sighing. "I'll check on the couch."

"Sofa," she corrected me. Couch was working class.

"I'll call him," I said, putting it at the bottom of my to-do list, lying. Englishly.

I couldn't do it, even in the name of living rooms and of scholarly endeavor. I wasn't drawn to the painting for its furnishings or historical framework, but for how it made me feel—less alone in my perpetual foreignness. I was interested in beauty and stillness because I'd lacked those in my life.

I did not make the call, but Kitaj became my symbol of cultural symbiosis and my cause. At the weekly cappuccino meetings, I kept suggesting the inclusion of his living room, gently pushing for a domesticity that was complex, crowded, nearly incoherent, for his empty chair that stood tall among the chaos.

"NOTHING FEELS RIGHT," I said into my cell. I was on the top of a double-decker bus, stuck in traffic around the Marble Arch circle. I'd felt so lost, so alone that day, that I found myself impulsively dialing my mother, even though I wasn't sure why. Perhaps, I knew she'd be by the phone. Perhaps, automatic numbers.

"You're young," she said gently, strangely calm compared to her histrionic calls, listening to my every word. It was better, I saw, when I called her. "Nothing feels right until your thirties." The bus moved an inch. Diesel seeped in through the windows. Hyde Park spread in front of me, but I felt closed in by the cars. "You need to be good to yourself," she said. "Treat yourself like a baby. The brain grows faster than the heart."

I imagined myself rocking my inner turmoil. I imagined Mom rocking me, now. "How did you and Dad find each other?" I surprised myself by asking something so intimate. Emotions were so fragile, could crack like thin porcelain.

"Love is a happy coincidence of moods." She chuckled. "It happens when two people meet at the right moment."

"Huh." I thought of Mom's poetry years, her haunted drawings, of how somewhere in her, she knew so much. Perhaps we *could* talk—talk about love. The phone line was a good connector. The distance was physical and so it felt less threatening. The medium was contained, deliberate, could be turned off. And I could command it, get her attention. "Thanks, Mom," I said, finally feeling a breeze on my face, wishing I'd thought of more questions and could keep her in this tender frame, this side of her mind, for just a bit longer.

On Evan's moving day, a dark morning in early December, I arrived early. "Don't stand there," he said, agitated. "Help me move that stuff."

Evan had a lot of stuff.

I'd been particularly stuff-resistant in my new apartment. I loved the open shelves and made neat piles of clothes and books. I used my old coffee table as a bathroom ledge and placed my cosmetics on them one by one. I kept my fridge only lightly stocked, and bought no decorative trinkets. The room partitions were bohemian beaded strands, but I'd tied them back to make crisp angles. My only adornment was a red sun decal that Evan had given me, stuck to my kitchen window under the brown slatted blinds, which made the sunlight blush across my gray counter.

When we arrived at Evan's new place, in Zone Three, I helped bring in the small boxes. Afterward, we sat in his dark front room. "The mover thinks I should marry you," he said. His gray eyes looked deeper, thicker, as if whole worlds swirled inside, making them the color of all color.

"Marry me?" We'd been together for less than a year! Marriage for me was a fuzzy notion, like looking at a pointillist painting up close: I knew it would make sense in the far-off distance, but was completely indiscernible now. But it was reassuring to know he felt confident enough to repeat it. I smiled, and turned away.

"Maybe he's right and I should marry you," Evan said, but not to me.

I moved boxes. *Play it cool.* I offered to leave and give him space like he'd done for me. He agreed. I left. I didn't call him. And he didn't call me.

For a week.

A horrible seven days. I checked my cell constantly, my landline for voice mail beeps. He'd mentioned marriage—marriage! I prayed I was giving him the space he needed to feel settled into his new abode. To think about next steps, future plans. Then, on Christmas, the world dark but lit red and green, he called. *Let's have lunch.*

On Boxing Day, we met at a curry house in Banglatown. He brought me a regifted bottle of Drambuie. My stomach heaved in waves. I couldn't fathom ingesting a calorie. Evan ordered up a storm—unusual for his home-cooking tastes and budgetary stylings. He dumped rice on his plate.

"This isn't working," he said. I used all my facial strength to blink back tears. My head spun. *Marriage* and now this? He had turned, flipped, spontaneous, quick.

"Why not?" I couldn't understand. I knew things weren't perfect, but not *this* not-perfect. Nothing was perfect. We'd both improved our lives, found our dream houses.

"They're on the opposite sides of London—doesn't that tell you anything?"

I shook my head.

"I'm looking for, well . . ." He paused. "You just don't make me feel comfortable. You have no throw pillows, no armchairs. No stuff to make me feel at home. I keep asking you, but . . ."

Then it hit me. "Are you sleeping with Honor?" I barely formed the sounds.

He didn't say anything for the longest second of my life. "She has matching plate sets," he finally conceded.

"You fucking asshole." I threw my biryani right at him. Then I got up, fled straight out the front door.

"It wasn't working out between us," he called after me, and then other words that I couldn't hear over the roar of my fury and shame. Honor, the middle-aged divorcée, had won. My youth meant nothing, my cool controlled style was worthless. I'd been trying to impress Evan with sophistication, my hipster neighborhood, moving bloody apartments for him, and what did he do? He cheated on me. With her. Suburban her.

How could I not have known?

I rushed up the creaky stairs to my solo abode, ready to call him and scream, but I stopped myself. Evan was right. He'd been asking me to cook him dinner, to help with his gardening, what I thought of marriage, but I'd played it cool. I'd been equating intimacy with neatness, maturity and beauty with minimalism and restraint. I thought getting rid of objects, being antihoard, would help me get close to people. But all Evan had wanted was for me to nurture him. Make him comfortable.

I looked around my living room, its blank walls, its cushionless couch. I was so good at purging, I'd gotten rid of my boyfriend.

My brain had paved my way out of Kildare, but it wasn't enough. All the domestic theory in the world couldn't teach me how to live.

· NINE ·

25 WEEKS: WHEN WATER BREAKS, ALMOST
New York City, 2011

I looked down at the water that crashed in every direction, underlying forces opposing one another for no apparent reason. My legs went wobbly—actually a nice break from the general aching strain.

"Why are my *legs* hurting?" I quickly looked up and asked Jon. "It feels like I run a marathon each day."

"Because you're carrying an extra twenty pounds," he said. "It's a real weight."

"Hm." He was right. A real burden. It was a blissfully clear Saturday afternoon, the sun bright but the air dry, the best of New York summer, and we were taking one of our weekly strolls through the city. Since we'd moved to NYC, we'd spent most Saturdays on foot, hiking from one event to another, always completing the full trajectory as pedestrians, committed to exploring the tucked-away shops and unusual offerings of Flushing, the Lower East Side, Harlem or, that day, Williamsburg, where we tried to take in every coffee shop and gadget sale, knowing that our daylong walks were numbered.

Now we headed back into Manhattan across the Williamsburg Bridge, an incredible and gargantuan structure with lanes even for walkers. The architecture was magnificent as were the views—enormous housing projects, buildings where tens of thousands of lives converged, their dreams and fears meshing and bumping into one another, reminding us of how small we are and how contained our physical existences can be, and yet our inner worlds can span continents, ages.

That was on top. Below, visible beneath cracks and layers of metal—the abyss. The bridge accommodated traffic on many levels, all of us—bikers, walkers, drivers, riders, mariners—suspended between boroughs, between land, taking our lives in our hands with no fuss at all, as if the state of hanging was banal, as if dangling in midair was par for any course.

"I can't take it," I burst out.

"I know," Jon said, "the weight is annoying, but I think you look super sexy." He squeezed me into his side. He was strong, a sturdy spectacular structure. I flashed to my sludgy walks home from school with Bubbie, my Sunday marches through Montreal with Dad, how intimate it was to step in sync with someone else, seeing the world from the same point, smelling the same scents, the same dust landing on our pores.

"It's not the weight," I said. "Well, not just the weight."

"What is it?"

You're the only person who's ever understood me, who enabled me to create the composed life that I so urgently needed. And now you're not on my side, but on the side of my insides. I can't even turn inward for refuge, as I've done for over thirty years, because my interior has been invaded.

"This pregnancy is hard for me," I said quietly. "I'm afraid of losing my space, my mind, all the ways I've learnt to cope with my past."

Jon was silent.

"Look at where I came from. What happens if I'm just not 'maternal'? What if I don't know how to hug or feed or play? Don't you feel that way? Aren't you worried?"

"No, not really," he said. "I mean, we'll figure it out. Everyone does it—how hard can it be?"

Damn reasonable Jon. He didn't get it, he didn't have the anxiety I had—despite his own background. But maybe that was better. One of us needed to be calm, a pillar of full breaths. He took my hand.

"I'm worried it *can* be pretty hard," I said. Aside from my messed-up past, there were other issues. Like, what did I know from kids? Almost no one in our social set was a parent. "I haven't *seen* a child in twenty-five years."

He chuckled. But I was serious.

"I've been trained in molecular biochemistry and continental feminist psychoanalytic theory, not home ec. I did internships in-stead of babysitting. I have no idea what to *do* with a baby. Or a child. Or, lord, a teenager." I reminded him of the weekend when my friends from Montreal came to visit with their two toddlers. Strollers, pouches, bedtimes were a language I didn't speak. Even Mones, our cat, hid in my closet and retched. The kids spent whole days fighting violently over chewed-up puzzle pieces. "Share, share, share," was the parents' mantra—*as if we all lived in a utopian commune*, I kept thinking. *What if they don't always want to share? What if a child wants to hang on to their stuffed musical octopus, keep it special, beautiful, under their sole control?* Then the toddlers left tangerine peels under our sofa. "I don't even know how to cook—how am I supposed to help another human realize their full potential? How do I avoid drowning the baby in my issues?"

"Well," Jon said, "at least you don't hold back."

I was able to be open with him, that was true. My concerns seemed concrete and surmountable when Jon and I discussed them, when I was willing to be seen for who I was. And I certainly hadn't always been able to do that.

"I have to pee again," I said, in the spirit of saying it all.

PUNCH LINES
London, 2004

"We better send someone out to get drinks," Andy said, pointing at the table with at least a hundred bottles on it. The house party was packed, but he was talking to *me*, a dazzling smile lighting his face.

"People will die of thirst," I played along, my voice shaking. I knew Andy from my new stand-up comedy workshop but we'd never spoken one-on-one. "And scurvy."

His lush lips stretched like elastics across his boyish Australian face, round and welcoming and topped with green eyes like jewels.

Nothing like Evan. After slowly recovering from my shame at being dumped, largely by talking about it with Charlotte, who was going through a divorce, as well as dodging him and Honor at the dance school by changing for class in an upstairs closet, I accepted my new singlehood. Eventually, in place of the heavy hollowness that would set in on Saturday mornings when I realized I had nowhere to go, that no one expected me anywhere, there sprouted an appreciation of my home. All four mini rooms were mine; I didn't have to live with depressives or drug addicts, with psychopathologies seeping through the walls. I splurged on a red-and-cream-colored shawl that I draped over the straight slat blinds in my bedroom, and a round red rug to spice up my gray wall-to-wall carpeting. I had savvy! I enjoyed how the sun filtered in through my window in the early mornings, casting a neat shadow of straight lines along my living room floor. I liked the smell of curry from the adjacent Pakistani men's club that wafted through my bedroom, reminding me of the bustling, globo life around me. I even cracked open a beginners cookbook and made some salad dressing.

Perhaps it was this new calm that enabled me to try out a pipe dream: stand-up comedy. Dad had performed Yiddish sketches, Eli worked in musical theater, my most exhilarating memory was my bat mitzvah speech. I'd always entertained people with my anecdotes and insecurities—why not bring them to the world! And if I'd been looking for answers in an academic way, well, here was the inexplicable, illogical art of humor. My first classes had gone well. "Funny." People gestured at me, serious, nodding.

"Let's get some air," Andy said. Was he flirting? He was six foot two, aqua-eyed, and everyone's crush. I was still the Woody Allen of women—self-deprecating, nerdy, insecure about my chubby body and mismatched features. Glasses galore. I followed him to the garden and we sat on a bench, his knees jetting out way past mine.

"Want a smoke?" he asked.

"Sure," I said.

"I don't smoke," he said.

"Me neither," I answered.

We laughed and he suddenly kissed me, tenderly, as if the jokes we'd shared in class now mingled in our mouths. Andy liked me!

"Come back to my place?" I couldn't believe I offered. He got our coats. "Let's keep this a secret," I blurted out, not wanting to confuse business with pleasure, not wanting to risk another public rejection.

"My lips are sealed," he answered. "On yours."

The next morning, he mocked me for having so many toilet rolls, and pretended to search my apartment for my imaginary husband. I cracked up. I didn't know what was more surprising—his advances, my compliance, or that he texted me sweet messages all day, especially considering we'd slept together on our first, well, conversation.

ANDY'S AND MY differences, which went well beyond the physical, were exhilarating. He was twenty-three, four years my junior, and was not only a charming Adonis, but dedicated to his art. He refused day jobs that didn't relate to his passion, performed every night, and was never rattled by failure. When we started going to see shows together, Andy schmoozed his way backstage to introduce himself to his famous comedian idols. I spent hours composing an e-mail requesting five minutes of stage time. I still worked at the museum and on my PhD and was chasing my dreams on weekends, stuck in the safety of classes. I wanted to walk in his extra-large footsteps. I longed to stand next to him and glow in his charismatic halo. When we met for drinks at a massive subterranean Aussie pub in Soho, it felt like the opposite of my world, as if, if one were to dig a hole from my parents' house down into and right through the earth, you'd end up at Wallabies.

Andy laughed loudly at my jokes in class—my stamp of approval. *When I was born, I pissed all over the OB. My mother was so embarrassed, she pulled me aside right there in the delivery room and said: Judy, if you're gonna urinate on the doctor, he's not gonna ask you out. . . . My father has reached an age where a lot of his friends are dying. I find it very sad, but he doesn't, because he's competitive. I'm like: Dad, I'm so sorry that your lifelong friend Mel died. He was only sixty-seven. He's like, Judy, I'm sixty-eight!* He encouraged me to try an open mic, listened as I over-rehearsed, gave me space as I paced the aisle (by aisle, I mean the vestibule at the entrance to this club, which was a cramped, beer-soaked, cigarette-infused basement room of a pub that used to be the meeting room of right-wing intellectuals during World War II) and then clapped through my set, assuring me when I worried I hadn't been good enough, happy when a comedy promoter approached me after the show. It was happening! I was happening! Together, we brainstormed and postmortemed, our clothes smelling like the alcohol-soaked floorboards of the pubs where we performed.

Andy became a fixture in my tiny apartment, which was larger than his damp room in a house share. He used my towels, dishes, pens, and borrowed thick handfuls of my CDs. I stocked food. He couldn't afford to take me out for dinner, or drinks, but I didn't mind. In exchange for his humorous aura I would finally be the Domestic Goddess.

MY OWN SPORADIC gigging led me to the heat of a women's comedy competition, the UK's largest. Sixteen of us were on that night, this time crowded into the back area of another subterranean pub in the "green room" that was curtained off by a sheet. Considering I was on twelfth in the lineup and having trouble schmoozing the drunk-on-rosé insurance company sponsors, my expectations were low. Indeed, when I was finally called up, the mic broke, hanging flaccid on its edge. I gestured to it in disgust.

People went crazy, guffawing. I couldn't believe it.

"Use the other mic," someone heckled. My stiffness appeared as nonchalance, and I shrugged and picked it out of its stand. I was totally exposed, no stand however tiny to cover even a slice of me.

"Well, that's my whole seven minutes," I said, not thinking, to uproarious applause. Somehow, my honesty in the moment had connected me to a crowd in a way I'd never before felt: so plugged in. Then I started: *Before I begin, I just wanted to remind everyone to please turn off your phones. Because if you don't, my mother will call.* Another round of applause. From there, my set—about living in the East End, types of joggers, a surreal piece about breaking up with my brain (*it's not you, it's me*)—just got better, the crowd clapping and whooping. I was attached, linked through gesture and laughter and in complete control. I created those seven minutes, managed the mood, set the pace, for everyone around me. In turn, the audience saw me, knew me, took me in. I was them and they me and I was in myself so much so that every cell of me belonged in the moment.

That night, Andy sat next to me on the top of the double-decker bus, our thighs touching, his enormous hand clasping my small clammy one. He cheered, his booming voice proud. We rode east, to my perfect little apartment, where I served Andy coffee like Evan had showed me as if passing on a wild sex trick, and my limbs were burning and even shaking in delight.

A WEEK LATER I got the call that I'd made it to the semifinals. "Congratulations!"

"Thank you," I croaked from my bed. It turned out those euphoric tremors had also marked the onset of a high fever, as if the experience of fitting in, of existing within my own skin, was too overwhelming to bear. Andy had come over to nurse me, and though I'd requested Gatorade and Tylenol, he'd arrived with ingredients for an Irish meat stew and three documentaries about vaudeville. I wasn't feeling particularly carnivorous from my drenched sheets, but hearing the clattering of pots and his humming, I reminded myself that he hadn't done a one-eighty or run away, that he was still here for me even in a difficult time, even when I wasn't fun or funny.

"Great job," the production assistant said over the phone. "You'll take part in the showcase next month. In Manchester."

Manchester? But I was too excited to question why, especially as they offered to pay for my train and budget hotel room. I was in the semifinals! My name would be on a Web site—as a comedian. Audiences liked me, Andy liked me. Life was making sense.

I ARRIVED AT the Manchester club thirty minutes early to find out I was on last, then walked ten miles in nervous pacing. Andy had decided a few days earlier that it was best he didn't come, just in case he got a last-minute gig, even though I'd offered to pay for his train. We didn't always go to each other's shows—he never demanded I come to his—and I reminded myself that this was work. But still I felt untethered—a new city, alone, as foreign as I could be (I couldn't understand even the poshest Mancunian accent). I tried to channel Andy's careerist bravado and confidence but knew no one in the Northern comedian clique and the MC pronounced my name incorrectly. The gig was not terrible—I did not die, but also, did not kill. *I'm unemployed, I have a lot of free time. Which is good, because I can't afford any other kind of time.* I held back tears as I left the stage, then ran from the club burning in shame.

I tried to reach Andy by text, and finally, after two large glasses of yellow white wine from my budget hotel's bar, I called him wailing. "I've ruined everything."

"You screwed up," was what he said, seemingly distracted. "Don't take it personally. Just do better next time."

I hung up feeling hollow. I'd needed him to say that I'd been great, the audience was stupid. But, I reasoned, he was probably right. I felt like I'd let the stage down, let him down, ruined his belief in my potential. I was so entwined with him, yet so alone.

It wasn't for a few days that I got the phone call. The ring itself was shrill. "Judy." It was the producer. "I mean, I love your act."

I knew it was bad.

"But you're way too Jewish for most of England. That's why we sent you to Manchester—to see how a Jew would go down in the North. I mean, if I was booking bar mitzvahs, you'd be first on my list." My ear burned into my cell. I'd wanted feedback, sure, but this was not in any universe what I'd expected. There was not a word in my set about my religion. I stared out my kitchen window, through the translucent red sun decal Evan had bought me, and saw the world in red shafts of light, as if it was revealing its true colors to me for the first time. "Plus, your face is much too Jewish for British television."

Too Jewish. All these years, I'd wanted to be seen, and now I was. But for being Jewish?

"Think about it. Tell me if you'd like to work with me on production, or finance."

"Thanks," I stammered as I hung up. *Finance?* I did Fine Arts.

I went to the mirror to see what the world saw, and found the Holocaust, Bubbie, my whole history, wrapped in my DNA, weaved into my skin cells, in my under-eye bags and dark, wanting brown pupils. I found everything I'd run away from appear right there, highlighting my every inch.

I placed my hands flat on my cheeks. If I didn't belong on stage, then where?

ANDY WAS BUSY making his mark, gigging every night, even if he was being paid largely in beer. He stayed over on weekends but stopped coming to parties. Instead, he'd spread his notes across my living room, sprawling out along my futon, his brown socks confidently poking out beyond the metal frame, stretching his arms like a cat settling in for a good lick. One night, it dawned on me that he looked more comfortable in my apartment then I ever did. "Have fun," he urged as I left for the evening. "I'll be here when you get back." *This is what it's like to date a real comedian,* I sighed as I stepped into the rainy night, leaving him to hone his art on my appliances.

The next day, my phone rang. She was breathless. "I can't go on."

I froze. "What are you talking about, Mom?"

"I can't see a way out of this."

"It's just an inheritance fight." I tried to calm her. "We'll take care of you. Please, don't talk like this."

"There's no point. I can't live anymore," she cried. "I'm going to kill myself."

I sat down on my blue wooden chair, gripped the edges. She was shrieking, hyperventilating. "Mom, please. Don't do anything. I'm going to help you."

"You promise?" She quieted, thank God. "You'll always be in touch?"

"Of course, I'm always here."

"For you, I'll live," she whispered. "For you. I love you so much."

"I love you so much too, Mom." My voice was firm but my hands shook. *I can help her,* I thought. *I'm far away but I can help her find a therapist, a good doctor. I can be there for her.* I called her back every hour that day. And the next. Until a few days later when she called me like this, again.

THAT SUNDAY EVENING, dizzy with nerves, I trudged up to a cabaret club hidden in one of Soho's secret winding roads. I'd been forcing myself to keep gigging, and was invited to perform at this West End show. I was both so excited to have been picked and also wished I was doing absolutely anything else than putting myself through this hellish anxiety. *Why do you do it? To be seen! Heard!* I entered the nondescript door to find a lush red lobby filled with golden chandeliers and a backstage full of pole dancers discussing their various affairs with Russell Brand while sizzling-on fake eyelashes. I took out my comb and haphazardly fed it through my strands and paced, waiting for my turn.

Only, as soon as I presented my intro line—"I'm a Canadian Jew, which means . . . nothing"—I heard a loud boo. "What?" I asked into the mic, shocked. I was thrown off. I'd added this first joke specifically to acknowledge my identity and show how not-important it was to my set, which usually worked. But tonight, the audience sniffed my fear, and the boos got louder. I might have assumed it was due to my demeanor or poor delivery and tried harder, but this response struck a chord. Since the Manchester disaster, I'd been experiencing increasing anti-Jewish sentiment. "Go Back to Hampstead," was heckled at me. "Jew play the Jewkaleleh?" was another clever one. "I don't really like Jews," a comic said to me—as a joke, his friend later clarified. I was awarded a scholarship from a British women's academic institution and their annual dinner was sprinkled with conversations about "the Jews who are in it for the money." The comments seeped under my olive-toned skin. Was I misunderstanding? Overreacting? Underreacting?

Even when I started commenting back ("um, since I'm here for an art history degree, I'm certainly not in it for the money"), I felt more and more like a visible minority, hyperconscious of how I was being seen—my nose, my American accent, my thick-rimmed glasses. In every interaction, every day, onstage and off, I began to guess at what the person I was with was seeing in me. Who was I to them?

Now, the audience started to chatter among themselves. I couldn't hold attention. They hated me. Under the gilded dome, in bright West End spotlights, thousands of miles from Montreal, from my history, old genetic terrors festered up. I thought of my fifth grade Yiddish teacher who had pulled me up to the front of the class. "Look at the eyes, the nose—if this had been Warsaw 'thirty-nine, Judy would have been the first to go." My pulse pounded, my eyes grew watery, the mic slipped in my hand. I ran off the stage at three minutes, straight past the curly girls, under disco balls, through the warren of Victorian staircases, in hot tears. The nineteenth-century walls might have been bedecked in gilded framed mirrors, but all I saw was a haze of brown stringy hair, running, running.

THE NEXT DAY, I noted Andy slipping two of my comedy how-to books into his man bag. "What are you doing?" I asked, as he made for my door.

"Just borrowing these." He smiled as always.

I stared at the gaping hole in my bookshelf. The remaining volumes fell awkwardly into the space on the shelf, which suddenly seemed vast.

"Have you borrowed others?" I asked, alarmed that I hadn't known.

"Just a few," he said, slinging his pack over one shoulder. "I'll bring them back, don't worry."

It was one thing to offer, but another to find out he'd taken. He didn't mind that I was upset. I scanned my minuscule flat—the unmade bed, his dishes in the sink, his pages on my sofa. Then I noted the blank space on my bulletin board. "Did you use the gift certificate I'd been saving?"

"I got comedy DVDs," he said. "It was going to expire."

My long-held tongue unfurled. "That was mine!"

"Whoa." Andy backed up. "You have anger issues."

"My anger issue is that I'm angry," I mumbled. I felt my boundaries being stretched, ready to snap.

I looked up at his glittering grin, his self-assured poise. He was eternally magnetic, driven, confident.

He walked out the door.

Motionless, I looked around my apartment—what else had I not noticed? Andy's papers sat in piles on the floor, as did mine. Books for my PhD, comedy, the museum, a theater project, Yiddish translations lined what was once my dining room table. My Hoover hadn't worked properly in ages, and parts of the carpets had crumbs on them, even though I pseudo-vacuumed every week. Free cosmetic samples—in fact anything free—was stocked in the now grimy cosmetics bags in my bathroom. I tried to keep it all tidy and neat, but items had tattered with time, with two of us camped and cramped in here. The sink was filled with dishes. The plant that an artist friend had bought me as a housewarming gift was completely dry but I kept it on top of the kitchen counter. I felt so poor, so financially vulnerable, that I couldn't bear to throw things away. I tried to be motherly, but Andy saw me as angry and aggressive. I offered too much of my home, my boundaries were too porous. I felt my jeans press right into my waist: I'd even gained weight.

I couldn't believe I hadn't noticed my own demise. Why couldn't I just work at the museum, be content? Why did I always want more, more, more? I thought of my mother's stuff, which seemed to be her dual attempt at both connection and protection. Was I looking for safety in the stuff and projects around me? I'd wanted to nurture, to be what Evan had dreamed of, but I was a mess. I was hoarding emotions, memories, doubts, self-perceptions, my ambivalent life cluttered with empty commitments and old selves I just couldn't jettison.

My fingers automatically dialed my mother, relying on that cord that bound us together while keeping us far enough apart. "How are you?" I asked.

"Terrible," she started, her voice trailing off like a coil of smoke.

I was going to interject and switch the conversation to me, a new strategy that was good for both of us. It got her out of her head, got me some attention. But she launched in first. "They're after me," she whispered. "Do you know anything about Fred's trip to Scotland?"

Did she mean Scotland Yard? And that her docile philosopher friend who I hadn't seen in fifteen years was reporting on her? "I can't deal with this now."

"Didn't I talk you through your problems?" she accused. "What about me?"

I sighed. She was right. "Fine."

She wanted to talk from the other room, people might be listening on the line. *They're coming to get me.* "All I ever did was try to help anybody, to take care of my parents."

Now I felt guilty, too.

"Would it be easier for you, for everyone if I was dead?"

"Mom, please." It was so tiring convincing someone to live.

"Why do you call, if you don't even care? Are you even my daughter?"

She didn't trust me, like Bubbie didn't trust her, screaming when

Mom had tried to get her help, forcing Mom to call ambulances to take her to the hospital.

"I don't know." I seethed and hung up, wondering why I kept seeking validation and what warped version of me she saw, if she saw me at all.

PASSOVER, AND ANOTHER trip to Montreal. This time, I could barely open the door to the den, let alone find a place to sit, let alone lie down and watch TV, escape into fictional worlds, as I'd done when I used to live here. It had gotten so much worse. The room was completely overrun with plastic bags of files, stacks of tape-recorded conversations, tomes about tax law. And then there were the dozens of clocks—bright blue and orange, pink and green, thick silvery hands and thin gold numerals, flashing digital and faux grandfather, each set at a different time, the congregation asynchronous and thus tracing not only the seconds, but the seconds between the seconds, one long allegro of passing, a blaring metronome with no pauses, calling to mind our internal clocks, the fragility of our rhythms, the ease with which it could all go terrifically wrong.

The sofa had been moved away from the wall and the seat cushions lifted so that items could be stored in and behind it. Even the furniture was exploding. My father's reclining chair was in a cleared-out patch by the window. He'd razed a thin path from the door and marked a place for himself like the outline of a victim at a murder scene. Now, he lounged in his nest, casually crossed-legged, reading his paper, glancing intermittently at the news, as if he wasn't sitting in what felt and sounded like a ticking time bomb.

"Here, why don't you sit on this?" My mother pushed a low-to-the-ground swivel chair toward me. Its seat was lopsided, hanging over on one side.

"No, thanks," I said. "I need a walk." I had just arrived that afternoon and already I was desperate for air. It made no sense how I often felt so homesick and yet at home, I just felt sick. Where was the home I was sick for? I walked to the door.

"Wait!" my mother shrieked.

"What?"

"I need to release the alarm," she whispered. She'd already enlisted the services of half of Montreal's locksmiths, with hundreds of locks throughout the house, but an alarm?

My mother punched a few buttons on a keypad behind one of the doors—I hadn't even noticed it amid all the junk. A loud voice bellowed: "System disarmed."

She thought someone would break into our dilapidated house? But I knew not to ask her. I did not want to be prisoner to her hour-long rants about the people she was convinced sat outside watching her so that she'd taped all the blinds to the walls. I felt sick. Each time I saw her, her grasp of reality seemed more undone. I noted the pink plastic container filled with Valium bottles perched on the edge of the dusty TV table. I looked away. She was dissolving.

I glanced at Dad, bedecked in the *Montreal Gazette*, and thought about his theory. Paranoia, he'd said, could be interpreted as a form of extreme narcissism, of needing to create a world in which you are at the center of everyone's attention.

But he never said: *Mom's* paranoia. Or *Mom's* desire for attention.

I looked at my mother's swollen face, her eyes reeking with melancholy. Screaming: get me out of here.

Get me out of myself.

I couldn't bear it. I stepped across the threshold.

"Let me in when I get back," I said, half joking.

MOM WAS CONSTANTLY on guard, ready for an attack.

Then one actually happened.

I was walking to the museum, just steps outside my front door, when people began to crowd the sidewalk, exiting the tube station instead of entering it. A queue appeared at the bus stop. An electronic traffic sign read: INCIDENT. The paparazzi arrived outside the nearby hospital gate. Then, the ambulances.

We'd been waiting. Ever since 9/11 everyone expected a bomb. It was a question of when, where, how. No one on the street seemed surprised; they moved quickly as normal. Brits rarely showed vulnerability, and, honed by years of IRA threats, they certainly did not panic. I, however, had less of a Blitz mentality, and more of a blintz one. "What's going on?" I barraged fellow pedestrians, energized by the drama, which made me feel like part of something. "What happened?" Sirens blared.

My fellows were, predictably, less fellowish. They shrugged, didn't answer.

They didn't have to. I went immediately into my genetically-garnered warzone mentality, even if I'd spent two and half decades running away from those implanted hydrogen bonds. I ran to the grocery store to stock up: water, scurvy-fighting pineapple chunks, calorie-heavy baked beans, and cash—as much as the machine would let me take. The shopping list I'd subconsciously rehearsed my whole life. I barely felt the ridiculous weight of the bags and quickly lugged them back to my apartment. As I got my passport ready near the door, I made the call I'd practiced for years. Despite the fact that it was five a.m. in Canada, my mother answered on the first ring (of course she slept by a phone—she had dozens).

"Something happened in London," I said firmly, confidently, as I'd learnt to talk to my parents, to not freak them out. I imagined their house, the gulag-style precautions, the hundreds of 1980s videocassettes stacked like brick walls to protect them, Billy Crystal on guard. "But I'm fine." With them, there was no room for me to be not-fine. "Don't worry," I repeated. "I'm really fine." I turned on the TV to watch the news anchor plot a map of the bomb locations; my mother turned on CNN in her attempt to connect to me. I told her of my shopping and waited for her to be proud, panicked and insane.

"I'm so glad you're OK," she said, shocking me with her calmness. "Thank you for calling." The woman who freaked out about hepatitis when I had a manicure and worried that at every meeting I'd be raped (*Erica Jong was seduced by a publisher,* she'd warn) was now a pillar of solidity and oneness. We stayed on the phone for over an hour, watching the TV together, Mom cool, reporting headlines, comparing this to other real and literary disasters. My unexpected lifeline.

"I'd better go," she said eventually. "Dad and I are getting new tires for the car."

"What?" I thought I'd misheard. Tires? At six a.m.? I was in a war.

"Tires. Thanks for calling, sweetie."

Of course, it had never really been about The War. Tragedy was no problem. The anxiety was all in the anticipation, preparation.

LATER ON THAT uncharacteristically sunny morning, already known as 7/7, double prime, odd, Andy texted to make sure I was OK. He wanted to see me; I smiled. On 7/8, we met for lunch near the museum. (Everyone, of course, had shown up for work. Blitz this.) I could hardly believe it had just been a day. Time swells with drama.

Andy needed to talk. About taking a break—from us. About this show we'd been planning to do together that just wasn't working out.

Wasn't. Working. Out. The words ran through my mind like a scrolling ticker tape newsfeed. "We just haven't found the right focus yet," I pleaded, referring to the show, to us. Deferring the inevitable. I knew things weren't stellar, but I hadn't imagined he'd actually turn on me, in an instant, now of all times.

"Just a break," he said. "Not a breakup."

He smiled at the blond waitress. I felt sick but ordered a salad and half listened to him, not at all concealing his good mood, as he described how he'd go on with the rest of his life—without me. I was afraid to speak, afraid of what might come out. I pretended to be at home, in bed, imagined the feel of my pillow on my cheek. My view drifted to a TV screen above us. A new incident. Police were searching buses.

My heart stalled. I tried to read the running headlines. I heard a rumbling around me, small whispers. I turned. The buses were on the street, parked right beside us. "Holy shit."

Andy was calm. "It's nothing," he read from the TV. "They're telling us explicitly that it was a false alarm."

Still. I wanted to say. *Still. It's all going on right here beside us.*

He offered to walk me home. Most streets were closed to pedestrians, so we were rerouted the long way around, and during our extended journey, Andy's phone rang. The comedy promoter who used to ask me to audition for competitions was now calling him. While everyone, everything was turning on me, he was being invited onto a radio show. "Of course!" He was elated, and bubbled along as we walked to my apartment, among alarms and police, plastic barriers, yellow lines of wavy uncertainty.

I TURNED ON the TV. It's what I always did in times of upheaval, of entropic, irreversible change. An inherited habit.

The set, a mere twenty inches, felt like it took up half my flat—it did. It showed fuzz. I stood and watched it.

Then I maneuvered my saucerlike antennae, waving it in the air, trying to pick up public channels until, at last, a picture emerged. Two men were being interviewed, but their talking heads were covered by scarves, disguised, like victims of hangings. Their muscular arms gesticulated, angry. I couldn't find a place to position the antennae so that the image remained still, so I stood and held it above the TV, surprised that the news was showcasing anonymous opinions.

"What is your feeling about the incident?" asked the journalist, whose serious white face was visible.

I balanced the saucer on the side of my tiny table. As long as I perched on the right edge of my futon, the reception lasted. I had to squeeze my expanding derriere in between piles. The provisions I'd picked up the day before filled my minuscule kitchen, and leaked into my living room, which was still stacked with papers: the towers of photocopied articles for my half-written PhD; the pile of notes for my eight-minute stand-up set that had taken me to the national level and taught me that my dreams could be curtailed by my nose. I reached up to touch it, and covered my face with my hand.

What was I doing here?

The reception on the TV wavered for a moment, and a trail of color swooped off the unvisaged characters' heads, as if their brains trailed behind them.

My brain trailed behind me. My apartment was starting to look a lot like my mother's hoarded mess. My comedy career was dreck, my relationship nearly over. *I* was blowing up. *I'm fine,* I heard myself tell my mother. *Fine.*

"The government must go down," said one young man in a British accent. "This country does nothing for us."

"Nothing," repeated the other. "I support the murderers!"

A chill helixed down my spine. This is what they meant by home-grown terrorism. The parasite within.

I stared at the anonymous voices and veils, and couldn't shake the feeling that there was something familiar about the Atwoodian image. Was it the uncharacteristic sunlight? The background? Yes, there was something recognizable about the blue door they were standing in front of. Its inner frame, its peeling paint, its slightly run-down edges. Where had I seen that door? Why would I recognize *a door*?

I felt the pulse in my eyes. I jumped up, opened my dusty front window, leaned fully out, and checked out *my front door.*

This interview about the end of Western civilization had taken place—literally—on my doorstep.

A bad joke. A terrible punch line.

The eternal sense that had always festered in my DNA rushed to my surface: Nothing is safe. The walls I'd tried so hard to build were collapsing on me. I might have been sitting at the center of my flat, wearing my snug one-bedroom costume, but I was still so far from being at home.

For the first time in years, I sobbed, cries deep and rich.

Please, Bubbie, tell me where to go.

· TEN ·

26 WEEKS: TUNA OR NOT TUNA
New York City, 2011

We usually think that events determine our emotions—that good things lead to happiness and bad ones to despair—but it can be the opposite. Sometimes our feelings come first, and determine how we react to events.

Walking up the grimy subway stairs, trying not to brush any urine-stained surfaces, I could hear my heart beat against the roaring Manhattan traffic, feel it pounding against my skin alongside the baby's kicks. *Excess blood, panic, or both?*

But as soon as I was tucked into my serene apartment, about to put my feet up, I noticed four missed calls. Before I could call back, it buzzed on its own accord. "Did you get my messages?" Mom asked, whispering, in that hushed tone that made her feel paper thin to me, like she could blow away or disintegrate at any second. "I researched tuna for you. On the Internet. It's serious."

My muscles tensed. Where had *this* dramatic turn come from? Mom had been thrilled about my pregnancy. She was the first person I told after Jon, and, as I'd expected, she exploded in screeches of delight ("This is the best thing that ever happened to me!"). Since then, she'd been excited during our calls, and diligently checking in to inquire about how I was feeling and how the fetus was faring. At first, I was resentful—she was suddenly interested in every detail of my well-being, and it wasn't even because of something I'd achieved. But with time, I began to appreciate her concern, grateful that she tried to curb her stress around me. Over the past few weeks, we'd been talking frequently and pleasantly, having long conversations about her pregnancy with me. "I also got pregnant immediately," she'd recently divulged. "I also had sore breasts, horrible cramps." I'd listened eagerly to these tales, reminding myself that we were genetically tagged—she was talking about *my* birth. But I didn't like today's panicked tone. And I probably didn't want to know what she found out about tuna.

A few days earlier, I'd received an urgent message from my OB. I called back during a meeting, pacing the edge of a coffee shop as I was passed along a network of nurses until I finally heard my doctor's German accent. (This one was German-Israeli.) "I vaz chasing out of ze hospital zis morning at your visit, but you didn't turn back. One test result iz not good."

Cardiac arrest.

"Your mercury is through ze roof. Enough with ze tuna."

It wasn't coffee, alcohol, or drugs that would get me and my fetus—it was tuna.

I could barely and yet totally believe it. "If there was one object, one metaphor through which I could trace my life, it's tuna!" I ranted to Jon that night about how our Kildare household had been swimming in tuna fish cans, how tuna had been the protein vunderfood. It made up nearly half my lunches, stinkily falling all over the place (my mother refused to mix it with mayo, just cottage cheese), or secretly appearing inside pasta (Mom, delicious spaghetti—oh wait, what the hell . . .). Stacked tapes of my earliest baby coos were filled with the background calls of my father: "Hey, where'd you put the tuna?" As a teenager, I rebelled and binged on raw tuna at sushi bars; tuna followed me as a rare steak into my African and European travels; canned tuna re-became my staple as a starving artist (not starving for tuna); I then hung out with Jon in Asian tuna markets as my yuppification began. Tuna tuna tuna.

"You have strong feelings," Jon had said, which I knew meant: hormones. "Let's lay off the fish."

Later, I'd mentioned the test to my mother. Not because I thought she'd console me (she actually replied, "That's crazy—when I was pregnant with you, I ate tuna subs all day!"; "Exactly," I'd wanted to say) but because we'd been connecting so well. She offered to Google mercury poisoning, which was the last thing I wanted her to do, but when I thought of her alone, in her self-bombarded house, using her online connection to do background checks, I hoped it would be a distraction. "Sure," I'd said. *She's just trying to help.*

"I printed out seventeen Web pages," she now added, breathless. "Let me read them to you." I could feel my cheeks get hot. "Tuna consumption can cause mercury toxicity . . ." I held the phone away from my ear and sighed. I'd told her to do it . . .

". . . neural defects . . ."

But what I really needed was someone to massage my feet, get me dinner . . .

". . . kidney tumors in rats . . ."

. . . be around in case I went into fucking labor . . .

". . . and foremost, fetal brain damage."

"Great," I said, sighing. "Thanks." I stared at my white carpet, my white noise. I'd handed her my vulnerability, asked for help in order to help *her*, and now I felt even worse. How was I supposed to care for a mom and a child? Who'd care for me?

I still felt like a kid who needed guidance and reassurance. I checked in with Jon about everyday choices, like whether to do yoga or go swimming or take on a freelance job. As a parent I'd have to make decisions all day. Who'd comfort me when I was confused? Answer my questions? I didn't have the kind of family that could just pop by in an emergency, or even in a nonemergency. I couldn't count on Jon for everything. I'd be so alone.

"Judy, it's the other line, I'll call you later." Mom suddenly hung up.

I stared at my phone. I *was* so alone.

CRACKING CODES
London 2007

"Vodka on the rocks." I ordered my new favorite drink from the bar, actually a few tables pushed together and covered with white crepe paper. I waited for the drink to arrive in its plastic cup and marveled at my surroundings: I was at a singles party at a northwest London synagogue, Purim-themed.

What had happened to me?

Drink in hand, twenty-nine years old, I stood quietly for a moment shaking my ice and watched other single twenty- and thirty-something Jews madly try to impress one another with witty banter, curved postures, pointy toes, and flashy leather purses. All of a sudden my funky fabric bag and red rounded flats seemed tattered and anachronistic. I had not come here on a marital mission—my friend Maya dragged me (I was shocked I'd even agreed)—so I felt strangely calm, an outsider watching the schmooze, expecting nothing.

The past eighteen months had been a social whirlwind. Andy and I had continued to see each other sporadically, and I tried to find ways to make it work, keep his love, clean his flat. Then I spent Chanuka with my family in Montreal; Andy stayed in London to gig. On a blisteringly cold New Year's Eve, I sat in a friend's living room, listening as girls received calls from their fiancés. I checked my phone, feigning a smile. But there were no texts. I knew I wasn't ready to get hitched, but still, I was crushed. It wasn't just that Andy hadn't called. It was that I was sitting with high school friends, hearing about their dream wedding color schemes, while he was *doing a show*. It hit me: I didn't want to marry Andy. I didn't even want to date him. I wanted to *be* him.

I drank a shot of Goldschläger, its spiciness zipping through me, thawing me, waking me up. I'd been confusing what I needed in a partner with what I needed for myself. I'd expected that one day Andy would come to my parties and shows. I'd connected his love with my talent. If I was funnier, he'd like me more; if he loved me more, I'd be funnier. I was such a good joker, I'd been kidding myself.

When I got back to London I'd asked him to meet me at a hamburger joint.

"Can you spot me a fiver?" he'd asked.

"This isn't working," I'd said. I'd wanted to prove I could be the nurturer and wasn't as substandard as Evan had deemed, but I'd simply gone to the other extreme. The opposite of academia was the comedy club, but in the end these endeavors were for me similar attempts to claim originality, get attention. Avoid emotion. I'd been performing, with Evan, with Andy.

"I guess." His grin radiated. Did he even care? I'd bought him a hot dog and fled. As my tears dried in the cool January wind, I felt invigorated. What I got from Andy—persistence, assurance, mojo— I could give myself. I began writing jokes on my own, talking myself out of quitting, and even calling my mother after bad gigs (at least she answered). I worked harder. When I bombed, I imagined Andy coaching me: "Next time." I mimicked the ease with which he networked. I lost weight, ridded my apartment of junk, and jettisoned layers of pretense. I began to admit my cluttered past, my troubled mother, the conditions of my formative life—especially to myself. I used the word "hoarder" for the first time.

I even dabbled in dating. When I had a fling with Eric the stylish architect—he could literally build our home!—who didn't show up on my birthday and then joked about being as inconsistent as Mr. Big, I knew sooner rather than later not to feel bad. When Richard the dashing dermatologist sent me a two-page e-mail detailing why he didn't think it would work out after our second date, I was sad, but I moved on. I barely spent an evening with the prestigious critic who always criticized; I'd become quicker to recognize when I went out with someone because I fantasized being like them rather than liked being with them.

Suddenly, new friends fell into my life, or perhaps, I decided to catch them. Arrivals from Montreal, Harvard, New York. Jewish friends with whom I could openly discuss my cultural discomfort and who laughed at my stories, but not at me. I admitted how alienated I felt. Just talking to them helped me crawl out of my embattled-foreigner frame of mind. I still couldn't explain why I stayed in London, the safe haven that had, in some ways, turned out to be threatening and cold. For the first time in years, I began to see that I *could* leave. I could go back, even if I wasn't sure to where.

One of those new friends was Maya, an economics student from Toronto. She'd schlepped me to this Purim party because she was on a serious husband-finding mission. *Was I?* I asked myself now, still planted by the bar. Though it felt entirely strange, on paper I belonged here. It was Purim, but I wasn't wearing a mask—well, maybe a slight I'm-doing-this-ironically one, but only slight.

"You're a real drinker," a man said as he sidled up to me.

I turned, surprised. "I've been in England for five years." I hardly believed it.

He laughed. He was taller than me and slightly overweight. He had dark features and sharp cheekbones. When had I last even talked to a Jewish guy?

It turned out his name was Ben. As in, short for Benedict! Why didn't English Jews just name their kids Christ? It would be less obvious that they were trying to fit in.

"What do you do?" he asked, eyeing my artsy garb.

"Whatever you need," I joked.

He smiled. "What brings you here tonight?"

"My finding-a-husband-obsessed friend."

He chuckled again.

"And you?"

"Guilt!"

The lights began to flicker and a disembodied voice announced the end of the party. Typical British classiness. Last call, rushing, fluorescent lights, discussions about train times, the buzz killed in an instant. Maya approached with her flock of friends and pinched my arm. "We're going to get our coats."

"I'd like to see you again," Christ said, taking out his phone. "Your number?"

I gave it. Why not? A synagogue date. A whole new old world that I'd never imagined would like me.

I rushed to meet the others, all buzzing with gossip; they lived nearby in the Jewish neighborhood or were heading west. I of course lived miles away. At the tube station, I asked the conductor when the last eastbound connections were running, and he assured me I'd be fine, as long as I ran for my final train.

I ran, and yet. My train had terminated. I had no choice but to follow the crowds up the mile-long elevator to an island in the middle of a highway that was the entrance to the Canada Water station. The irony: the familiarity of Canada and yet the total strangeness of this industrial landscape in southeast London. (Not sure what the Canada or the water referred to except for a sewage stream.) It was definitely not safe to walk anywhere in this pitch-black, sidewalk-less neighborhood. I searched for information about the nearest night buses and car services but when I called, no one answered. Worse comes to worst, I calmed myself, I would stand here awake for five hours until dawn . . . I'd call someone . . . Mom?! . . . Then I noticed another woman reading the poster boards. "Are you trying to get out of here too?" I asked.

"Yes," she answered in a heavy accent.

Just then a black cab with its light on emerged from the obsidian horizon. I never took black cabs—the outrageous expense was prohibitive—but what could I do? I ran into the highway and flagged it down, forcing it to stop in the middle of a lane. "Come with me," I called to the stranded foreigner; for once, that title went to someone else.

As our car sped through the dark night, I pondered how well I knew the bulk of London's winding geography, how intimate I'd become with its neighborhoods and parks, its radio programs and urban systems. Yet I still felt so out of place. Crossing the iconic Tower Bridge, I wondered whether it was my fault, if I harbored some internal flaw, a wrongly flicked switch that never allowed me to feel a fit. Or, I questioned, watching the Thames jet out from two sides under me, if it was the city's fault in its ambivalence, its hunger for and antipathy to us aliens.

I DIDN'T HEAR from Pope Benny for three weeks and forgot about him. But then he called, engaging me in a long conversation about his entrepreneurial work in holistic medicine based on a family inheritance (a businessman?! . . . A self-starter? . . . Strangely frank about his life? . . . This, now, turned me on). "You sound like a spiritual person," he repeated, and though I had no idea what that meant, I kind of liked it.

The next night he picked me up in front of my tiny apartment in a massive BMW sports car, himself posed against the convertible as he waited for me to come down. The car of assholes, I thought, but I also liked it that he drove and, admittedly, that he made money.

"Interesting neighborhood," he said, raising his brow.

"Interesting person," I answered, getting in.

We went to a local Vietnamese restaurant. He ordered everything on the menu. "Why not?"

Back in the car, he leaned over and kissed me, his strong lips warm on mine.

"How old are you?" I asked, eyeing the crinkles at the sides of his eyes, not wanting to beat around any bushes. I figured he was almost forty.

He paused. "Forty-five in a few days."

Whoa. Crazy. But then I thought, I'm almost thirty. An adult. And so is he.

"I'm going to Montreal next week," I said.

"I'll call you there," he said.

Yeah right, I thought. But it didn't matter. I'd had fun.

"GET UP," MY mother pleaded. "It's nine a.m. You said you'd help me." She spoke from the threshold to my old bedroom. The floor was a storm of stuff, impervious, ominous like quicksand.

I'd arrived from London the night before and was jet-lagged. I sat up, groggy. The room was a disaster, laden with her mushroom-ing collection of swivel chairs, reams of printer paper, growing stacks of remainder hardbacks about Canadian modern art and Italian ghettos. My luggage took up the only remaining place on the ever-grottier pink carpet. The ceiling fan provided circulation while pouring dust, probably the same shed skin residues that had been there for years. My pillow pile—I needed to use many because each individual one was thin, a bargain basement purchase—was held upright by two large lamps and a stack of printers on what was once a night table. It struck me that my mother's home office was like the British Home Office, scouring for terrorists, protecting the country's borders. I felt the piles poking at the back of my neck. Now they seemed less my mother's barriers than her whole being, as if her stuff was what imposed on others, proved her existence. *See,* they were saying to my nape, *I touched you.*

"I called the taxi already," she said. "It's here."

"Here?" My mother was perennially late. But not for this. She'd never let me take a taxi, she'd never wake me. Unless it was about her houses.

"Please go. I need you to be there, to see what's going on at the open house. Please, for me, your mother." I knew the rental property was up for sale because her brother wanted to retrieve his share of their inheritance. She thought the real estate agent was in cahoots with my uncle and wanted me to listen in on his conversations.

"You want me to follow the agent around as he shows people the property?" I reiterated her seemingly crazy request.

"Yes! That would be excellent. Follow him closely. Wait—I'll get you a tape recorder."

"I'm *not* taking a tape recorder," I blared. Then, "Welcome home," I mumbled under my breath.

I pulled on a pair of jeans that I fished out of my suitcase, my anger mounting. When other people went home for visits, their par-ents took them out for dinner and planned family get-togethers; they didn't ship them off on espionage stints.

Then again, I knew how this house—which she'd cared for meticulously, lovingly for years—connected her to her parents, her past, her purpose. I could feel my chest tighten, feel myself slip into her world wholly, stepping into its vestibule, its winding hallways, cramped rooms, tugged against my will. "Hurry, Judy, please," she begged, standing at my door as I changed. I turned away from her, but knew it didn't matter—she wasn't really looking.

It was an early spring day. The sun was vibrant, the rays reflected off cars, off surfaces that had long been covered with snow, happy to do some reflecting. I arrived at Hutchison Street, noting the irony: the only neighborhood where in the 1950s my refugee grandparents could afford to buy a house was now the center of artsy, haute-boho Montreal, filled with artisanal chocolate bars and Latin American bruncheries.

I'd been inside this triplex only once, years earlier, and only in a small front room in which one of the tenants—an alternative medicine man/plumber—diluted homeopathic solutions. Now, I walked up to the third-floor flat, where my mother's family had lived decades ago, climbing the outdoor spiral staircases, *the DNA strands*. I was nervous as I opened the door and introduced myself to the agent, who sneered. Perhaps Mom was right.

I looked around me—wood floors, hanging plants, retro red-and-white sofas, an antique coat rack that looked like a cubist tree. It was hard to imagine how this chic space had become so firmly tied to my mother's identity. I wandered through the small rooms, spying. Not on the agent, but on my mother, trying to transpose stories onto spaces, to make sense of snippets of narrative. This was the first house that my grandparents had owned. After their escape to Russia, they journeyed back to Poland (Mom being born on the way), where they lived for several years, trying to find their families and reassemble their lives. My grandfather became a successful furrier in postwar Wrocław, my mother's first home, which I knew from a black-and-white photo of her clutching her one doll, smiling, holding hands with a governess, surrounded by pigeons. *You had a nanny after the Holocaust?* But they soon left on a boat for Israel, where they lived in her uncle's hand-built garage. Away from the death of her younger sister, whose life had lasted only a few months. They couldn't take any more death.

Two years later, when my grandfather's heart condition proved too difficult for the work of pioneering, and with my mother's baby brother, they all left the Middle East for Montreal, where my grandmother's one remaining sister had opened a fruit store, just a few blocks away. Finally, with their work as furrier and seamstress, Bubbie and Zaidy had been able to buy Hutchison, the house that made them part of a new society after theirs had been ravaged before their eyes. It was here, I thought as I touched the wooden windowsill, that my mother lived when she was a top student in Quebec. Here, she was the pillar of potential.

The old windows let in the bright light. The 1920s moldings cast shadows on slivers of the ceiling.

I moved to the kitchen with its black granite countertop. Bubbie never chopped kosher meat on *this*, I knew. I tried hard to feel her bunioned, sturdy feet in my steps, but my toes just felt cold.

A couple dressed in black, both wearing tall black leather boots, walked in.

"Welcome," I said, gesturing around me, as if I was a host.

In England, I recalled as I checked out the storage closet that hosted expensive bikes, people lived in the same neighborhoods as their ancestors. No one was obsessed with questions about their pasts or their heritage, because they lived the answers.

Then I climbed down one flight and stood on the balcony, watching people headed to fancy bistros and organic bagelries for brunch, remembering that lunch at the Greek restaurant. A woman with a young son came to tour the building. How oblivious they are, I thought, to this house's past, to the role it played in psyches and psychoses.

"I'm the sellers' daughter," I explained to the woman when she turned to stare at me, wondering why I was following her around.

THAT AFTERNOON, I stood in front of the coffee shop where I'd just bought a Frappucino—one I could never afford in London—my hands shaking. After going back home and reporting to Mom the day's nonevents, describing in detail every viewer I'd seen, I'd taken the metro back to this neighborhood, trying to relive the missed moment of the morning. Instead I felt lost, bloated with too much time and no direction except "not home." I'd watched Montrealers who sat for hours in funky coffee shops. I'd wandered between artisanal soap boutiques and vintage clothing stores, trying to be in the present, but my mind raced. My mom was not OK. Not OK. Today had not been normal. This wasn't just anxiety and stress. Her rage and fear that her houses would be taken from her were identical to what Bubbie experienced, why Mom had had her hospitalized and medicated. Mom's case seemed worse, especially since Bubbie had not been depressed, but aside from that, wasn't it the same condition?

And what was I supposed to do?

Then, my phone buzzed. Somehow I'd missed a call. It was a voice message from Ben. He was thinking of me. "How's the French food?"

My head rushed. A way out. The potential of a different life, a different love.

Maybe I could make something normal after all.

THEN AGAIN. HE took me to a twenty-four-hour restaurant in Chinatown. "Cheap and cheerful" as the English said.

I wasn't sure how much I cared. On the one hand, I was growing tired of the casual rencontre. I stared at the plastic menu of options, moo shoo dishes swimming in front of my eyes, tired of choice. Ben was open, older, established. I'd been hoping for something more solid, but . . .

On the other, stronger, hand, I was excited to see him and was feeling fresh and alive, the new spring air coiling its way up to my brain, pushing my neurons to fire too quickly in odd directions, reminding me of his passionate embraces, his strong arms. I was ready.

I'd put on strappy pink sandals—cheap ones that made me look cheap, in the right way, I hoped—and met him downstairs, still not allowing him up. I was not about to give up my home so easily, to expose my space, not like with Andy or Evan, and especially not to a high earner who was probably used to much fancier digs. Ben leaned against his Beamer. I tried to stay balanced on my shoes, then leaned into his body.

"Whoa, you're looking sassy tonight," he mumbled. I knew he knew that I knew that tonight he would know me.

And then I found myself here, at a corner table, in a near empty dive off Leicester Square. "This place is particularly good," he said, as if their drenched fried noodles were more outstanding than their neighbor's.

I ordered wine. It was sweet. Syrupy sweet. He drank tea.

Then he tried to show his big-spender status by ordering copious amounts of fried rice. "And let's have the bamboo shoot foo yung! And the sweet and sour dough balls!" The waitress scribbled like a courtroom scribe. "Judy, is there anything else you want?"

"No, fourteen varieties of lo mein should do."

He laughed, kind of.

"I'll have another glass of the dessert chardonnay. Actually, make that a carafe."

I kept drinking, staring at the moving water-fountain wall art, wondering what was considered kitsch in Asia? Old Master portraits? Abstract black canvases? He went on about how spiritual I was, and how he'd had a terrible weekend with his ex in Cornwall, explaining that I shouldn't feel threatened. I didn't feel threatened. I felt frisky. "Let's go," I said.

"Really?"

OMG. For several dates, he'd been begging to sleep with me, and now this? So life. "Really."

In his car, he kissed and grabbed me as he drove, only stopping between red lights to move forward at record speeds.

"Back to yours?" he said.

"No! Yours."

"What? Why?"

"Yours." I had never been so firm in my life. But there was no question: I'd rather open my legs than my front door. I wanted to see his first, to know who I was dealing with. "YOURS." I panicked for a second. I should never have told him where I lived.

"I'm going to yours," he said, between gearshifts and cleavage.

"I swear to God." I threw his arms off me. "If you drive to mine I will not let you in. I will not!"

"Yeesh, fine," he said.

I felt strong. I knew what I wanted. "Drive!"

The problem was that he lived in the suburbs, and not only was my liquored personality and liquid courage wearing off, but heavy making out at traffic light intervals was draining my energy.

I was pleased when he finally pulled up to his home, which he'd more than once mentioned was worth over a million pounds.

He opened the door. "Welcome."

I walked in, teetering on my heels, ready to plop myself into this dazzling new domestic life.

Which is why I was particularly startled to trip on a slick of papers. A whole pile of unopened envelopes. There were boxes everywhere. The kitchen table was lined with old food. The furniture was covered in sweaters, blankets. The image spun. He shut the lights. Thank God, I said, shutting my eyes.

Was I drunk or was this house a disaster? It looked like no one had been here for months.

I kept telling myself that the upper echelons were messy, as a way of showing they didn't care. But messy wasn't dirty, and no one should not-care this much, right?

"Come upstairs to the bedroom." He grabbed my hand. I kept my eyes nearly closed, opened only to a squint, trying to focus inward. I didn't want to see this. He threw things out of the way, lots of things, and threw me onto the bed. He pulled up my shirt, and pulled off his clothes, rolling on top of me. I couldn't breathe. His weight pressed down on my small frame, he felt like a truck. He would suffocate me.

"Move over," I said, pushing him with all my might.

"Sorry," he whispered. Then, "Damn." Business was shut. And, I took a peek—it was a small business to begin with.

I sighed. After all that begging . . . I pulled up my pants.

"Going to the bathroom," I said.

"It's just on the right," he said. "Don't mind the mess."

The mess? It was more of a tornado. T-shirts, towels, used razors hung from all ledges. Caked toothpaste like cement covered each edge of the sink. I couldn't find soap to wash my hands, just traces of yellow dishwashing liquid. I felt sick. At least I'd asked to see his apartment first, I reasoned to my spinning self. Now, I could walk away.

Except for the fact that I was stranded. "I need to put my head down," I said, crawling over sweatshirts and onto his mattress, or at least, what I thought was a mattress. I pulled a bit of blanket over my face wanting to hide, to separate myself from this scene. As soon as my head stopped spinning and the sun flirted with rising, I was getting the hell out of here.

I must have fallen asleep because the next thing I heard was a panic attack.

"I can't do it," he said, quickly. "I just can't do it."

"Yeah, I know you can't, it's fine," I said. "I just need to sleep this off for a few minutes."

"No, I can't take it, I can't take you being here, with me." He paced in and out of his room. "You have to go to another room, sleep downstairs. You have to go."

I looked at the clock. "It's three a.m., and we're in buttfuck London."

"I can't!"

He felt trapped?

"I'm just sleeping; I don't want anything from you," I said, surprised at my growing candor.

"I'm calling you a cab."

"I'm a cab," I said under my breath.

"What?"

"Nothing." I got up and started getting dressed. "I'm fucking tired and this is ridiculous."

I wobbled downstairs, and began lacing up my pink heels, embarrassed that they had to see such a disaster on the floor. Junk was everywhere.

"Give me money," I said, realizing I sounded like a prostitute.

"What?"

"For this ridiculous middle-of-the-night cab ride."

"This should be enough." He handed me several bags of coins.

He even hoarded change. To think *I* had been worried about inviting *him* over.

"Call me?" he asked in a high-pitched voice, as I walked back down the garden path.

"Yeah, right," I actually said out loud.

"What a loser," I said to the cabdriver as I climbed in, my pink shoes shining in the dewy night. I couldn't believe I'd been out with my mother, again.

A week later, Maya schlepped me to another synagogue for another singles event. I'd told her that Benedict and I had had our last supper. "Aren't you upset?" she asked, scanning the room for the future father of her sure-to-be-hyperanxious children.

"No," I said. But for the first time, it wasn't because I was hiding my feelings. It was because I really wasn't upset. I didn't *want* that relationship. When I got to my apartment that evening and locked the door behind me, I settled down on my clean futon in my organized living room and felt relaxed. I'd left my Montreal house ten years earlier. Finally, I'd built a foundation.

It was weeks later, sitting on a comedian's toilet, that I found my bible. Though I'd heard of it, certainly, I'd never actually perused the sacred text word by word. Somehow, seeing them on the page, so matter-of-fact, especially when I'd picked up the book out of boredom and was looking forward to denigrating it (*how could such atrocious schlock sell?*), they called out to me a greater life lesson than any I'd received in my now six years of "emotional college" in England (much longer and more difficult than regular college, even Harvard).

"*This* is funny," I said, holding up the tome as I returned to the living room where three of us had been rehearsing sketches. Of course I meant, "this book is brilliant and changed my life in an instant," but "funny" was the highest—and only—accolade among comic folk.

Mel, an Australian, looked over at me holding her copy of *He's Just Not That Into You* and smirked. "Yeah, it's a pretty good read," she said, but then I recalled how she'd been endlessly confessing her woes about a Shakespearean actor who'd been inviting her to the Globe but never anywhere out-of-this-world. To me, however, the authors' insight was simply incredible: if a guy didn't call you back, or dumped you, it was because—well—he didn't like you. That was it! It sucked, maybe, but, it didn't really matter; there's nothing you could do, so move on. This frank honesty, this blasé discussion of not-being-liked and being-OK, blew my mind, disabling me from concentrating for the rest of the rehearsal.

Before I left, Mel said I should borrow the book, and suggested I also take a pop-anthropology hit, *Watching the English*. I shrugged (it looked so long) but took it anyway, unused to reading anything that wasn't PhD-related. But on the tube ride home, with glances at just a few pages, more wonderment and salvation began. Sure, I'd deduced some "class rules" at the museum, but I'd had no idea that hundreds more standards existed. All the crazy yet intimidating oddities of British social behavior were laid out in chapters like a high school textbook: Food Rules, Road Rules, Play Rules, Sex Rules. Privacy and indirectness reigned (never request a tour of someone's house). Middle-class English folk did not introduce themselves by name (why should anyone care who *you* are). One did not compliment because it meant too much *noticing* of the other (aha!). One did not speak to their neighbors because it meant putting pressure on them (asking to borrow sugar might lead to—gasp—years of forced hellos). "Negative politeness" was the British way: assuming people were most comfortable not being seen, it was most polite to leave people alone (versus American positive politeness, which was founded on enthusiastic inclusion and, well, being nice).

There was a clear system to this craziness, a logic that I could decipher. And, like the guys who didn't call, it wasn't all about me. If a comedian I'd known for years crossed the street instead of saying hi to me, it was just British politeness. It wasn't about me! If a guy texted me nonstop, asked me to hang out at the pub to watch the football with all his friends, invited me to move in, and then told me he just wanted to be friends, it was just crazy English *and* male behavior. It wasn't me! Or, it was me, but it didn't matter that much. And, it was possible for me to try to understand.

This newfound sense of detachment followed me home that night, and into my stage life. When I finally got a spot at a popular gig on a boat, only to arrive and find it was miles away from the tube station at the East London docks and en route I saw a series of teenage girls fist fighting, not to mention the deck was covered in Union Jack flags (a symbol of the British far right) and I was the only woman, let alone foreigner, let alone Jew on board, and the drunken audience of three was seated behind a pole, and I was nearly attacked by a Rottweiler while onstage, and the performance didn't go so well, I did not beat myself up like some of the other comics, but simply said, *that was not about me.*

As I walked back to the train, watching out for any unusual violence, I marveled about how when I first got glasses, their effect was so apparent: trees were no longer a composition of green clouds but I could see each distinct leaf. Nature, I'd realized, was intricate and beautiful! I felt like I was wearing similarly thick lenses now, distanced from my surrounds, whose intricacies I saw clearly. These codes showed me that there were boundaries between me and Brits, me and men, me and the world, and that those differences weren't lonely, but empowering. Even interesting. Taking wide steps, despite my unfashionable rounded shoes, I felt in control.

Two weeks later, R. B. Kitaj, my heroic drawing room painter, committed suicide.

At the museum, first thing in the morning, my coffee still too hot to drink, the BBC Web site glared at me: my middle-class hero—the Royal Academician, this English art success—had suffocated himself with a plastic bag. His obituary, which I read immediately, my cheeks tingling, explained that he'd always been attacked for being an outsider with unfashionable intellectual opinions on art, implying his insecurity had led to his self-destruction. I should have called him, I kept thinking, struck by the brutal finality of this news. It was as if I'd unexpectedly lost, not a friend, but an ideal. *He killed himself. Even Mom hadn't killed herself.* Everything was frail, paper-thin. How could the creator of this striking living room, the bearer of a life I wanted to use as a model, have vanished? My hands shook as I Googled, binging on the headlines.

When I gained some composure, I stood up in the middle of the office to share this news. But suddenly Helen swept frantically by, followed by a horde of harried assistants. "Is everyone all right?" I asked, suppressing my update.

"It's urgent," Charlotte explained, sighing, as if art history was a field rife with emergencies. "The construction workers didn't understand. One of them urinated in the eighteenth-century toilet. And sat on the furniture."

"I'm so sorry about the *sofa*," I said, apologizing instinctively while reminding myself not to demonstrate excessive compassion.

"You mean, chaise longue."

"Right," I said, but just then I knew: I would never get it right.

I had no class. I too was an outsider, deeply unfashionable. England had been my cherished escape, and I'd learnt a lot here, but, Lord (and Lady), I was so not English.

· ELEVEN ·

COMMENCEMENT
London, 2007

We woke to the powdery London light that existed only in the mornings, before the days became gray and smoggy like a Dickens Christmas even in July. Mom was nestled into my pillows, her elbow propped up. My parents had come for my doctoral graduation, and were staying with me. It was fun to have them here, sharing my space, even if it meant they'd had to take the shelves out of my tiny European fridge to fit their stash of budget groceries.

I'd woken once in the night to listen to the chorus of breaths. Her breathing, Dad's breathing from the futon in the next room. Little blusters and burps; a symphony of genealogy. Would I ever hear this again? I always wondered if it was the last time.

"I just don't see why she dumped him," Mom now said. "Aiden was so good for her."

"Maya recently broke up with a guy who was like Aiden," I said. The night before, we'd met Maya for dinner at a gastropub. Minutes before Maya's arrival, Mom had disappeared into the bathroom. I'd feared the worst—a mood swing, an inconsolable episode—and had to distract Maya while I figured out how I'd manage the rest of the evening. But just as I was about to go looking for Mom, she appeared, fully made up in cosmetics and a scarf, neither of which I had any idea she owned. I hadn't even changed, and there she was, a surprise transformation, a soft smile adorning her visage. I was relieved, but also upset that the grin wasn't for me. Maya had thought she seemed incredibly sweet.

"Why?" Mom asked, turning to me in the bed. "Maya seems smart."

"Maybe she's not ready," I said, enjoying our chat session in this SATC pidgin, feeling like we were two teenage girls who kissed pillows and did must-increase-their-bust exercises. I'd reported several of my recent dates to Mom. When I didn't know how to progress things with Tim, she said, "Drink some red wine." When Ian had been aloof, canceling dinners but inviting me to his choir recitals, she'd said: "He sounds gay." Now she smiled. "Aiden was so grounding," she said. "Carrie needed it. Does Maya?"

"Good morning," Dad called to us from the other room.

"Morning," I called back. "How did you sleep?"

And then.

The person shifting in an instant, as if clicking on a new effect in Instagram, immediately changing the tone, the coloring, the sharpness of the lines, and thus, the whole meaning of the picture.

I felt Mom's body tense on the bed next to me. The sheets became taut. "What do you want to do today?" I asked, generally, to the stifling air around me. "The Globe?"

"Sure, the Globe," Dad answered and closed the door to the bathroom.

Mom rolled away, her back to me. She pushed the blanket between us. "Sure, the Globe," she mocked.

I breathed, trying to stay calm. My tiny apartment felt like it was shrinking. "What's wrong?" I asked. "Why are you mad? Are you mad at me?" Could just talking to my father have set her off? She wanted something from me that I just didn't understand, couldn't give.

"I'm not mad at you, Judy," she hissed, now frantically dressing herself.

I went to the kitchen to give her space.

Within minutes she was slamming doors, then yanking open my fridge, pulling out the margarine tub and the knife, then, they left her hand. Swerved toward my arm.

"Stop attacking Judy," my father screamed. "What the hell did she do to you?"

I halted frozen in front of the sink.

"We're here for her PhD graduation," he continued. "We're guests in her house."

My limbs tingled. I was shocked by Mom's actions, but even more so by Dad's. I'd just turned thirty years old, and this was the first time he had defended me.

"Stop it."

His voice boomed into my brain. He had acknowledged the dysfunction. He had acknowledged me. I was not hidden and transparent, but real, tangible. When he saw me, I saw myself. I saw the situation.

"Get out," I said quietly. I looked Mom in the madly glinting eyes. Her hands were full of plastic containers. "Behave yourself or get the fuck out of my house."

My house. There it was. Our houses were separate. We were separate. She was not me.

"Fine," she mumbled, and I stumbled back, my hands trembling, shocked at her easy capitulation. "I'll behave," she said in a quiet voice, aping me like a schoolchild. Then she sat in my chair and began spreading cheese on a roll. As if nothing had happened.

She was ill, really ill, and it wasn't just in my head. But it didn't mean I had to be the victim of her illness.

That afternoon I wore a cap and gown. I was finally ready to graduate.

THE NEXT DAY, I dropped my parents off at Heathrow. "I have too many things going on with the houses," Mom had said. "I need to get back."

"So go," I said. How many times could I convince them to come, to stay, to enjoy themselves, to enjoy me?

The day before, Mom had arrived at the graduation ceremony alongside Dad, gleaming with pride. Like a professional ninja photographer, she left her seat to follow me as I processed, skidding down the church aisles with each of my formal steps, contorting to take snaps of every moment of my ascension in the academy. ("Wow, your mother's really into this," a peer mused. "American style," I'd answered, knowing that's what she'd been implying, strangely proud of Mom's lack of British restraint.) Mom's mood had remained buzzing through the champagne and strawberry reception in the institute's courtyard and even in the galleries, as she giddily examined nineteenth-century French cabaret and café scenes. I was careful to balance my time and introductions between her and an increasingly drunken Dad, who pulled me aside, a toppling glass in one hand, wiping tears from his eyes with the other. "Your grandmothers would have been so proud," he said as he pinched my upper arm. I'd imagined Bubbie, her strong warrior arms clutched around my gown, her checkerboard cheek in my neck. "I always knew you'd become a doctor," she'd say, not caring that I was a doctor of sculptures.

Now, at the airport, Mom was frantic, packing and repacking her important documents, while Dad, hands-in-pockets, whistled an off-key tune and stared into the terminal's distance. No trace of his former recognition.

I did not worry this would be the last time I'd ever see them. I did not worry. Instead, I pushed them through security and waved good-bye from behind the black rope. My cheeks were dry. My throat, lumpless. I did not know where my life was going. I did not know where I belonged in any grand sense, but for now, I was going back home, to my solo apartment. I had created my own protective walls, even if they were made of cardboard in a radical enclave in East London.

There, I opened my new laptop—a graduation gift from my parents—and started to write my first one-woman show. At thirty, at last, I could be alone.

3RD TRIMESTER:

The Bedroom

———•———

· TWELVE ·

27 WEEKS: LINEA NIGRA
California, 2011

I walked onto the dining veranda by myself, slightly worried that I'd have no one to eat dinner with, but only slightly. This writing conference was particularly social, especially—and to my shock—to someone with a bump de bébé.

"Mama Judy!" a table of voices called and I turned, flushed with pride at belonging. "We're saving you a seat." These writers, from across states, ages, and religions had become my crowd; we often discussed children. My pregnancy reminded them of their own. People were rarely bored talking about their kids, or providing advice about mine in utero. Instead of *Bird by Bird*, my new friends and I would write *Burp by Burp*. I'd been so worried that a fetal mound, which preempted me with its allusions to sex, rattles, and milk stains, would alienate colleagues, make me seem uncommitted, not serious, tracing for the world my diminishing cerebral capacity and identity. Instead, pregnancy turned out to be the one universal topic that connected me to strangers. Plus, I had the strongest identity of all. Everyone knew who I was. The moment I'd arrived the man who was helping people unload suitcases beelined to my massive torso and exclaimed: "You're the pregnant one!"

"No," I'd answered. "Just kidding."

Then he lugged my luggage first. People had never been so nice.

Even my roommate, a forty-year-old housekeeper turned genius novelist with a husky cigarette voice and a following of doting adolescent gay men, completely uninterested in the world o' child, was intrigued by my maternal ambivalence. "I'm not that into it either!" I confessed, to her surprise and endless questioning.

"So why did you do it? How will you manage?" Being pregnant, an utterly private experience, meant very publicly doing a thing that most people had strong feelings about, evoking passionate memories and opinions, coaxing them to share—even their doubt. I was the catalyst.

I breathed in the fresh air, focusing on the vista of wiry thin trees that extended to the sky, the rugged brown mountains that glistened in the leaking red sunset. The land felt old, ancient enough to inspire new age ideas. I'd never been to Northern California before. Here I was, pregnant, and lo and behold, I'd traveled alone to a fresh place. I was still growing, and not just around my abdomen. I motioned to my callers that I'd be with them after visiting the buffet. I hadn't known a single one of them before this week, I mused. I was still free, able to do new things, meet new people.

If anything, the conference had been the most enjoyable of my career. I did not feel the need to attend every lecture, schmooze every success story, or provide rehearsed speeches about my incredibly keen interest in Victorian asylums. Finally, I thought, I was ready for college. I was constantly reminded that there was life outside my brain.

Life inside me. I put my hand on my belly and felt a little foot ram my ribs, darling kneecaps smash my kidneys, my insides twisting in new ways. Being fused to another being had its existential and physical ramifications, including that I was never alone. I was always part of a pair, a member of a team. And yet, still me. Even more in tune with my desires and instincts.

"Don't eat that," a woman who I'd not yet met whispered as I hovered over the tiramisu. "Fetal alcohol syndrome," she said, enunciating each word.

"Thanks for the warning," I replied, flashing to all the people who "tsked" me in the past few months. Diet Coke, coffee, yogic inversions, C-section anesthetics, public toilets, bending down—all verboten, worthy of public shaming. Suddenly, though, I really didn't care. The California air brought out my inner confidence. And my good old brashness. "Good news is, I've cut down on my heroin use, so the baby should be OK."

GO WEST
London, 2007

The first thing I thought when I saw Jon across the crowded British pub was: what a Jew. He was short and bald, and, Dan had been right about his condition. A few weeks earlier, Dan and his girlfriend Lara had taken me to a nouveau British nose-to-tail restaurant for my thirtieth birthday, ordering up a storm of nostril fricassee and tentacle-inspired small plates. As I tried to hide my half-eaten (completely uneaten), insanely expensive foodstuffs under my particularly airy bread (why did the holes have to be so big?) I shocked myself by blurting out: "Hey, don't you guys know any single Jewish men who are nice, somewhat normal, and solvent?"

"Well, I do know one," Dan had said after a moment's pause. "But I have to warn you, he's very hairy."

"So what?" I'd replied. "So am I."

It hit me later that evening: "Nice, somewhat normal, and solvent" was what I wanted, clean and clear. I could be open about it and not seem pathetic. Besides, I wasn't even really looking. My PhD was done, the museum exhibition over, my visa and lease soon up for renewal. I was working on my one-woman show that had recently been commissioned to be performed in Edinburgh! Combining comedy and research, it was a story about Jewish identity in England, and felt like the culmination of my London experience. After that, I would go home, as soon as I figured out where that might be.

In any case, I hadn't been particularly concerned about Jon's hirsuteness until now, in the bar, as I, fashionably late in a pink pea-coat and retro glasses, approached the table where Chewbacca was waiting.

"You look like you said you did on the phone. A fabulous Anne Frank." He laughed snarkily. "That was pretty obnoxious."

"Thanks," I responded, annoyed that I'd bothered shaving my legs. He was even more crass than he'd been when he'd called, weeks after Dan passed on my details, going on about how he knew Montreal for its superior strip clubs.

"You don't look a day over thirty-two," he said.

I was thirty. It was sparks from the start. Nuclear sparks.

It was my turn. "What do you do? What's your passion? Your dream?" The words crashed out of my mouth. I wouldn't normally have launched in like this (in England, no less), but there was no time to waste. He had booked us tickets to a show about to begin, and apparently, I was aging rapidly.

"I don't have ambition," he said.

Great, I thought. A real winner. Then I learned that the show he planned to woo me with was a ukulele concert. We made our way to the venue upstairs. He started panicking. "Since you were so late, we might not get seats."

"Chillax," I said, plunking myself down on the floor. I could already tell this was a wasted evening. There was no point maintaining pretenses. Forget ladylike leg-crossings. Forget the list of preplanned conversation topics and selection of witty anecdotes demonstrating savvy yet vulnerable sides of myself. Forget breath mints.

"I'm not used to being in the audience," I said, surprisingly insufferable. "I perform."

"Wow, that's odious," he said.

"Thanks." What was this—a date or a fight?

Between sets, he leaned into me. "You're brutal, you're honest, you say what you mean. You're so not British."

"No-duh," I snapped. "I thought the white teeth gave it away."

"What are you looking for in relationships?" he asked.

"Here's my policy," I said, speaking curtly over the ukuleles like I never spoke to anyone. "One stray and you're out. I don't forgive infidelity. EVER." Why would I say that? I amazed myself with my unfeminine frankness, with the clarity of my protocols.

"So you know what you want," he said, smirking.

"You lack ambition and don't." I smirked back.

"Fair enough." He looked at his watch. I assumed it was because he wanted to go, but it turned out he was freaked out about missing the last tube. He had come to the dangerous cool east of London, and he needed to get back to his suburban-mama-boy west. "Where's the train? How long will it take me to get there?"

"You can't take a cab?" I asked. "How cheap are you?"

"That's my rule," he said. "No cabs. We all have rules."

"Fair enough."

I tried to describe the route to the station, but he was so annoyingly nervous that I walked him there. We arrived just in time. "I wouldn't want you to feel worried," I said, noticing he didn't seem worried that I now had to walk home alone. This was antichivalry.

"I'll call you." He ran to catch the train.

Good-bye, weirdo, I thought, as I bounded down the street. The brutality of our conversation had left me strangely energized. I'd survived plenty of rejection; a date that climaxed in the guy dashing for public transportation didn't send me into a spiral of self-critical depression. I was pleased with my lack of disappointment. I was fine on my own.

So it surprised me when I arrived home to find an e-mail from Jon. Apparently, he'd had a great time. Really? I went to sleep.

THE NEXT DAY, Maya and I conducted a postmortem, giggling over the lack of courtliness. I felt good about not feeling bad. "What did you write back?" she asked.

"Nothing." I was proud of my restraint.

"Are you crazy?" Her tone changed to serious. "He's a single Jewish guy who likes you and isn't totally insane. Give him another chance."

Aware of her unluckiness in love, I had to admit she had a point (not to mention, a rather low opinion of my romantic appeal). That night, I semireluctantly texted Jon a thanks. Then, I didn't hear from him.

That was fine. I was busy with my one-woman show, and about to go on a second date with David, my ultimate match-on-paper. An American pursuing his successful social justice career, he had an Ivy League degree like I did, yet was better-looking—chiseled, built, serious with an underlying smile. We saw a Pinter matinee, for which he called me *twice* to make sure I was on time. The three-hour play was about a 1950s dysfunctional abusive asylum for suicidals. It made me want to check in. After the curtain fell, I was about to mock the depressive tone when David exclaimed: "Genius! A fascinating representation of cultural malaise." Then he added, "I'm on a cleanse, so let's just sit outside and chat."

I followed, careful of how my legs were crossed so my calves' fatness careened away from him. He semireclined his muscular physique and launched into a full-scale analysis of his previous relationships with "powerful-yet-insecure/push-pull" women. He mentioned he was going to a hip East End club that evening. I was about to begin my usual spiel, to impress with my savvy knowledge of hot spots and get myself invited so I could show up late and coyly grab his attention that I would never fully have, eventually seducing him while not seeming like I cared. But as I looked at his "Yidonis" figure, aloof, checking out his surrounds, glancing at me intermittently, explaining his "tendency to recycle intimacies," it just felt like so much work. Andy, Evan, Christ the hoarder. I was too tired.

So when I retreated to the restroom and noticed a missed call from Jon, I was pleasantly surprised. I sat on the toilet listening to his voice mail. "I know it's last minute, but will you come see a comic poet tonight? That is, if you can bear being in the audience.

If not, let's make another plan. I'd like to see you again—soon." His message was direct. Fresh. His voice felt alive. For a second all "the rules" flashed through me: a last-minute date? But thinking of David (probably still talking about himself), I realized: who cared! Our first date *had* been fun. I *felt* like seeing this guy. His brashness brought out my own, a quality I had desperately tried to conceal in this repressed country. I texted him right away. "See you there."

"Great," he texted back.

I didn't even go home to change.

"Twice in a week," Jon said, his eyes sparkling, greeting me at the theater door. "People will talk."

"So let them," I said. "Nu, where's my beer?"

"At the bar," he said. "Go get it. And get me one too." He smiled and went. As I waited for him in the audience, I thought about the backwardness of this Jon situation. No chiseled features. No save-the-world. No romance, chivalry, flirting, mystery, or any of the usual titillation. Not civil and choreographed, but candid and chaotic. No polite beating around the bush, but a burning bush. No flirty self, but more of myself. Less Carrie and Mr. Big, more Homer and Marge.

That night, after the show, after we decided to look for hot food (not an easy task at ten p.m. in London), after I loved the all-night clubbers' hamburger joint ("You're so not British," he repeated), and after I asked him about his greatest weakness and he answered, "Gambling" (*what!?* I'd thought, that sounds like a neon red flag, but then reminded myself that at least it was honest), he dropped me off at my flat. There was no kiss, not even a hug. "See you later," he said.

"Call me," I answered.

As I walked up the stairs, it struck me in a flash. "I don't even *like* this guy," I said aloud. "My luck, we'll get married."

DATE NUMBER THREE was fairly good. After I'd expertly suggested a hit French film about breast cancer, infidelity, and funerals, and Jon had met me at the cinema only to inquire as to whether perhaps I'd want to do something that sounded a little more, well, fun, and said he'd booked two seats at the bar at a nearby swanky restaurant, and after I wondered if that was controlling but then realized that yes, of course I wanted to do something more fun, and after we'd sat at the bar, joking, eating fifty-dollar salmon and zucchini blossoms like they were an afterthought, and then after we took a walk to Waterloo station, and a vagrant saw us holding hands among the day's commuters' debris which looked like a light snow littered across the stone floor and called out, "Take care of each other forever," and then, in the tunnel where my train was due, he suddenly pulled me into him and kissed me quickly on the lips, a staccato gesture, conversational, invitational—after all that, I thought, that wasn't too bad.

But now two weeks later, I wondered if maybe it was. Why'd he ask me to pick an outing if he had his own plans? Did he—a lawyer turned business advisor—shun high art? Hate my taste? He'd said I should come to his flat tonight to say good-bye before he left for a month of traveling and that he'd call me to finalize, but I hadn't heard a peep. Maybe he wasn't as plainspoken as I thought. Then again, he'd never been quick to call. Then again, I wasn't looking for love. I needed to leave London. *Who knew?* I told myself, as I wandered into a liquor store to pick up wine for Maya's first annual summer barbecue.

My phone buzzed with Mom's name. "Hi," I answered, happy for the distraction.

"Judy." She was breathless. "There's no point in my going on. I can't see a way out of the mess I'm in. I should just say good-bye now."

"Mom." I sighed. *This is a disease,* my memory calmly whispered. *A family disease, our coat of arms.* "You need to get help."

I could have told her how much I loved her and needed her and didn't want to hear her talk that way. I could have changed topics to distract her and shift her mood. (The other day, I'd immediately swerved her into a monologue about how I should date men who read fiction because they were empathetic, but not men who wrote fiction, because they were overly sensitive and self-involved. *Lately*

I've been telling Dad, she joked, *"If you don't do what I say, I* won't *divorce you!"*) I could have told her I'd met my Harry Goldenblatt, asked her why he hadn't called, whether I should call him.

But I didn't want to. I didn't want to talk about Jon just to soothe her rage.

I also realized that I knew the answer: I shouldn't call Jon. Not because of the Rules or playing hard to get, but because I didn't want to. The truth was, I was shy, and he'd said he'd call me. I needed to be with someone reliable who could ease my anxieties and make me feel comfortable, not make me pretend to be the extrovert I really wasn't.

"I've gotta go to a barbecue," I said instead. "You'll find a way out of the mess."

Then, just as I walked into the party—Jon. "Are you coming over tonight?"

"Oh, OK," I said, acting surprised, not-saying *Why didn't you call yesterday* or *Dude, do you even like me?* Was I being too passive? Not honest? Or was some game acceptable, as long as it was fun?

Again, I didn't go home to change. He met me at the station and suggested we go to a local café for dessert. I was disappointed not to see his flat, not to mention that this wasn't an invitation to steamy smooching, which would have at least confirmed that he was at all attracted to me, but fair enough. One thing at a time.

At the café, which I'd passed many times before (Nigel used to live in this very neighborhood, and every step I took felt double, as if the old me and new me were both walking down these blocks), Jon got us an outdoor table. I very un-Britishly ordered cheesecake—calorically and financially decadent. We chatted excitedly about his upcoming trip to the Balkans and mine to Scotland. I was upset when the bill arrived.

And even more so, when Jon declared: "Since I've paid for everything so far, I think it's your turn."

Of course I would have offered, as I had every other time, but it was another thing to be told. Besides, this reeked of Andy, of Evan, even of Ben's bags of money. And besides, it wasn't even true. I *had* paid for the late-night burgers, for several drinks. I was always careful about that, overly conscious about the appropriate giving of gifts.

"Excuse me, but I like to be treated like a lady," I blurted out, my cheeks hot. "Try to be a gentleman." Then I got up and fled to the tiny bathroom at the back of the restaurant. I locked the creaky door and stared into the mirror. What had just happened? When had I ever run out on a date?

"Sorry for blowing up," I said as I sat back down, "but I felt like I was being falsely accused."

"My last girlfriend felt that I controlled our relationship because I made more money," Jon said. "I didn't want you to feel that way."

"Let me get this one," I offered, picking up the check.

"Next one's on me," he said. "Le Gavroche, here we come."

"You'd better believe it," I mumbled, noting our cheesecakes cost the equivalent of half a day's museum salary or roughly twenty thousand stand-up gigs.

"So a fight on our fourth date," Jon said as he walked me back.

"Guess so." Just like our first, I didn't say.

"The important thing is, we discussed it and made up."

At the station he kissed me again, quickly, on the lips. And then he was off. And so was I.

DAYS LATER, I phoned Eli. "We have to do something," I said. "She's going insane."

"I know. She's been calling me at least five times a day, threatening suicide." I nearly dropped the phone. I hadn't realized she called him as much as she called me—even more. Her condition was getting worse. *It was real.*

"We need to get her on meds," I said. "I'm gonna call Dad."

"OK, keep me posted."

I breathed. I had an ally.

But Dad was less of one. He didn't want Mom to listen in on the call, so I had to ring him at work, at a predetermined time, like we were part of some larceny scheme. "Eh," he pooh-poohed. "The medications don't help. Besides, she's not gonna tell the doctor what's wrong with her. She'll play it normal, that's the killer. She *knows* it's insane." He went on about how hard it was to be caught up in her daily rants, how he tried to stay out until she was nearly asleep each night. I pictured him creeping down the dark hallways of Kildare, casting long, thin shadows on the stacks.

"Go stay at Carlton if you need," I pleaded, feeling guilty about my own escape.

"It's not so easy," Dad said. But, I thought, even Bubbie got shots. There *must* be something—some psychiatrist, hospital, therapist—that could help.

THE NEXT WEEK, I'd just completed my round of London previews when I got Jon's text. "Sitting at a riverside cafe in Ljubljana. Eating seafood. How's your show?"

Not the most gushingly romantic serenade, but I liked it that he was thinking about me.

Then I headed home to pack. For the first time, I was going to the Edinburgh festival not as a struggling performer but at someone's invitation. After years of begging for audiences and panic attacks about reviews, I was ready to do the festival on my own terms, with my solo show, which I'd created, directed, composed, designed, and performed. When I'd sat down to write it, I kept thinking about a passage I'd read that explained it takes four generations for trauma to pass through a family. I framed my show around four generations of mine. What had I learned from my history? In the show, I played not only Bubbie, who told a story about swimming with her sisters in the Vistula, but also my fantasy daughter, a thirty-year-old woman who, one hundred years after the Holocaust, felt settled in her Jewish identity, living a calm and content life in California. I didn't play my mother; instead I'd had her record her lines. In the opening scene, a discussion between the various voices inside my head is interrupted by her. "Mom, what are you doing here?" I ask. "I'll always be in your head," she answers, light and laughing. "Even after I die, I'll be here."

Packing my gear, I looked around my apartment, which now served as my rehearsal hall, studio, workshop, and chill-out lounge where I watched TV late into the night. My quiet, safe space in here allowed me to better deal with challenges and rejections outside. Telling my own story of danger made me feel safer, even happy.

As I worked on this culminating show, a farewell to England, a fantasy of Lublin to LA, my childhood dream of moving to New York City—the land of liberty, a place where many old friends now lived, where I felt that standards and measures meant something and weren't just a rehearsal for life—was increasingly tenacious. Being "foreign" had given me an excuse to be temporary and tentative but, I knew, it was time to make my home.

· THIRTEEN ·

28 WEEKS: DREAMING IN OFF-COLOR
New York City, 2011

Jon and I were finishing our Saturday brunch at a Belgian restaurant, imagining how dining would work when the baby arrived—would we bring the stroller to the table? Wear her in a papoose? Would she cry hysterically the whole time, making us take turns walking up and down the aisle like the couple next to us was doing? How would we know what sauce she preferred on her mussels?—when the calls started. "Dad can't get into the house," Eli said from L.A. "Mom's not answering the door. He's locked out."

"Dad doesn't have any keys?"

"No one but Mom has the keys."

"Where the hell is she?" I asked, thinking that she hadn't left her house in over a year, trying not to think of her latest spate of panicked suicide calls.

"No idea."

"Fuck," I said, my chest tightening. "We have to call a locksmith."

"Dad doesn't want to," Eli said. "He wants to drive to Carlton and wait there."

"Wait for what?" I wanted to pull my hormonally lush hair out.

Someone has to *do* something. How could he just hide out in his maternal abode? But, combing my strands with my fingers, I also understood his fear. I wouldn't want to enter that house alone, either, and discover a horror scene. Wasn't I just hiding out here?

Eli and I made calls. The police would take a missing person report after twenty-four hours. The Vermont border patrol could not disclose who crossed without a medical letter. The bus company had no record of her buying a ticket that day.

Where the hell was she? I'd gotten used to Mom being a shut-in, a permanent anchor lodged in my old home. It meant Kildare was always inhabited. It meant I could monitor her. The idea of her roaming free—or worse—made me feel unhinged, exhausted. My mind whirred. Not sure what to do, Jon and I decided to go ahead with our plans and, after a nap, we walked over to a friend's garden party. This is what regular people do on weekends, I kept telling myself as we zigzagged across warm city streets, as my two realities zigzagged along each other. "Where the hell could she be?" Jon asked.

"Ha," I blurted as it hit me. "She's probably coming here. Get ready!"

We both chuckled, but as the sounds of my words ricocheted through the humid air, it struck me that my joke could be the truth. Of course! That was exactly the kind of thing she'd do. No promises, no commitments, no forewarning; just a spur of the moment decision to come visit, possibly to off-load money so it wasn't in her name and subject to whatever home-heist she thought was taking place, but also because she wanted to see me pregnant, to bond over this thing that was and wasn't me, that was and wasn't her, that was and wasn't us both, separate and together. I knew it in my stressed bones.

"Where will we put her?" I asked, but had already made plans. She'd stay in the office for now, for the rest of the pregnancy. She'd be there in case I went into labor when Jon was out. I'd take weeks off work and she'd hang out with me in the city—markets, bookstores, doctors' appointments—telling me stories about when she was pregnant with me as she did on the phone, but instead in the flesh, as we walked along the High Line or nibbled on freshly imported Viennese pastry in the Neue Galerie café.

Jon and I said hello to our hosts, and as guests stood around their lush midtown garden tippling cucumber cocktails and chatting about apartment renovations, I mentally planned the route to pick her up. She'd come into Penn or Port Authority, I worked out. Neither was far.

Then, over the verboten hot dog course, I felt a buzz in my pocket, jumped off the picnic bench and made my way to a corner of the darkening patio, watching a cat dart between the bushes and the back door.

"She called," Eli said. "She's in Ottawa."

"Huh?"

"She's visiting Barbara."

"Barbara?" The urban topiary spun, geometric vines jetting in all directions.

She'd spontaneously decided to visit an old family friend.

No one is coming. I stared down at my belly, now occluding my toes, prompting my sciatica. The baby, I could feel, was pushing on all of me, in all of me, ribs, bladder, heart, kicking me senseless from the inside out. "But she hasn't left the house in years," was all I could say. *She's alive and fine,* I told myself, but instead of feeling relief, envy soaked me like sweat. She had left her house—to visit Barbara?!

I watched the cat jet behind the garden wall, spurred on by the scent of rodents, the thrill of the catch. Even after all these years, after all my running, I just wanted to be with her. I still dreamed of her coming over. I was waiting for her, like she was waiting for me, each of us expecting the other to deliver things that we just didn't, couldn't.

"Sorry. I can't meet you for dinner tonight," Jon says. We are at a fancy hotel in London, with a grand bar and white barstools. I know it's a bad sign, even before I notice that he is holding hands with— wait—a team of Russian prostitutes?

That night I woke up and found myself drenched in hormonal sweat. I was used to first trimester dreams of nursing coyotes and rekindling old flames, second trimester ones in which I had to manage streams of cats attached to me with long umbilical leashes or steer race cars from the backseat, and even the sporadic insane nightmare where I found myself on an NFL team in front of TV cameras with no understanding of how to be a quarterback, letting down my team, guilty that I used pregnancy as an excuse to get out of scrimmaging. But lately, I'd entered an even more troubling nocturnal world than that of professional sports: the land of deception and Lifetime movies. A world in which Jon died of brain cancer, or changed his mind about wanting children, or simply left me because I was no fun anymore.

I turned over to his side of the bed. It was empty.

Oh God. How would I do this alone? Having a baby was not my thing, it was our thing. It wasn't just the physical reality that wouldn't exist without Jon, but the possibility. I couldn't do it—practically, emotionally, spiritually—alone. I just couldn't. Where the hell was he?

I found him in the den. "What are you doing in here?"

"Um, you threw me out. Snoring."

"Oh," I said. "Sorry." I left the room so he could go back to sleep. *But how do I know he will stay?* I felt palpitations. Jon's greatest gift to me had been consistency, but what if life was never consistent again? People flip, turn wildly at the drop of a wrong word, a cry. Each time I let someone in, I opened myself to the risk that they'd make a mess and then walk back out, run away to unpredictable places. Even the baby could turn on me. She was in my stomach for now, but what would happen when she inched into the world, no longer relying on our connection? When this part of me, my literal flesh and fluid, was free-floating in the universe? The cord was thick, but was snipped off in a second.

SKELETONS IN THE CLOSET, AND EVERYWHERE ELSE
London, 2007

I was more nervous than I cared to admit as I stepped over the foot-bridge to the Tate Modern, focusing on placing one appendage in front of the other, on not looking down or thinking about how flimsy the structure was or about my general fears of suspension and deep waters and, well, dates. The bridge swayed and I reminded myself that it was supposed to. The side-to-side motion was its net; the give would save me.

It had been nearly two months since Jon and I had seen each other; one month since his crustacean message. He'd surprised me by texting two weeks after I returned from Scotland, asking how my show had gone and saying he'd love to get together. I hadn't chased him, and yet, he'd remembered me. I was about to type back a snarky reply about his awakening from the dead, but my mind flashed with my mother's advice: "Be nice and straightforward. Show men clearly that you are interested. Make it easy for them." I'd replied that I'd like to see him too, anticipating we'd meet for romantic drinks that evening. Jon suggested "next Friday."

Next Friday? Why not next year? At this rate, I thought, it would take a decade before we got to second base. This guy might drive like a *meshuggener*, but he was a slow mover. Or perhaps, I suspected, he wasn't all that into me. Oy, I wanted an indication of where this was going! I'd suggested we go to a global cities exhibit since I knew he loved travel and figured it would give us material to discuss. But as I hit the museum's lawn, for the millionth time fiddling with my hair, pants, mind, I saw Jon approach, shaking his head. "The show closed yesterday."

He leaned in to hug me, his warm body soft and familiar. "I don't know this area," he said, "but I saw a tapas place on the way."

My high-art plans did not seem to be serving me well in this relationship, but at least my knowledge of East London could help. "Let's go to Baltic," I said. "It's Russian." Would he like it?

He did. The dim, cavernous restaurant with its Soviet-inspired menu and jazz soundtrack was modern and romantic. The waitstaff was mildly nice. "I find this place normal," I said. "Like New York."

"I love New York," Jon said. "I used to live there."

My interest surged. We talked about cities, but not based on an exhibition. He told me about his summer in the Balkans and his various solo trips around the globe. Jon wanted to see everything, meet everyone. He could analyze a joke, but his conversation ranged wide, his political opinions fluid and not necessarily popular. While I moaned about how my local crafts market was shutting down, he thought it was best to see the positive in gentrification, to accept that change was inevitable and newness was exciting. He was up for discussion and debate, which I appreciated. His eyes twinkled and his smile became ever more attractive as the evening went on. I was glad our plan was improvised, that I hadn't donned a costume, rehearsed.

Over sweet blini, he held my hands. I used the restroom, cleaning my teeth, straightening my bra. Tonight, I finally felt a real connection, that sizzling energy, sprouting between us. Tonight, I knew, was it.

I returned to the table to find that Jon had paid (we simultaneously joked about me slipping out at the right time—we could even joke about our fights!) and was grabbing our coats. I followed him outside, waiting for him to suggest the next move.

"Let's find a cab," he said.

"I thought you didn't do cabs," I teased.

"For you, I do."

"Ah, your inner Romeo finally makes its appearance."

"I can do gentleman. Especially when specifically asked." He winked.

"Touché," I said as he flagged down a black car.

He opened the back door, and I crawled into the large passenger area.

Then he shut it.

Before I even had a chance to gasp in surprise, he explained through the window: "I need to take my friend Kate's two kids to buy rabbits in the morning."

Who? What? *Rabbits?*

"Why don't you stay over for the night?" he offered.

I was about to say, well, yes, but to do that you have to get into the cab, when he continued: "Next Sunday?"

Wait, I thought. You're asking me to have sex with you, for the first time, a week in advance?

He leaned all the way in the window, and gave me a final peck on the cheek, before telling the cabbie my address and exactly how to drive there.

I WASN'T FEELING well that Sunday, but I certainly wasn't going to cancel. After months of confusing rapport with Jon, the ambiguousness was causing me serious existential itchiness. I wanted a yes or no answer.

I arrived at his apartment with my packed overnight bag only to be confronted by a massive bronze cow door-knocker. "This is quite something," I said. The flat was the type of Victorian shabby chic conversion that everyone swooned over, but never appealed to me with its crowded rooms and quirky detailing, its stained glass and heavy drapes. Jon's was spacious with large windows, but modest, Britishly filled with mismatched heirlooms, oddly stacked books, an alarming number of CDs, French country tables, and awkward empty spaces, seemingly unfinished. Upper-middle class, I assessed. At least it's clean, I thought as I smelled fresh lemon.

Jon said a curt hello and took my bag, then invited me to sit on one of the two couches (or was that sofas?) that made an L-shape. He sat down on the other one, on the other side of the room.

"So," I bellowed across the echoing space. "How were the rabbits?"

As he spoke I slowly inched my way along the couch so that at least I could be closer to his piece of furniture. He didn't budge. I turned to glimpse my tattered overnight bag on the shiny floor and suddenly a panic arose in me: he didn't really want me there. I remembered my friend Claire who I'd worked on a play with years before. "Sure, you can store the entire set in my basement!" she'd offered. A friend and I rented a truck, only to turn up and find out that she had no basement. "You should have told me you hadn't *seen* the basement," my English companion explained on the way back. "English people offer. We offer to have you over for dinner, to make you tea, to store your furniture. We don't *mean* it." She chuckled at my naivety. "It's just our way of saying we like you." Did Jon— English Jon—like me?

"What would you like to do tonight?" he asked.

Um, you, I wanted to answer. "My stomach isn't feeling great," I blurted out.

"Let's go to Golders Green and get you kosher chicken soup."

Granted, a nice offer, but he seemed a bit too eager to get me out of his house.

"Why don't we go for a walk first?" he suggested. "I want to show you the architectural detailing in the neighborhood."

Outside, we stepped side by side, not touching, the gap between us palpable, reminding me of artist Rachel Whiteread's solid resin casts of the normally invisible spaces beneath chairs. As Jon pointed out the local aesthetic features, I learnt that he was passionate about domestic design and was involved in house refurbishment projects in various countries. I liked that about him, of course, but what the hell was going on?

"Listen, can I ask you something?" My brashness now shocked me. "I'm not English, as you well know, and so I don't understand. I mean, do you like me? Like, *like* me? Are you attracted to me?"

Pause.

Idiot.

"There are two types of women," Jon finally answered, rounding a corner. I followed, my heart hammering wildly. I hadn't planned to put him—or myself—on the spot. "The kind that you want to be friends with. And the kind that you like romantically."

All I could feel was that space between us, my hand unheld, waving free-fall in the evening breeze. I knew what was coming: the "we're-better-as-friends" soliloquy. Well, I needed to leave England

anyway and this would give me the final push out. *It doesn't matter,*
I told myself.

"And you." He paused. I held my breath. "You are both."

I was both? "So you *do* like me." I turned away and smiled.

"Yes," he answered, still marching at a clip. "I'd rather not con-
tinue this now."

"OK." That was fine. He was English, this was uncomfortable for
him, I respected that. Besides, I had my answer and felt good. Great,
actually. "Tell me more about the value of Victorian stained glass,"
I said to change the topic.

"OK," he said. "And then let's go get you that soup."

That night, I crept (perhaps dashed) over to Jon's side of the bed,
but was rebuffed. "Spending the night doesn't need to mean sex," he
said. "Let's take this slowly. I like you."

Frustrated, still confused, I nestled beside him instead.

"Um, can you move over?" Jon asked.

"Over where?" Was this another Ben, kicking me out?

"To your side." He gestured to the empty half of the king-size
bed. "I need room to sleep."

I rolled back along the dark blue über-masculine sheets (did I
mention the iron metal headboard?) all the way to the other end of
the mattress, to my own hemisphere. No snuggling here, but lots of
snoring. I listened to Jon's snuffling, trying to relax to its rhythm,
sinking into the soft bed, thinking that this wasn't that bad. After
all, I had a stomachache. Why had I even rushed it?

The next morning, Jon made me coffee and drove me home. I
still didn't know what was going on between us, but for the first
time, I felt that that was fine.

The itchiest thing of all, I reminded myself, was the act of healing. I didn't always need to scratch.

WHEN I INVITED Jon to my Rosh Hashanah dinner, I expected him
to decline. He didn't.

It would be the first time he'd see my space. And my friends. The
first time I would envision "us" through their eyes. Not to mention,

the first time he'd try my food. I panicked, and made sure Yolanda, an American performance artist who lived in a semihabitable industrial plant, was coming over to help cook. What did I know from honey-baked chicken and kugel? Yolanda was hands-on, confident at everyday things.

"Your place is cute," Jon said as soon as he came up the rickety staircase with his overnight bag, which he slung on my bed. I followed his gaze as he gave himself a tour of my triple-cleaned space. "Really cute." I breathed a sigh of relief, hoping he meant it, that "cute" was good, and that my mismatched cutlery and plates would also fall under its heading.

Yolanda had been busy hacking chicken thighs in my minuscule kitchen while I'd been preparing the one salad I knew how to make. Jon followed me into the room and watched. "I wouldn't do that," he said as I sliced pears. "You'll slash yourself." He mimed a different cutting technique, then he gave me a peck on the cheek. I blushed in front of Yolanda, whom I'd not told about our courtship.

He stood behind us, peering. "You should really put the cheese in last," he said. "It'll get soggy."

"OK, thanks." I was curt. Enough with the critique.

Then he turned to Yolanda. "Way too much breading," he guffawed. "You're sure that will cook? I'm not in the mood for kosher salmonella."

She expertly ignored him while rolling her eyes so that I could see. My oven was starting to heat and I too began to fume. Is this how a person acted when invited for dinner? More than that, I was getting whiffs of Evan. Was I once again going to be shunned and dumped for my domestic fallibility?

Fortunately, the doorbell rang with my final guests. "I'll get it," Jon said, clearly wanting to be useful.

"OK," I answered cheerfully, and waited for the car crash. The arrivals were a couple of reserved and highly intellectual avant-garde Israeli architects. How would brash Jon talk to them? Serves him right. I watched him plop himself down on my futon as if he'd been here a thousand times.

I finished the salad, Yolanda continuing to roll her eyes whenever we heard him make a joke about the chefs taking their time, and my heat grew until I was burning up. Domestic chores were the end of me. I could not do this, could not fail again. I didn't want to be with someone controlling, condescending, obsessed with home, with cooking, judging me the whole time. I decided: I would end it that very night.

But as I brought out the first course, I saw him talking to the couple. They both seemed so at ease, smiling, drinking in his words and then responding with enthusiasm—about their work, architecture, Jewish identity in the UK. He filled their glasses. Jon's openness was what had attracted me, I remembered. It comforted me. I loved his frankness, for better and for worse. I had to calm down: it was me, this time, who was shifting moods, black and white. "Delicious," he said, biting into my salad, into the chicken.

When he went to the bathroom, my Israeli friends gave me the thumbs-up.

When everyone left, I was brash back. "You were rude in the kitchen."

"Sucks for you," Jon said. "You'll have to put up with me."

"If you're lucky," I mumbled. He kissed me, a sweet one, for a sweet new year.

THE NEXT MORNING, we were woken by his phone. "Sure, I'll come get them," Jon offered to someone who I assumed was his mother. I was about to make a crack about being a mama's boy when he told me he was picking up Kate's kids from the train station.

Kate? Of the rabbits? "Who is she?" I asked, forcing myself to sound calm.

"Just a friend," Jon said, then got up to shower. I decided to file away this troubling information for later.

That night, he called to see if I was free. "I'm too tired," I said, as I walked up Islington High Street. It was the truth. And, it was starting to dawn on me, he wasn't going anywhere fast. I too could take my time. Jon wouldn't suddenly forget me, or dive into an incomprehensible mood in which I didn't exist. He wouldn't retreat into his head, or turn his caring attention to rage and so I didn't have to grab and squeeze it hard. "But thanks for coming over," I said. "I'm glad you liked my flat."

"It's sweet," Jon said. "Very you. I admire that you support yourself. Just one thing. You really need nicer towels."

"You're so not English," I said, noting that I was not offended, did not take his comment as a criticism of my being, just of my linen. I also felt proud: he'd noticed what was probably the most significant accomplishment of my life thus far. Not wild success but self-sufficiency. His frankness made me trust him. His openness made me candid in a way I'd never been—with anyone. I was about to laugh off his request, but then recalled Evan and his desire for comfort. Back then, I hadn't been able to hear his demands, which seemed selfish, beside the point. But now I could listen. Sure, I couldn't really afford nice towels, but some things were an investment. I turned around and headed straight for Marks and Spencer.

That night, I noticed that Jon had left a green travel toothbrush on the sunk edge of my sink, in a little toothbrush bed.

NEARLY TEN DAYS later—the ten days of forgiveness between Rosh Hashanah and Yom Kippur, the days of cleansing, honesty, renewal— I walked up the stairs to Jon's flat. I'd been visiting an art historian friend in Spain for a long weekend and Jon had texted me, punctually, reliably, every twenty-four hours. I liked it. It was as if he'd been Ferberizing me, teaching me that he'd return at regular intervals, so I could relax and let go. No surprises. Then, on the last day, I checked my inbox, and found he'd e-mailed a few days earlier, asking me to come over the night I returned to London. He'd signed it "Love Jon."

It was now that night, and we began to set out tea and cake on his kitchen table, when more words skidded from my mouth. "I need to talk to you about something," I said, cringing at the girlfriendliness of it, careful about proceeding. How I hated we-have-to-talk talks. "It made me uncomfortable when Kate called the other morning, asking you to pick up her kids." I braced myself, ready for him to yell, tell me I was being unreasonable, critical, selfish, that in fact, he loved her. "If we're going to take this seriously, or going to date, then I feel like you need to make some boundaries—"

"OK," Jon said, cutting me off. "Let me think about it."

Two days later we sat on a bench in a small park near a gathering of my art historian colleagues. Jon had burst into the awkward crowd boisterously, trying to change the conversation from critical theory and the fluctuating position of the contemporary London art scene to sports cars. At first I cringed in shame, but then I just laughed. That was him. Not me. He wasn't my spokesperson.

"I talked to Kate," he now said. "I told her that you were my girlfriend, and it wasn't appropriate for her to call me at all hours and expect me to care for her kids. I said we had to make boundaries."

"Wow. Thanks."

"I was so taken by how you told me. You were calm and considered, and not huffy and histrionic. I was able to see that you were right."

"There's something else I need to tell you," I said, inspired by my emotional success, proud of how I'd been handling things, not even realizing I'd been mature, and especially, attractive in my maturity. I had spoken my mind, been honest, and managed the problem. I took his hand. "I can't stay here."

"The park?"

"No, London. I just don't think it's where I really belong. I can't see a future for myself here."

"Good to know," Jon said. "I'd move to New York in a flash."

Could this be true? "Speaking of which, I'm going to Montreal in a few weeks," I added. "I'll be gone for a month. What do you want to do?"

"What do you mean?"

"I mean, I totally understand if you want to, you know, take a break. I mean, I don't want to make assumptions—"

Jon laughed. "Let's just assume we'll be together until we aren't. Also, I'll come to Montreal. I haven't been in ages and I want to meet your family. Speaking of which, do you want to break the Yom Kippur fast at my parents' house?"

"Of course," I said, wondering if this too-good-to-be-true scenario was a joke, a slice of unreality that would disintegrate into crumbs at any second. But then I stopped myself from thinking, and instead, suggested we go get dinner.

JON PICKED ME up in his convertible, the roof down on an unusually sunny London afternoon. I got in and leaned over to kiss him on the lips.

"Do I look OK?" I asked. I was excited but also nervous. It had been years since I'd been invited to meet the parents. And even longer since I'd been invited to their house, my boyfriend's childhood abode, the site of his formative years, where his dreams were constructed, his personality crystallized, his perspective honed, his template for intimacy sizzled into his psyche like a panini press.

"You look perfect," he said. "For someone who claims to be fasting."

"I *am* fasting," I stressed. "Some of us have willpower."

"Bo-ring."

We drove up the hilly streets of Hampstead, right past Freud's house—a shared landmark for us, I thought. Jon, like most British Jews, had spent most of his life living in that neighborhood; I, like most North American Jews, had spent most of my life in psychoanalysis. This was the house Freud had fled to from the Nazis, the house to which he'd brought all his collections. His tchotchkes were still there, but now, displayed as a museum, behind glass, organized, safe.

I took a deep breath and tried to relax in the warmth. But the wind blew into my face, screwing up my eye shadow. Jon was a ridiculous driver. He swerved through the winding roads that barely fit his car, let alone the oncoming traffic. Compared to all my artsy boyfriends, his sports car seemed manly and independent, and so his crazy driving didn't generally bother me. I liked how he pushed his way through the crowded city. I admired how he wasn't afraid to take risks—most of the time.

"What the hell are you doing?" I cried as his tires came to a screeching halt in front of a Victorian hedge.

"Listen," he said, turning to me. "There's something I need to tell you."

My heart stopped. This wasn't like him. He didn't do drama.

"What?" I was ready for the worst. He was turning around. Taking me somewhere else. He'd changed his mind about sharing this most intimate of relations and spaces. It was over. This was the end. He was dying. He was already dead. I was dead.

"My mother has a lot of stuff," he said.

"Huh?"

"My mother. She has a lot of stuff."

"Whatever," I said loudly. A lot of stuff? Ha. He had *no idea* how much junk it would take to impress me.

"No, I mean *a lot* of stuff," he stressed. "Vases. Plates. Newspapers."

"Just drive already." I shivered and cut the conversation short. Was this some kind of joke? I had—for sure—kept my childhood home a secret from him, from everyone. Had he somehow found out? "I'm starving."

"All right, then," he said, pounding on the gas. The car jolted back into action. "Don't say I didn't warn you."

Warn me? But before I had time to think anymore we arrived at his house, set back off the road. It was much larger and more exquisite than my childhood home, but my eyes were immediately drawn to the circular driveway. It was filled—with three rusted Volvos. From the 1980s.

"I told you," Jon mumbled as we walked up to the front door. He rang the bell.

His mother answered. She was short and thin, with died pinky-orange hair and svelte lips outlining an angular but large smile. "So nice to meet you, Judy."

"So nice to meet you too," I answered, my own lips doing yoga stretches past my ears. But I was no longer paying attention to her face. Instead, my eyes were darting around, taking it all in. Next to her was a human-sized tower of junk mail. Behind her I could make out a long line of Tiffany lamps. Farther back, a whole room piled with wooden dining room tables.

My mother has a lot of stuff.

"It's time to break the fast," she said.

"It certainly is," I barely eked out. My pulse pounded. Everything I'd run away from was now in front of me, closing in on me. *I could still run,* I thought, *catch the bus on the corner.* I eyed a heap of yellowing newspapers.

Jon saw my stare. He gestured to the stack. "That pile is structural."

Huh? In my dizzy state it took me a second to realize he was referring to it as if it was a wall. Ha! It *was* structural, I thought. The crux. The core.

But more than that, it was a joke. All these years of kidding around, and yet the one thing I never joked about was the home that I came from. Never. Not once.

"Come in," Jon's mother said.

I held my breath, inched my way inside, looked around me at a real live version of my childhood angst and, for the first time, exploded into laughter.

JON'S FAMILY WAS wealthier than mine, so their hoarding comprised a different class of object. The dining room, bigger than any of my parents' rooms, had antique chairs stacked on their backs, boxes from Sotheby's, collector toasters, and chandeliers salvaged from synagogues across Europe. But what surprised me even more than the extensive Edwardian decanter collection was Jon's attitude. Before we sat down to eat, we wandered through their sprawling four-story Victorian detached, as he pointed out a full-sized library card catalogue and a population of ceramic tumblers. "Just in case we have sixty-five guests for dinner," he joked.

As we explored, I barraged Jon with questions. I wondered if his mother's hoarding emerged from her immigrant experience (she had come from Africa to London) and if attaching to objects was easier than to foreign English people . . . "Your mother is so petite. Is she afraid of losing her husband and being alone in this big space? Is she filling up her house prophylactically?" Jon chuckled at my blunt overanalysis. He didn't know why his mother was a hoarder, but what ultimately stood out to me was that he was OK with it, with exposing his family's craziness, aware and confident that his mother's mess wasn't *him*. Not even ashamed.

I'm not my mother's house, I remembered. I was here, thirty years old, someone's girlfriend in London. *My mother's mess isn't me.*

As we walked up the final flight of stairs, I felt amazed at the extraordinary coincidence that two children of hoarders had found each other and could no longer hold myself back. "My mother has stuff too!" I was panting. "Reams of it. Thumbtacks, onesies, laundry baskets bought on sale. Tupperware, Play-Doh sets, wall calendars from the late 1970s. My childhood bed is currently a warehouse for fax machines. My friends complain that their inheritances are being spent on cruises; mine is being spent on hole punchers. My mother's house," I confessed, pointing all around me, "is even worse."

"Worse?" Jon stopped.

"Worse." Now I worried I'd gone too far, that in coming clean I'd made a mess.

"Wow," he replied after a pause. "I can't wait to see it!"

As he opened an attic freezer filled with ten-year-old kosher turkeys, I suddenly understood. Like me, he had grown up in small pockets of affection surrounded by record players and hotel-shampoo collections. Our forthright rapport countered our worlds of hidden secrets. Being open about our past messes, even joking about them, helped clean them up. His successful detachment from his mother's *mishegas* could help guide my own. My attraction to Jon was propelled by his ability to face the ugly and the odd, to accept it without judgment or fear.

But most of all, I understood that after three decades, I had finally found someone I could bring home.

· FOURTEEN ·

BUILT-INS
Montreal, 2007

Jon once told me that his parents had never picked him up at an airport. I was going to do everything imaginable to make him feel at home here, in Montreal. *He's actually coming to meet my family.* My brain froze over. What would he think? And they? Thank God he'd booked a room in a hotel.

I paced in the arrivals lounge, surrounded by layers of winter fabrics, all of us waiters playing bumper cars with our fluffed-out bodies. It was a particularly harsh day, gray and blizzardy, the snow rolling across the city so that two-lane streets had shrunk to one, vehicles nestling up to one another as they pushed in their own directions.

When Jon emerged, I gulped and waved.

"No fanfare?" he asked and kissed me. "Let's go meet your family," he said. "And let's see how *you* drive."

"Driving in snow is its own story," I said, as I turned the key. "Get ready, bitch."

As a warm-up, I took him first to Carlton, where Dad had convinced Eli to live with Uncle Moishe and keep an eye on him—and maybe to justify never selling this parental hideaway. Though Dad advertised it on par with the Mandarin Oriental, the building was infused with whiffs of urine, the pipes were rotting and the infrastructure was collapsing. Having said that, he had redone the flooring, and Eli had created a funky, retro-designed interior, which is why I felt more at ease showing it.

I parked in the snow heap outside. The temperature had reached minus twenty-five. I braced myself as I opened the door to the windchill factor, feeling the fragility of my small physique. The cold made it impossible to dawdle, so I ran up the snow-filled stairs. Jon was elated: the extreme frost, the unusual mounds of white, all an adventure. "I can't wait to do some ice driving!" His mouth emitted streaks of steam.

"Hello?" I called as I opened the door to the upstairs flat.

"Hello!" Jon called up, giddy.

"Hi," my mother's and brother's voices made their way down.

My mother?

I hadn't prepared. There was so much to say, to warn Jon about, still. I'd planned to assure him: she was not the future me. I'm not her. *Not her.*

But Jon pushed in behind me and shut the door. I held my breath as I walked up the stairs. This was it. Well, I consoled myself, Mom is easier to meet than her house.

"Jon, so nice to meet you."

"It's brilliant to meet you too."

They hugged. Full-blown, all-physical, total-contact embracing. I turned away, moved and scared by this breaching of boundaries.

"Let's see this place." Jon excitedly noted Eli's guitar collection. I'd warned him that some rooms were disaster zones, but he happily pranced around the shining new parquet, leaving traces of dark slush, as if tracking his journey into my family.

"Ay, Jon," I called, both annoyed and relieved that here, the mess was his. "Shoes off in Canada!"

"Oops, sorry," he said, looking down. He slipped them off and went to chat music with Eli while I wiped up his marks. Jon had always been socially comfortable, the kind of person you could take anywhere. Even here.

"He's friendly," I whispered to my mother.

"Certainly!" She was smiling widely. Could they be getting along? Could he have simply taken my mother for who she was, despite everything? Was there no problem?

Thank you, Mom, I ESPed to her. *Thank you for being so normal today.*

AFTER A DAY of traipsing through piles of snow and Jon repeating that he couldn't believe the city functioned as usual when people were skiing down the streets, we had fish at the diner with Dad. "Do you like him?" I asked when Jon went to the bathroom.

"He seems like the kind of guy I could hang out with," Dad replied. "That's all I can say," which I took as my father's closest admission of love.

But all this was only part.

Jon drove this time as we headed across town for the moment I'd feared my whole life. Bringing him home. We parked in the driveway.

I reminded myself of his mother's Volvos.

"Jon!" My mother immediately greeted us at the door. "Come in."

I shut my eyes as we entered, afraid of what I'd find, but was relieved and grateful to see she'd made attempts to tidy up. The boots and rubbers had been lined up on each side of the vestibule; the hallway leading to the kitchen was clear of the usual plastic bags stuffed with two liter Diet Coke bottles. The floor looked, at least, dirt free.

"Do you want a hot drink? Coffee? Tea? Juice? I have cheese Danish, cinnamon Danish, prune Danish–"

Prune Danish? "Mom."

"I never met a Danish I didn't like," Jon said, heading straight for the kitchen, not even looking around. "It would be rude not to."

My mother heaped pastries on the table (which had otherwise been cleared of crumbs—thank you). "How about pickles? Should I order Chinese? Wait! I have a cold pizza in the fridge."

"Mom." I glanced at Jon, who seemed content being fed. "I'm going to show Jon around," I said, as soon as I saw him finish a pastry and before my mother could get another one in. I had to get it over with.

Jon followed me into room after room as I introduced him to the piles of laundry baskets, the commercial-grade stash of Manischewitz and newspapers dating back to the 1980s, when people still read newspapers. I tried to joke like he did, but the lines weren't coming out. "Here's the Chinese laundry factory," I said, my tour de maison nowhere near as funny as his. Instead, I became earnest, trying desperately to prove that we had class. "Check out these Rosenthal dishes that my mom bought on sale in the seventies." I opened a credenza door to reveal a mountain of never-used factory-second plates.

"This *is* worse than my mother's," he agreed. "The great thing about you is that you make me feel like the family I come from is normal."

My tour eventually landed in the basement, where my father had recently carved out a section for a single bed. His undershirts and pants were draped on every surface, like graying flags of surrender. I tried not to notice that the old pullout couch I used to crawl into at night was completely covered.

"Check this out," Jon called. He was not examining my father's frightening nest, but instead, excavating something from under a landslide of vinyl records. "*This* is worth keeping."

He'd not run, but gone digging, and found my parents' 1970s Danish modern teak dining room table. "We should refurbish this," he said, as he fondled joints and felt surfaces, checked for inscriptions. He had not only accepted the junk, but had found a side of my parents that I had long forgotten about, a side that was stylish, worldly.

"Wow. Amazing how a sense of fashion can turn into this," I said, gesturing around. "Scary." But my own fear was diminishing, hearing his "we," his commitment and acceptance. Like Evan, he had a domestic streak, but Jon found it charming—and not lacking—that I was not, as I called it, a domestic eater. *A chance to try more restaurants!* he'd happily conceded.

In any case, Jon was excited, blowing dust, pulling wooden legs out of the jumble, seeing value in the junk. *Thirty years, and I can finally show myself, share myself.* "A twentieth-century classic."

That night, we slept at a chic boutique hotel that had a screenlike fireplace emanating two-dimensional flames. It was the first time I'd stayed at a hotel in my own city, never mind such a luxury room (Jon's ability to self-soothe was extremely not Batalion). I was a part of here, and not a part of here. An inhabitant and a visitor. When I'd told my parents, they were fine with it. Maybe it was too much for them to host Jon too. Maybe they saw me, noted what I needed.

I breathed in the crisp white linen sheets. For five nights I'd been buried under my mom's junk, and then Jon came and whisked me off. My Prince Churlish.

Before dozing off, I thought of his green travel toothbrush, perched in my bathroom. I knew, it fit.

"MY LEASE EXPIRES at the end of April," I said to Jon over the phone two months later as I leaned on the pillars of the staircase at the Art Institute—the same staircase that had been the subject of an e-mail a few weeks earlier instructing everyone not to use it on a particular Tuesday due to a royal visit. "Who knows what will happen? The new landlords may want to evict me."

"That sounds like a good time for you to move in here," Jon replied, as I expected. For a while, he'd been hinting that he wanted me to (it would mean so much less time driving; so financially convenient; hey, move in here already) but I'd stayed quiet. Spending my life with someone, sure. Getting married, even, that I could now begin to vaguely see, a reality in the hazy distance whose contours were beginning to emerge as solid lines. But living together? And in *his space* with the golden calf? Still a mirage. He'd said he loved me, but I was scared. How could I—who had worked so hard, over decades, to painstakingly cultivate my own place, build my own walls—share them? I felt ready to merge my life, but my home?

"Let me think about it."

And I did, for three hours, until on my way home I noted that my favorite local hole-in-the-wall bar, a dimly lit secret, overflowed with trendy twenty-two-year-olds.

Jon and I set a date: the week of my thirty-first birthday. We used the Volvos to move me, and were done six trips later—six trips during which I traversed the same streets as always, but this time, from a novel perspective. I'd been the young art history student on the bus, the aspiring comedian in the tube, and now I was a thirtysomething Jewish girlfriend in a car. On these new urban treks, I saw not cool pubs, but interesting ethnic restaurants; not single smokers congregated around inside jokes, but midcentury architecture. I no longer experienced the winding streets as dark and mysterious, full of potential and loneliness, intense with my raw inner life. Instead I saw traffic lights and alternate routes, litter and shaded benches, simple conversation.

I'd been in London for seven years—the figure of wholeness and renewal. Seven days of the week, days of mourning, years of sabbatical, of the fat and the skinny cows. In seven years, your body's cells completely regenerated so you were an entirely new person.

"WHAT IS *THIS*?" I pointed to a drawer in Jon's desk overflowing with old ticket stubs. Busy unpacking, with boxes of my own stuff piled like human-sized cardboard ghosts around me, I was flummoxed, caught off-guard. How had I not noticed this before? "Are these yours?" I called into the next room. Were there other things I hadn't known? I'd never wanted to pry, to suffocate: but what else was concealed?

"Jon," I called more loudly. Why wasn't he coming? "Jon!"

Now he came running. I pointed in revulsion at the first drawer.

"Tickets to every gig I've ever been to," Jon said quietly. "I love music."

I pointed to another drawer. Paper bags. And another one—holy shit. Old empty boxes. Not just thousands of CDs, but cassette tapes. Pens to supply a small country. I felt nauseous. I'd thought we had no secrets. But Jon had hoarding tendencies.

He saw me go white. "Don't worry," he said. "I don't *need* this." He immediately began emptying a drawer into the trash. "I can let go."

I sighed with relief.

I'd traveled across the world to find a relationship that was familiar, like the ones I grew up in. But, I thought as I watched him dispose of designer shopping bags, one I could finally have some control over. One that had a logic to it, room for negotiation. "I want my own open shelving," I said. "I need it."

"I'll call the contractor tomorrow," Jon said. "We'll make you some built-ins."

Built-ins. Permanent, clean, steady. Punched right into the very foundation of the space. My childhood dream.

"And that part of the office is yours," he continued. "I cleared those drawers." He gestured toward a closet that I opened to find half empty. My clean, glass slipper. We both knew our baggage impacted those around us. He was giving me room to breathe.

"Thank you so much," I said, turning up the volume on Jon's stereo, even though I didn't care for the song. I carefully placed my files in piles, respecting Jon's already filled areas. Spaces create the people who live in them, but sometimes, to fit to their spaces, people have to morph too.

"But it's like ninety-five degrees," I whined to Jon. It was the one-year anniversary of our first date, that memorable evening where we fought the whole time and he ran for the train. He was taking me out to Jerusalem's one nonkosher high-end eatery, and insisting I wear a cocktail dress that we'd picked out together a few months earlier. "I never wear dresses."

"Please. For me," he said, putting on what looked to me like exceptionally comfortable shoes.

After spending a good part of our relationship traveling the globe from Toronto to Montenegro, Liverpool to Chennai, Jon and I had ended up in Israel. It felt like the right time for us to spend a week here, in this whirring axis mundi, a place where it all met, the original foundation. Jon's distant relative was having a bar mitzvah, and he'd always made staying in touch with his extended family a priority, which I liked. (I hadn't seen my cologned relatives in years.)

We'd spent the day before wandering through the city of gilt and guilt, sightseeing in the old quarter, reminiscing about the visits we'd each made in our adolescence. I remembered the cool nights walking home from the Wall, and flirting with boys (or more like, fantasizing). He remembered arcades, and knew everything about Jerusalem's churches—which I had never even seen.

I slipped on my short polka-dot Betsey Johnson dress, which made me feel self-conscious. I did not love my knees; my joints always seemed larger than the parts they needed to bring together. "Let's go," I said.

"Can you just grab this?" Jon handed me a crumpled bag from Boots, an English drugstore. I'd seen him schlep it around before.

"I have to wear a party dress *and* carry your plastic bags for you?"

"For me," he repeated.

Jon had informed the restaurant that it was our anniversary; they kept the champagne flowing. Due to migraines, he didn't drink, so it all flowed to me. As did the more adventurous dishes, as did the bread, which I was picking at to avoid drowning in alcohol, as did the jokes that Jon was expertly cracking. Which is why I was surprised when he pulled a straight face.

"Where's that plastic bag?" he asked.

"Oh, *le plastique*; *très* bag lady chic!" I was drunk, my shoes off under the table, my underwear digging into my bloated belly. I flung it over to him.

"Judy." He lowered his voice.

I leaned in. "Yeeeah?"

"Remember a few months ago when I said I wanted to spend my life with you." It was true, he'd mentioned it once on a holiday weekend when we'd been lounging in bed, passionately reminiscing about each meal we'd eaten that week.

"Yeeaah?"

From the plastic bag, he pulled out a velvet box.

I barely had the chance to sit up straight before he opened it. A ring.

But—it was not an engagement ring. It had diamonds embedded in its side, forming a curvy pattern. Was he proposing or offering me jewels from a pharmacy?

"Jon," I said slowly, thinking back to that walk we took when I asked him point-blank if he liked me. "What exactly is going on here?"

"What do you mean?"

"What do *you* mean?"

"You need me to spell it out for you?" he asked. "Will you marry me?"

"Yes," I said. "I need you to spell it out. And, yes. I will marry you."

He slipped the ring on my shaking finger. "I bought one I can return," he said. "I wasn't sure if you'd like it."

I. Was. Getting. Married.

Me.

Awkward. Nerdy. Me.

"You schlepped this for a week through Israel?" was all I could say.

He kissed me. We held hands, my new stones pressing dents into both our skins. "We're getting married," I finally uttered. The biggest decision of my life thus far, made without a line of neurotic dialogue. Not even a second to think. "Can you believe it?"

Then we both said, "Let's call the mothers."

Jon's asked to speak to me. "Wise decision," she said, Englishly. "Congratulations. Good choice."

I knew mine would not react in quite the same way.

"Mom, there's something I have to tell you." We were both silent for a moment before I declared the news: "Jon and I are getting married." I braced myself for the cries of joy, the thank gods.

Instead, she gasped. "Are you sure?"

"What?"

"How do you know?"

"What do you mean, how do I know?"

"Did he ask you?"

"Yes, yes, he asked me." Christ, could she not be happy, trusting, responding to my reality, for one fucking second? (And I wondered why I second-guessed everything.)

"So you're getting married."

"Yes."

"For real?"

"Yes!"

That's when my mother began to wail—for twenty minutes straight. For the first time, her howl sounded a little less like a bomb-shelter siren, and a little more like life.

· FIFTEEN ·

SMALL STEPS
Montreal, 2008

"We need to go to social services," I told Dad as I got into his car, my lines rehearsed. I was in Montreal to help my parents get outfits for my wedding, but my priorities had shifted. "Now." For years, I'd wanted to get help, sure there were medications, therapies, solutions. Dad continually dissuaded me, claiming it was all useless, that these interventions often caused more harm than good. But I *had* to do something. "This is getting insane."

I looked over at him watching the road. He had enormous bags under his eyes, the wrinkled skin sallow and dark. "OK," he said.

Really?

"They're open until eight p.m. for urgent drop-ins," I explained, my words tripping over one another. I was in no way prepared for this response. "Let's see what they have to say."

Dad put his foot on the gas, pumped the pedal.

I clasped my hands, squeezed tight.

This was actually happening.

"COME OVER IMMEDIATELY." That morning, Mom's voice was shrill over the echo-ey budget phone. "It's critical."

Just a few months after our engagement, Mom's suicide calls had become constant. I was always calling back, checking in, the bad Samaritan hotline. This, interspersed with dozens of daily phone sessions planning a wedding: heavy hors d'oeuvres or a smoked-meat station? Should the breadbaskets have a napkin inside and if so, would you like it to match or contrast with the tablecloths? Diamantés in the stamens of the corsages or just the bouquet? (Do I look like I know? I never even thought I'd have a boyfriend!)

On this visit, Dad had asked me to stay at Carlton to keep an eye on Moishe, as Eli was out of town. Though I found it hard to be at my parents' house, now I felt rejected from it. I'd always assumed that I was shunned for leaving, but suddenly I wondered if my demands for cleanliness had been difficult for them, that they'd actually wanted me to go.

But not this morning, when Mom called me first thing, waking me up, demanding that I come over so she could talk to me. I managed my way out through piles of snow and onto the 161 bus, the one I used to take the other way, escaping from my house to downtown, to anywhere. I recalled the bus-lady my mother had been, plonked between Filipino housekeepers but with more bags and less makeup, embarrassing me in front of other kids whose mothers drove Jeeps. Now it was me freezing alongside cleaning ladies and elementary schoolchildren, my socks wet within my London shoes that were by no means a match for this weather. The rubber floors were wet, covered in a brown-gray slush like toothbrush foam, the dreaded liquid of my youth, leaving salty traces that you'd notice only after it had dried; rings that circled right around your pants, higher up than you'd ever assumed the water could reach. I'd never visited my house before as a guest and wondered where I'd sit, to where I'd retreat. There was no space, nowhere to settle, nothing to do but lounge in Mom's kitchen, be lulled into her story, her world.

The bus rode along Fleet Road and I thought of the real Fleet Street in London, the one of newspaper fame, lined with pubs from the 1620s. Canada always struck me as a movie set, a place where everything was too new; the oldest restaurants advertised that they'd been in business "*depuis* 1995." My new world felt old, my old one, new. I lived a split screen, confused about my position in both, wondering what of me remained constant.

The bus trudged on, tired against the weather. Fleet connected Carlton to Kildare, the only two family houses left. Both Hutchison and even Campden had, to my shock, eventually been sold—my mother had had to let them go. The triangle had deflated to a line; the whole business of the inheritance should have been over. But as I'd had a hunch all along, it wasn't and wouldn't be. Because it wasn't about the inheritance.

I was relieved to be in Montreal alone. The last time Jon visited, Mom had bolted all the doors and even many drawers inside the house. She'd locked Jon upstairs, and the next night, the door to Dad's bathroom. This was Dad's last straw and he exploded in a way I'd never seen, lunging at her across the table, nearly throttling her in our kitchen. Jon fled to my old room and closed the door; I had to physically pry Dad's hands off Mom's throat, and then calm him by telling him I understood how frustrating this all was. Then, Mom screamed at me, accusing me of taking his side. She was right, I conceded as I headed back to reassure my traumatized boyfriend.

And I'd been worried about the hoarding.

Now, the bus swerved along old familiar roads. The ride home. I recalled my old feelings: *I pray no one is there.* But of course, today I wasn't going home, I was going to see my mother, and she was definitely there.

I trudged down the street as quickly as possible and up her stairs, my anger mounting as I pressed the doorbell repeatedly, aggressively, until I saw Mom's eyes peek out from behind the blinds. I heard various clicks and the unchaining of bolts, and finally Mom let me in, hugging me quickly, then leading me to the kitchen for the talk. I forced my frustration under my skin.

"Where are my glasses?" my mother screeched as we sat down. "They're taking things from me. And all my papers." She ruffled through piles and files along the table. "They've made everything a mess. I can't find anything."

They made a mess? I thought of my lost bat mitzvah checks, how months after the event I was still begging her for the guests' addresses so I could send thank you cards, and how months after that, Mom had made me write each one a full essay apologizing for why *I* had been so late in writing. I'd been devoured by her disorder. Now, there were crumbs everywhere. The beige linoleum tiles peeled off the floor. Food and grime covered the counter. The chair fabric was sticky. My mother's hair had gone completely gray and was piled in a bun atop her head. She'd locked herself into her house, a shut-in, shutting out, melding with the building, her mind's mess stamped on every surface.

"You look like you lost weight," I said.

"Who knows? I'm probably dying," she said. "I need to talk to you."

I felt my neck stiffen, my guard shooting up. But then I looked at her face, the terror wild in her eyes, fear like shining flames in her dark pupils, her whole being possessed by this all-consuming dread. "Fine," I said softly. "For one hour."

"Fine."

It was as easy as that. I could make a limit. Instead of entering her world wholly, I could meet her at the threshold.

Not to say that the hour was easy. "Let me start at the beginning," my mother said, now that she had an audience. "It was the spring of 1998."

"Mom, I know—"

"You gave me an hour!"

I reheard the story, literally biting my tongue so as not to constantly disagree. But the conversation took an unusual turn. My mother was now convinced that people were breaking into the house, looking for her secrets, rifling through her files. "That car parked in front of the house," she said, "is spying on me. The children next door too. The neighbors." Then she pointed to a pencil. "I've heard they put cameras in the erasers," she whispered. "They're coming to get me. How can I possibly go on?"

I imagined this world of hers, in which every molecule was

attacking her and she was a 24/7 victim of massive threat. She built bigger and bigger walls around her to protect herself but all she was doing was creating a smaller and smaller, deathly dangerous universe inside. "Maybe the car's just parked—" I tried.

"For days at a time?" she shot back.

I shut up, tried to keep calm, examining the stale food on the counter, the residues of sauce and bread on the dirty plates covering the table. The tea bags so old, so dry, that the paper came undone in hot water, leaving leaves floating around your mug. It made no sense to me how people could live this way, how my parents, warm and alive, intelligent and educated, could live in what was no longer mess but dirt and debris. I'd stopped asking to hire a cleaner (or repairman, or plumber, or doctor) as I knew I'd only be met with resistance—from fear of the intruder, but perhaps also from shame. *It's not my dilapidating house, it's not my mess,* I kept repeating to mute my feelings. Finally, I couldn't take it, the intensity, the bizarreness, the victimhood, the wretched sadness that was for nothing. I exploded: "You're not rich. You're not powerful. Why would anyone be after your stuff? Who would care? I don't understand what reality you're living in right now, but it's not mine."

I'd gone too far. I cringed, waiting for her explosion, but again she surprised me. "Thank you," she said softly. "Thank you for not being against me, for listening to my side. That's all I want—for you to acknowledge my story."

Maybe, I thought, that's all anyone wanted—someone to see us.

THAT AFTERNOON, I phoned Maya, who was now back in Canada and who was also—hallelujah—getting married. After a discussion about designer ketubahs and her oocyte prenup arrangement, she asked how my family was. She knew my mother wasn't well, though not the extent of it; she herself came from Holocaust survivors and refugees—though ones who were more functional.

"She's just not getting help," was what I said. "It's so stressful to see her suffer, to see the anxious, obsessive thinking that's taken over her life." I didn't say more.

"It's so hard," Maya said. "I'm so sorry."

"I'm thirty-one years old, and can barely deal with this now: how did I cope when I was a child? When I didn't understand psychology, when I was defenseless, needy?" I recalled my pig-lined credenza, the Bonimart panics, the terror of each stride into the store that was going to eat me up. The unnecessary anguish of every weekend. "Each time I interact with my mom, it's double: the pain of the present and the past, when I was vulnerable and had no one to protect me."

This was ridiculous. Calla-lily bridal bouquets, kosher-style menus: even in a foreign country, I could plan a grand fête. I was making my own family. I had fashioned a new, better life. This craziness was not acceptable.

I was strong enough to make Mom a better life too.

AND SO, THERE we were, Dad and me, driving along Fleet, my heart beating wildly. Dad had spent decades complaining about the endless stop signs on this street, but they'd never been as annoying as now, when at each pause, at each release from the gas, I was sure he'd change his mind. I was too nervous to talk anymore, and recalled the time a few years earlier when he picked me up from the gym, and out of nowhere, turned down the volume of his talk radio show, stopped the car and said: "Judy, marriage is hard enough when you're from the same religion." At the time, amid my total surprise (this was the closest we'd ever come to any discussion of romance, and one of his few acknowledgments of my adulthood), I'd thought he was judging my particularly un-Jewish lineup of boyfriends. But now I wondered if it was his way of telling me, even ages ago, that he needed help.

A year earlier I'd been in Montreal when Dad got sick. His lungs. The clouds on the X-ray ranged from light to dark black, not yes malignant or no malignant but literal shades of gray, amorphous silhouettes that had no place inside a man of thick tennis soles and bold one-liners, of hardened perspective and solid structures. The doctor had asked him to undress and I got up to leave. "No, stay," Dad had said. *Stay?* I was repulsed, terrified, by his need. In front of me were all the things I didn't want to know. Dad's saggy flesh, his sunken chest, his pale lower back that curved inward. Soft flab hanging from his thigh, bones jetting out like broken umbrella wires. I thought of all the hospitals we'd been to together for my colitis. How he'd raced to the emergency room when Eli hit his head on the monkey bars, his shirt soaked in his son's blood. Each time, he was the leader, the belligerent advocate saying, "Tell me *what you see*." But that day, the pulmonologist shut off the light box, and Dad's whole lungs went black. "Wait," I'd insisted, but my voice had wobbled and I said no more.

Not this time, I vowed. Today I would be fierce, bellicose. In charge.

We soon arrived at the Cavendish Mall. Social Services was in the small office building above the main entrance, across from where Pumperniks had once resided. Dad, who'd made a full recovery from what turned out to be pneumonia, drove right up to the door.

"I'll wait for you in the entrance while you park," I said.

"Oh no," he said. "I'm not coming."

"What?"

"I'll circle."

I wanted to scream. *For how long will you sit in your car, circling, waiting for Mom?*

"Judy," he called, before driving off. "Don't use her real name."

THE CHAIRS IN the office were plastic, the desk was imitation wood, and the social worker, probably in her late thirties, had brown hair. Books and files were scattered around her station; I saw no names on them. She smiled, but not too wide. This was my moment, I thought. The solution to the main suffering of my existence was here, behind a blue ceramic flowerpot with two cacti.

How to begin? I had no language for this discussion. Dad and I never talked about my mother in any way except to joke or complain about the melodrama. Now I had to let facts and vignettes drip out, including the Valium addiction and the suicide threats and the alarms. *Don't use her name. Don't use your name. Don't let them trace us.*

The social worker nodded and hmm-ed. She seemed familiar with "bad cases" like mine. My excitement was growing—perhaps she could help. "We'll need your father's permission to enter the house for an assessment," she said.

I was silent.

"Your father wouldn't agree?" she asked.

"I don't know."

"Typical," she said. "The partners of mentally ill people often become slightly ill themselves. After years of cohabitation, their reality shifts, their normal is skewed."

My mind flashed to Dad's car, the trunk of which had become a worsening mess of plastic bags and tennis balls. I thought of his clothes piled all over the playroom. Forever, the family drowning.

Then she handed me a stack of papers. "Don't worry. Fill out all these forms. Go to court. Stress that your mother is a danger to herself and others—a life danger. Remember. That's important. They might then keep her in for a few days."

A few days?

I took the slew of pages, thinking: hell will be a room where they make me fill out government forms.

And that was it.

I walked out, my head spinning. I'd thought coming here would solve the problem, offer guidance, reprieve. I sighed. I was always looking for quick solutions, but it was going to be a long, long process.

I walked out of the mall into the night looking for my circling dad, reminding myself: small steps.

· SIXTEEN ·

30 WEEKS: RECOVERY ROOM
New York City, 2011

I clutched my notebook as I sped—as much as I could at my bloated
size—through the long white hallway of the maternity ward. Motherhood might not have come naturally, but school did. A couple of
months back I'd found out one uptown hospital ran a whole roster
of parenting classes; I'd signed up for a semester's worth of seminars.

First, Jon and I participated in the "Babies and Pets" workshop.
On Jon's urging we'd adopted a rescue cat a few years earlier—a
process that was much more complex than getting pregnant. I'd
grown attached to Mones, who was an elegant but misanthropic
tabby who vomited every time a child was near. Jon and I had arrived early and were first to express our concerns during circle time.
"Our cat is so neurotic and anxious," I announced. "I don't know
how she'll ever adapt to having a baby around." The other expectant
parents then declared their worries, which were largely about
whether or not their fifty-pound schnauzers would accidentally murder their newborns. After the session, Jon and I laughed at our ri-
diculousness. "Oh yeah, other people seemed concerned about their
baby not being *killed*, not their pet's complex emotional backstory."

At the newborn fundamentals class, where I took a dozen pages of notes—with diagrams—on how to treat cradle cap, I chuckled when my attempt to swaddle a doll ended in my accidentally breaking off her head. At the Infant CPR class that I took with a pregnant acquaintance from Harvard (I suggested we bond over brunch and prenatal massage; she thought perhaps a first-aid class might be more useful), I was blown away by all the anti-SIDS recommendations. "You have to sleep in the same room as your baby for *a year*?" Then Jon took the dads' class while I went shopping at the Upper Breast Side and found out I was imposing horrors on my ducts with my underwire bra.

And now here I was again, panting my way into Breast-feeding 101. I took a seat in the circle, noticing the equipment spread on the table: those easy-to-decapitate dolls, a variety of crescent-shaped pillows and an extra-large plush nipple. "Today's special guest will be an actual breast-feeding woman," the lactation nurse proudly declared while setting up a giant flip chart. "She'll show you how to get a latch." A what? And, did I really want to see that live? "But before that, let's go around the room and everyone can say for how long they plan to breast-feed."

Wait. This was supposed to be an intro to nursing. Since I didn't know anything about it yet, how was I supposed to know how long I wanted to do it?

"One year," every single woman declared and the nurse nodded vigorously as she scribbled numbers next to their names like they were scores.

I thought of Tina Fey's line: *Breast-feeding was amazing; the most gratifying seventy-two hours of my life.* "I don't know," I mumbled when it came my turn. "Maybe three months."

"I'll write down six plus," nursie said with a saccharine smile. "My goal is for everyone to be feeding for at least twelve."

Your goal? Argh! I was so tired of everyone else's opinions. My splicing abs, the tiramisu toxins. I'd recently been chastised at a party—where everyone was downing delicious-looking margaritas—for ordering a special-treat Fresca. "Starting her on the aspartame early . . ." Just the other day a waitress at a hummus bar insisted I was having a boy. "Actually it's a girl," I said. "But your belly is round." "But the sonogram shows female genitalia." "No!" Um, yes.

I'd been biting my swollen tongue, but now I was starting to wonder whether—with my last chance for hormones to take the behavioral blame—I should let my larynx loose like my ligaments. I fantasized replying, "No, I will not be giving birth in an organic sink in the Park Slope Food Co-op followed by a placenta barbecue! The prehistoric water-loving women you are emulating in your back-to-nature water births were fourteen, not forty-two! And many of them died! Your insistence that your entire household—including your doula and her rescue dogs—all sleep together in a single futon bed is more dogged than any doctor's prescriptions! You are insane for naming your child Timothée! Lethem! Bon Jovi! And doubly insane for doing baby-led weaning with your endive ragouts and single-origin garlic cloves marinated in bone marrow *jus*!"

The nurse rambled about terms I didn't know, and plugged the almighty boob. "Around the globe, the average length of time that women breast-feed is four years."

In cultures where women work? I didn't ask. I wanted to breast-feed—that's why I was there—but I inwardly rolled my eyes. Enough with the "breastapo" tone.

"The American Academy of Pediatrics recommends exclusive breast-feeding for six months minimum, but note: one year is preferable." Huh? The AAP said that too? I sat up in my seat. She read their statement: "Human milk protects against infant disease . . . diabetes . . . bacteremia . . . leukemia."

Cancer?! It was one thing to be contrarian, another to disregard serious medical recommendations.

What is wrong with me? I grabbed my water bottle, feeling faint. The cat panic, my inability to diaper a doll, my ridiculous sartorial choices. Why didn't I care about my child? Why didn't I want that fuzzy, nurturing experience that everyone else craved?

What if I just couldn't love her?

I got up and dashed out of the room. Shaky, I wobbled through a maze of anonymous hallways. I was now one of the giant women from that yoga class who I imagined held sacred knowledge, only I had none of it. I looked around: I was going to be poked and prodded, cut open again, and then, one of these post-natal beds would be for me. And her.

My overworked heart raced.

Then, as I turned a corner I saw a gurney parked outside a room. A woman lay on it, smiling, a man's fingers laced around her own. I smelled a familiar alcohol-like scent and clenched my puffy fists as something hit me—a memory of my colitis surgery I hadn't recalled in decades.

IT WAS MY mother's hand I felt when I awoke into a cloud of noise and pain, the most excruciating, bone-busting, all-body aching I'd ever experienced. I'd never before felt such a surge of desperation, of wanting to escape my physical being, crawl out of my organs. But just then, my mom's smooth palm, young like a twelve-year-old's, younger than mine, flowed up and down my cheek. In that moment of torture, she was at my bed, stroking me. "Squeeze my hand whenever it hurts," she whispered into my ear. "As if you're passing the pain to me."

VERITY ON THE VISTULA
Poland, 2008

"I think you should go a little faster," I chided Jon, as my childhood friend Nadia's eyes bugged out of her head. It was dark by the time the four of us, including Eli, approached the German-Polish border in our rented German minivan. We were the only car on the autobahn, which Jon took as a license to drive at light speed.

Days after our engagement party at the Freud Museum, I was schlepping Jon to—of all places—Poland. Despite all my travel, I'd never been to the land where all four of my grandparents were born, raised and married, where after the war, my mother spent her formative years. I thought of Bubbie's stories about being the only female tutor in Puławy and how she took her younger sisters swimming in the Vistula, the river that brought sparkles to her eyes. I recalled the photo of her with her mysterious beau on the banks of that river, the largest in Poland, running right through it like an arrow in a heart, imagining Bubbie falling in love here, more than once.

Now that *I* was in love, legally linking my heritage to another—and one who came from generations of knighted barristers—I wanted to connect to my roots. My background always felt so hazy, the stuff of myths. All I knew was that I came from Polish peasants and joked that if it wasn't for the Holocaust, I'd be a farmer in the Warsaw–Lublin corridor. I wanted to know that Jon understood my origins, the dark skies and warped-wood shtetl huts that were part of my maternal narrative.

We approached the border. I was genetically programmed to feel nervous at the prospect of showing "my papers" at Eastern European checkpoints. I pretended not to notice that Jon was having fun weaving between lanes. My stomach tensed as we drove up, only to find no border patrol. It was completely open. "I guess the problem never was getting *into* the country," I said, as Jon sailed past the empty booth. Or, as much as he could until we hit Polish soil, which was literally soil. The autobahn became a crumbly country road. Even with Jon's carefree driving, it took hours more to reach Wrocław, the place—the very real place—of Mom's first home.

IN THE MORNING, we walked into the brightly colored medieval town square that I recognized from photos, though the black-and-white images had concealed the magnificent pastel shades of the buildings. I touched the side of a structure, my fingers grazing over its dusty paint: this place existed, for real. How strange it must be for Mom, I thought, that the site of her earliest memories and formative experiences had been off-limits, even dangerous, for so very long, becoming an image in the mind rather than in the world. I rubbed my fingers together, like an archaeologist investigating clues in the granules of pigment—how long had it been here? What had it wit-

nessed? Covered up? The buildings, colorful like sidewalk chalk, like
the squares in Candy Land, felt confusing, more surreal than real.
Later, later this will make sense, I told myself, hoping, wishing I had
more stories to draw on, more collective memories to trace.

We found a bakery and Eli, Nadia, and I cackled at the similarities—challahs, blintzes, cheesecake! *This* is where it was from. This
shop could have been located in my neighborhood in Montreal.
"Cool," Jon said, stuffing himself with meat pie. Then he took a
photo. *He's having fun,* I told myself, sensing that we were not quite
in sync.

That afternoon, we visited parks, museums, and shops, wandering
through cobbled streets. Mom did not know her old address, so I
could only imagine which building had hosted Bubbie's cooking and
Zaidy's furs, Mom's nanny, her one doll. Mom had been so young
here, remembered so little, and despite all of Bubbie's stories, I'd
missed so many details. As I shielded my eyes from the bright
sunshine—even the weather didn't match my image of the country—I chided myself for not having asked the right questions. Now,
I kept asking myself if I felt a connection, a sense that this was my
past, my ancestral home, possibly for dozens of generations. My
motherland. But illiterate in the language, I felt more like an anonymous tourist in a land that didn't even know it held my secrets.

UNTIL I CHECKED my e-mail. The week before, I'd contacted friends
of friends, hoping one or two might have time to meet. I had not
expected to find an in-box inundated with messages from Polish
curators, professors, and tour guides, all eager to rendezvous.

The very next day a Polish scholar met us for breakfast at our
Krakow hotel, welcoming us as if we were a UN committee. We
wound through the medieval streets in and around the former Jewish quarter, looking at old synagogues but mainly this new, hip
neighborhood of Jewish-themed bars and contemporary art galleries,
of molecular borscht foam and digital photography. Very little reminded me of Bubbie or Mom.

That night we went to a "Jewish restaurant." The Klezmer band

belted out *Fiddler on the Roof* classics as my cholent was followed by
a dessert of hamantaschen—not Bubbie's brisket and Kit Kats, that
was for sure. The crowd laughed and clapped along. While this
might have been a standard scene at my elementary school's annual
Purim carnival (in a particularly good year), it was less expected on
a Tuesday night in November in Krakow. Especially when the energized throng consisted of a busload of retired Germans. I gestured
at Jon to get some video of this troubling sight, not sure whether I
had a rational reason to be disturbed by German tourists enjoying
an evening of ersatz Jewish culture. Jon, on the other hand, seemed
pleasantly amused and clapped along. That disturbed me even more.

Amid the strains of "Tradition," notes which all of a sudden
tingled with foreignness, all sorts of things about Jon that I'd repressed came flooding back. The way his bubbie's name was Gwen-
dolyn, how she skied, went to finishing school in Switzerland, talked
about sports cars, and served roast lamb topped with mint sauce (my
bubbie had never even *heard* of mint). How Jon had attended a fancy
Christian school, how his *mamahloshen* was Latin, and his founding
myths, Greek. It wasn't just our demeanors and jobs that differed,
but our heritages, our family's defining incidents. Generationally, I
was just minutes removed from terror.

That night, I was woken after midnight by a text: the senior advisor to the mayor of Lodz, saying he'd be delighted to see me. Me?
"Cool," Jon muttered, between snores. How could he not see how
crazy this was? The next day, at an über-trendy café, the advisor told
us of his overwhelming interest in Lodz's Jewish history. "I'm just a
fucking goy," he repeated, as we all sipped macchiatos. A twenty-
something tour guide then showed us the town, and explained that,
like many youths, he'd decided to become Jewish, certain he had
hidden Jewish roots. He told us about dozens of youth organiza-
tions, a whole Jew-cool movement. Jon thought the city looked like
Liverpool and asked him questions about the local film industry. I
nearly fainted. Was he not *listening* to this guy? If I'd once thought
it cosmic that both of us had been raised by hoarders, it now began
to seem like Jon and I had absolutely nothing in common.

I tried to tune in as we wandered around, stopping to see a night-club with see-through bathroom stalls as the guide told us about how a third of the city's population was Jewish before the war. I rinsed my hands in the fluorescent sink, staring at clubbers right through the walls, convoluting all my expectations. I'd thought I was going to Poland to find a missing link, but it seemed that Poland was missing me too.

THEN I INTRODUCED Jon to my actual family: we dined with distant cousins—the communist branch of my clan—who'd stayed in Poland after the war for political reasons and whom I'd never met. Their tiny apartment with a makeshift kitchen and cramped living room filled with trinkets and mismatched glassware but also magazines, newspapers, passion, finally fit my mental image of Eastern bloc existence. I stared at their ornaments, wondering if Bubbie and Zaidy's home had been similar, back in the 1940s, but figured that they hadn't had the time to amass such a stash. Yet.

In Yiddish, I told my cousins about the amazing stories of a Jewish cultural renaissance. "Are you crazy?" my otherwise soft-spoken cousin's husband suddenly barked. "Bullshit." He insisted the Poles only pretended to like Jews for American money. "They are anti-Semites to the core."

Jon sat quietly, eating cold potato salad, taking random footage of the flags on their credenza. When I translated, he shrugged. *But do you not see how bizarre, how troubling, this all is?* I said with my eyes. He ate coleslaw. I felt so empty that it made me nauseous. I had no idea what to believe.

The next night at a hotel in Lublin where, apparently, Nazis used to stay (in my bed?), Jon complained to the front desk about the pillows. I tucked myself in, my head spinning. Jew love, Jew hate, home, Holocaust.

I dozed off, thinking of Mom's doll, which she clutched fiercely with two hands in the black-and-white photo. Even though it was her most prized possession, the object of all her adoration, she ended up giving it away to a neighbor. She'd wanted so badly to make friends, to be liked, that she handed it to a brusque girl who'd asked to hold it. I'd heard the story before but now pictured the handoff, one arm lifted, the other lingering, fingers wrapped around the doll's elbow, not wanting to let go, to lose contact with what she loved. While Bubbie and Zaidy had been searching for their parents, siblings, cousins—finding out one by one that they were dead— Mom was giving up her imagined friend, the warm fabric baby she rocked to sleep, who kept her company day and night. *Good-bye*, I pictured her saying, wide-eyed, holding back tears as her fingers slowly unfurled, the rough girl pulling, pulling, as if pulling Mom's soft skin right off her body, until the transaction was complete. *Do widzenia*. Mom watched as the Polish girl hugged her doll, *her* doll, knowing at that instant she'd never touch it again. She'd made someone else happy, but she herself had been turned inside out. The beginning of her black hole.

IN THE MORNING we met our local guide, Lukasz, an intellectual with a man bag. He hopped in our minivan and Jon drove us all east. That's when we saw the road sign: CHELM. Eli, Nadia, and I burst into applause. The legendary city of Jewish humor folklore— the town of fools—featured in half our high school literature. We couldn't believe it actually existed as a real place, with a train station and drugstores. "What's Chelm?" Jon asked. He didn't even know!

The town's synagogue was now a bar; a swastika was spray-painted on one wall. But the Jewish cemetery displayed a sign indicating that an organization of people who'd "come out" as Jews were dedicated to preserving it. I was totally confused. Did Poland like Jews or hate Jews? I stared at Jon as he fiddled with the GPS and wondered if I was marrying someone who didn't understand where I came from or how much had been taken.

Freezing, we got into the car. Lukasz told us that his grandfather was from Kraśnik, the same town mine had come from. Lukasz was thirty-four, an academic. He'd grown up across the street from Majdanek death camp, and became obsessed with the Holocaust. Was it *he* and I who were *beshert*, soul mates?

I stared into the back of his calm head, while out of the corner of my eye I watched my fiancé violently meander across lanes, insensitive to the situation, to the passengers, to everything. He didn't get it, didn't get me. Who the hell was I marrying?

THAT EVENING, WE drove to Puławy. On the small roads in the Lublin–Warsaw corridor, we passed tall thin trees, forests just as I imagined them from stories about Partisans. In town, we saw the small wooden houses that were implanted in my mind from every Sholem Aleichem folktale. "Drive around this block again!" I commanded Jon, desperate to see every abode, trying hard to imagine which one might have belonged to my bubbie and her tales. Her family had made paper bags. They'd been robbed, once. Something about a roof? The details didn't add up to a story.

After our third trip around the residential streets, Jon was annoyed: "Enough already. Where to?"

"The Vistula!" I ordered, angry at him for not knowing. Though it was below zero, I wanted to walk the paths near the river, Bubbie's river. The banks of the Vistula were where I was sure I would finally feel the sense of connection that I so craved.

Jon parked in the lot, near the riverside park. No one else wanted to get out of the warm car. I was relieved. I threw open the door and ran, right for the paths I wanted to recognize from Bubbie's photo. It was arctic, and I wrapped my zipless coat around me, hugging myself as I leapt through the trees, trying to get close to the water, which I could now make out was down a slope, in a ravine. I wasn't sure how I'd get to the shore, but with the water in view, I continued to speed along, feeling my feet step in spots that her shoes might have touched, repeating to myself: this is the place. Her stories. Her soul. My fingers lost feeling. My nose was running. I came to a dead end and became teary. Not because I felt so much, but because I didn't. Here I was, in Bubbie's footsteps, and it felt like nothing. Like a random park, in a random town, on a road trip in Eastern Europe. I felt thoroughly frozen.

I stopped and heard a rustle. I turned around.

It was Jon, silent, standing a few feet behind me. His arm was outstretched. He was holding out my bright orange wool hat, which appeared like a flash of life against the darkening Polish sky.

I looked at him and saw not the man I'd been angry at, but my chauffeur, documentarian, protector. He did not share my history, did not understand every element of my past, but accepted it and me, and helped me find my own meaning, offering warmth when my journey got cold. He was not affected by the things I was, or scared by the same threats, but that was a *good* thing. His coolness, optimism, and detachment were traits I could learn from, and enabled him to be a pillar for my experience and vulnerability. Our difference was our strength. I ran to him, realizing I hadn't come to Poland now of all times because I had cold feet. I came because he was the support I needed in order to make the trip.

I stood by Jon as my bubbie had stood by her fancy suitor. Poland was not my missing home, and I was not Poland's missing piece. I was not my heritage of trauma and terror. Poland and I had both been seeking something intangible. But Jon was real. He was my home, which I now understood was not about a certain place, present or past, but between us. It was the ability to be yourself around those you loved.

I took Jon's hand. Only then did I sense my bubbie looking down on me. "You did *gut*, Judaleh," she was saying. "Now put on the hat, and go eat something."

SIX MONTHS LATER, I walked down the aisle of Bevis Marks Synagogue, built in 1701 near my old Whitechapel neighborhood. I felt kinship with the shul less for its orthodox Sephardic service than its incredible Queen Anne architecture, its chandeliers lit by real candles. My toes were stuffed into white heels like a Chinese virgin; my layered-silk beaded dress and calla lilies tied me all together. I'd spent that past half hour in the basement as Jon and Dad performed an eighteenth-century-style negotiation of my dowry and now Dad's arm was hitched around mine as I carefully advanced toward the altar, where Jon, in a pink kippah and matching vest that took about seven fittings to get right, waited with his parents—and Mom.

Eli had told me that she wasn't leaving the house at all anymore and I'd feared she wouldn't make it. At first, I was mortified, imagining the shame I'd feel at stepping out in front of two hundred people with my mother a "no show" for my own wedding, and I offered to do anything to help her get here. But the more probable her potential absence was, the more I realized that her not-being-there would in some ways be a relief, serving as a coming-out: my mother is not well. She can't be here. *She could never totally be here for me,* I would have announced to the world. I'd still marry Jon.

At the last minute, though, she showed up, having put her important papers in a friend's locked basement. Only afterward did I hear from Eli how—while I was making final arrangements for my premium makeup artist and high-end videography—Mom, a mess of bags and keys, had accidentally locked everyone out of the house, forcing the fire department to chop down the front door less than two hours before their flight. But then, unaware, I was relieved, so happy to meet her at the boutique hotel in the flesh. She spent the weekend putting on a giddy face. At least she'd let my hairdresser do her up. *She's always wanted to be present,* I saw, as she desperately tried to paint her own nails at the last minute. *Even if she couldn't be in the way I needed.*

But now, as I, shaking, ascended the stairs to the altar, she reached for me and squeezed my hand. Unlike the rest of her, her fingers were slender, elegant, made for being poised on the ridges of a teacup, for long white gloves. Fine, dexterous, in control. It was as if they told a truth about her, referred to a self that she could have been, should have been, had she not been plagued by her history or genetic materials, had nothing taken hold of her synapses, tainting her thoughts with turmoil. Tears rolled down the creases of her eyes along her puffy wide cheeks, her face beaming brighter than the candelabras. "I love you," she whispered as I took my place next to Jon, alongside all our parents—each one born on a different continent, though most of our grandparents were likely from a five-mile radius. Here we were, together again under our chuppah, a structure that was exposed on all sides, symbolizing, I hoped, our future home—airy, open, welcoming, with nothing to hide.

Later, at the reception in the grand, gilded Victorian hall nearby, I could just picture Bubbie looking down at me, at my couture dress, upscale flowers, the haute hors d'oeuvres and designer cocktails. *Judaleh,* she would have said. *You call this food?*

· SEVENTEEN ·

VOYAGEUR, ENCORE
New York City, 2010

"Are you driving or are you reading?" I barked at the cabdriver who'd taken out his newspaper at a red light one too many times. He grumbled and folded it back up. I buried a smug smile. It wasn't so much that we were finally moving along Fifth Avenue, but that in that one instant, in that utterance that crept out of my mouth unedited, I knew I had reacculturated. I was back in New York.

A few months after our wedding, Jon and I had actually made the move that we'd discussed for ages. We arrived in NYC, a city away from both our parental homes, with nothing but four suitcases. Empty canvases, blank slates, minimal and organized. I'd felt lightened, elated (easily pretending our massive storage piles back in London didn't exist). At first, however, the non-British ease and comfort that I'd been dreaming of for so long didn't manifest. We viewed twenty-seven apartments in three days, and when we finally called the broker to tell her which one we wanted, she laughed and said it was long gone. The delis overflowed with options—What kind of salmon? Which piece? What toppings? Which plate?—and I hadn't been ready to know what I wanted and loudly—loudly—

call it out. I'd become used to British dawdling, to awkward hem-
ming and hawing, to quieter volumes, to fewer stores with fewer
products and fewer daily decisions, from condiments to careers. But
in New York, possibility, individuality and responsibility were in
every breath and sandwich.

With time, though, Jon and I worked it out. People always ordered the same thing, we deduced. We turned up our volumes, and
shared opinions and exasperations with fellow pedestrians. We selected our apartment—a temporary one while looking to buy—after
having been inside it for less than one minute. (The New York Minute?) Layers of self-consciousness slid off me like old scales.

The cab pulled up outside our building and I walked through the
large, high-ceilinged beige lobby, waving hello to the doorman, having friendlier interaction than in an entire day in London. I took the
elevator up to the eighteenth floor—eighteen for luck, I'd noted—a
level that was still human-ish: I could see people on the street, even
if I was closer to the people in the next building over. Life in the sky.

Our apartment was small and almost entirely empty; we'd
bought one sofa, two desks, three chairs, a bed. Who needed night
tables?! Every item purchased—from soap dish to garbage can—was
a project, each object precious, agreed upon by both of us. A small
bookshelf held a few tomes. Aside from that, the walls were windows, and whether from my desk or bed I could see all the way to
Central Park, even across the Hudson River. I loved that there was
nothing in the corners, nothing hanging on to me.

Tonight, a few writers I'd already befriended—fast friends,
American style—were coming over to share work. I'd left both academia and comedy behind, secure in my home with Jon, no longer
needing to feel at home in school or on the stage. At first, I'd been
embarrassed when people walked in—our apartment seemed too
slick, out of character for me. I was uncomfortable in my comfort. I
should have been living in a rickety building, in an artsy neighborhood. But Jon, a real foreigner, had wanted to live centrally in order
to feel centered in his new country. Of course, I understood that. "If

it wasn't for you, I'd live in Brooklyn or Queens," I'd said to him when we were looking.

"But it is for me," he'd answered. "I helped bring you home."

He was right. We were an us, and, for now at least, I'd rather live near midtown than in England. I felt refreshed here and wondered if it was the move, or if cities really did speak differently to different people. Was it that I had more friends in New York who knew me from my youth, more cultural similarities, more opportunities for the kinds of work I wanted to do, more affordable food? Or was it that the energy of the place, its fabric and geography, its scents and sensual landscapes, appealed more to my corporeal being? I'd take tall buildings and clean vistas over London's winding roads and damp corners. Cold sun over warm rain, brashness over reserve, the widespread availability of smoked fish spreads over dinner party anti-Semitism.

And so, for all of that, I lived where Jon wanted, recalling that my identity was less rooted in an address, more in my family.

Just then, Jon walked in, tailored in his suit. Even his career had improved here, thanks to being closer to the powerbase, as he put it. "Hi, powerbase," I teased as he came over. He kissed me and we paused life for a moment to hold hands and look out at the pink sunset that crescendoed across New Jersey. Finally, I was starting to feel at home.

THE NEXT MORNING, Dad called. It was only the fourth time he'd called me since I'd left home in 1996. "She's really planning it," he said. "The details. She's asking about the cemetery. She's making me promise I'll bury her inside, in the plot we bought, and not outside, with the suicides." He didn't make jokes. He didn't laugh.

There was no time to book airline tickets, no time to plan, to think.

I ran to the bus.

· EIGHTEEN ·

32 WEEKS: FROM GIGGLE TO TEARS
New York City, 2011

"Ready?" Jon asked.

"No," I said, but opened the door anyway. It was time to enter a new discomfort zone: shopping for the anticipated roommate.

My father had repeatedly told me not to buy anything. It was a Jewish superstition that if you even mentioned the fetus, much less buy it a wardrobe, the pregnancy would terminate immediately. "We didn't have a crib until you were ten—years!" he would joke, though I always wanted to point out that perhaps that was the beginning of my constantly feeling like an uninvited guest to my life. I hadn't put off this shopping spree because of superstition, however. It wasn't the loss of my baby that I feared, just the loss of my home office. But I knew Jon was right: it was time to start.

Though there was a massive baby store a block away from our apartment, I insisted we browse at Giggle, the exclusive store all the way downtown where I knew we'd never end up really shopping. I hadn't even done "the research" yet. This was just a reconnaissance mission.

"Can I help you?" A heavily made-up middle-aged woman approached me before I even got across the threshold. I looked up, but my gaze pranced right past her. The store was bedecked floor to ceiling with infant snowsuits, monkey-shaped first-aid kits, heated bubble baths, and sedan-sized fluorescent strollers equipped with GPS systems and headlights. "You look like you could use some help," her lipstick said.

"I could," I barely eked out. "I need to sit down."

"Of course," she said, obviously thinking this was due to the fact that I was one hundred and forty percent my normal body weight, and not All This Stuff.

Jon escorted me to a collection of velvety chairs. "Gliders," she said. "For breast-feeding." You need massive armchairs with foldable footrests just for nursing?

"We need to make a registry," Jon said. "I assume we need an appointment?"

"Why don't you just do it now?" The woman smiled. "I'll help."

"But we don't know anything," I whispered from my seated position. "I haven't done any research yet. I'm only seven months pregnant."

"Seven months pregnant!" she exclaimed. "You need to order your crib, like, yesterday! In fact, like four weeks ago."

"But we're Jewish," I squeaked. "There are superstitions. What if we buy it all and the baby, well"—there was no other way to say it—"what if the baby dies?"

Who talks about their baby dying? I chastised myself. I should be concerned about buying things to keep her alive, to satisfy her needs, to make her safe.

"We can hold off delivery until your delivery! We have a storeroom for just that purpose," she said cheerily. "Many of our customers are Jewish."

They had a special room for Jewish neuroses? God, I love-hated New York.

"Let's begin with furniture," she said. "Do you want the organic changing table?"

"Should I?"

"It's what people are getting."

"Screw them," Jon said. "That's ridiculous." My eyes bulged.

"You look uncomfortable," lady lips said to me. "Can I offer you one of our new quilted French pillows? It has three green certifications and won two eco awards."

"No, thanks."

"A baby book might make you smile; or a digital frame with LCD night-light—"

"I'm fine," I said, my hands now hovering near my throat. I started to gag.

"Oh, are you sick? Have you tried our vitamin-infused organic candy selection? We also have a whole new collection of unscented mom and baby creams!"

Now I *was* nauseous. "You take over," I pleaded with Jon. "I need a minute."

I was so grateful that Jon—in all his bald, manly glory—adored shopping and was the great housewife that I wasn't. I watched the saleslady show him cribs, bumpers, carriers, tubs, and then a series of towels with tiny elephant-shaped hoods. Where would I put all this? I imagined the hoard in my apartment, stacked on sofas and counters, creating a barricade that tumbled on top of me, suffocating me, anschlussing the space I'd so carefully carved out for myself, a space ringing with shrill screams, the wild rants of my red-faced daughter. Teething giraffes. Clown mobiles. *Stacks and stacks of molded tuna cans. Stale Danish. Fuck!*

Suddenly I heard with clarity: these were not infant cries, but the screams of my mother. Hungry curses. Unsatisfied pleas. I imagined myself sinking under the whole stash as in quicksand, writhing between my two cords, past and present, like a charm dangling off an endless umbilical bracelet. I couldn't breathe. Would my baby be a rebirth of my mother: needy and unhinged? Is parenting a child the same as parenting a parent?

I scanned the room for some empty space to calm me down, and settled my eye on the firm geometric lines of the windowsill. I focused on my skin, its surface and underside, envisioning stacks of soft organelles, reminding myself that outlines had layers, that I could breathe within its thickness.

"Judy," Jon called. "Do you want the video monitor with wireless access or the one shaped like a sheep?"

I turned to look at him across the mass of bright pinks and orange, smiling moms in Lululemon, sheets with adorable Japanese cartoon characters, and baskets full of fair trade baby rattles. Everything, everyone seemed so happy.

"Breast-shaped bottles with saliva-mixing technology? What about this halogen sunlight lamp for the corner of the office? I mean, nursery?" he added.

Office to nursery. No more clean. No more boundaries. No more me.

How was I supposed to nurture, to protect a constantly crying baby, and what if I couldn't satisfy her needs? For thirty-four years I'd tried to learn how to take care of myself, and just barely made it. How—in the next seven weeks—could I figure out how to save a child?

"I don't know." In the middle of Giggle, I was bawling.

WHITE WALLS
Montreal, 2010

"I can't believe you're doing this to me!" In the emergency psychiatric wing, Mom is screaming.

I am running madly, trying to find orderlies to help me keep her in the hallway where they asked us to wait. Mom has realized what's happening and she's trying to escape. Thank God she brought four massive bags filled with files that weigh her down. This is what I've been waiting for, I remind myself, and yet, every part of me winces. I don't want to be here, and certainly not with her.

After the bus ride, I spent the previous night on a stain-drenched kitchen chair while she ranted wildly, threatened suicide, and I withdrew, nervously making plans. Each step needed to work. We had to convince the judge, ensure that the police transported her, then persuade the doctor to admit her, even just for twenty-four hours. That, according to the social workers, would be a great victory. That morning, in the beige *People's Court*–ish courtroom, we won. The judge shook his head in pity. Afterward, Eli, Dad, and I—finally, on the same team—marched through the sunny morning, the cut-glass rays, to the local police station. We took a number. *Just here to incarcerate our mother,* Eli and I repeated over the shrill radio alerts about handcuffs. I wore black pants and a purple sweater to show I was reasonable, all business. *Will I have to watch while they tie her down?* I had wondered. *Will I have to watch when the ambulance guys first see the house—the alarms, the piles, the filth?* Even after all these years, even amid all this drama, I was embarrassed.

But in the end, we didn't have to call 911. Eli's gentle voice was magically soothing, turning her wild pupils soft. The two of us managed to convince her to come with us to the emergency psychiatry ward. (Dad hid in the basement.) She hadn't left her house in years, and yet, she came, dragging her duffel bags like guard dogs. *Somewhere inside her, she wants help*, I try to convince myself. *That's why she agreed to come.*

"You captured me," she yells.

I did. *Just because you're paranoid doesn't mean they're not out to get you.* Her delusions had become reality. I was now the criminal, the SS trooper, she'd always feared.

Luckily I am asked to move to another room. Eli goes to make calls and I walk, my legs helping to soothe me, as always. I find myself wandering through the basement of the Jewish General Hospital where I was delivered. (*Being born was difficult,* I used to joke in my stand-up act. *Not only did I go from the warm comfortable womb to the cold dangerous world, but I was naked, wet, and the very same day, I found out I'd have to move in with my parents.*) I'd traveled the world, through Egypt, Israel, the DMZ in Korea, and yet here I am again. A boomerang to my birth. Death and birth are all splashed together in these white walls.

I pass the room where my brother had his bris, thinking of the parts of ourselves we lose before we even know we're losing them. The hospital's basement is like a warren, a web of unexpected corridors. They must disorient us on purpose, I decide, hoping in our confusion we'll consent to undergo things we wouldn't do even in our own bathrooms.

They let me see her in a triage room.

"Get the fuck out!" she yells before I even cross the threshold. "Do you know what you've done? I will die here and it's your fault. You should know that you have ended my life."

"I'm just trying to help you," I say quietly, firmly, to convince myself despite the hard bed and metallic instruments. What *am* I doing? Am I giving up on her? Have all these years of pleading for someone to help me been a mistake? Maybe Dad was right all along. Perhaps I should not commit so fiercely to committing.

"Get the fuck out of here."

It's her disease speaking, I remind myself. It's her disease that can't stand me.

But I get out.

A nurse calls me over: "So." She's chewing gum. "Like, she told us she's homeless." Homeless? "And, like, that she has no family."

"She has homes. Several." I don't even begin to get into the fact that she hoards houses, that her whole disease plays out in the home, as she fills and barricades it, locks herself in.

"Oh, also, in her bags we found dozens of keys. And thousands of dollars."

I hope this can help convince them to keep her in. "You must listen to my version of the story," I say. "She's extremely clever, but not seeing reality."

"Super interesting," the nurse says, lowering her tone, like this is gossip. "Like, make sure to tell the doctors."

We are interrupted by an orderly. "She's resistant. We have to restrain her. We'll use ties."

Ties. *My mother.* My own limbs go numb. There is life in her, even if it's buried deep. My mother, who told all the good stories. At Great-aunt Gittel's house, she'd leave the adult table and sit on the floor with us in the den, my second cousins all entranced by her improvised worlds where good reigned over evil, while I sat next to her, my elbow on her knee. These concrete moments are so far away, covered over, photos at the base of a collage, occluded by more recent images. When was the last time I saw my mother's knee?

Dad finally joins us, and Eli sits with him in the relatives' room. The vending machine offers Kit Kats. They remind me of Bubbie, and suddenly it dawns on me that this is the very same emergency room where Mom used to take Bubbie to be treated for the same *mishegas*, as Dad called it. But my mother cannot see the parallel.

What about me? How can I know that *I'm* not deluded too, that my own reality holds weight? A part of me is constantly on edge, waiting for these damaged genes to express themselves in my own cells, metastasizing through my consciousness. Not that I would even realize.

I unwrap the top of my Kit Kat and crack the lines, parallel, neat and crisp. I take a bite, ready for a moment of bliss, but instead the taste shocks me: it is bitter. I look at the package and am enraged. Who the hell wants a *dark chocolate* Kit Kat? If you want dark, buy Valrhona, Jacques Torres, Godiva, even, but Kit Kat? The bitterness burns my insides, and I feel vacant, reminding me that at my center I am a hollow core.

For a second, that image calms me.

Which is good, because the psychiatrist calls us in. We shuffle into her tiny office. I motion for Dad and Eli to sit on the metal chairs. I stand, face her. It's my turn to talk, to present the case of my lifetime, the real performance that I've been rehearsing for all these years. It suddenly dawns on me that I've never told anyone except Jon the whole story. No other friend, no lover. Even the social workers have gotten only half versions. I have honored my mom's wishes, kept her secrets. Perhaps it's because I'm afraid they will consider me crazy by association. I should have done more, and sooner. Now I must convey it all, convince this woman to keep my mom here. To save her.

But before I even open my mouth, the doctor speaks: "Paranoid delusions. Severe depression. Acute intelligence, but no emotional insight. A bad case. I do not know how you've managed." She looks up at me now from her file, speaks gently. "I do not know how you've managed for all these years."

There! There it is! The sentence I've been waiting for for a third of a century. Warm tears marathon down my cheeks, hot, soft, so heavy I could hear each drop.

We are in the open, skeletons out of the closet, along with keys and cash. The truth is out there, scientific.

Someone else will take care of Mom.

"Go home," the doctor orders me. "We are treating your mother now. I'm going to keep her here for eight weeks. Go home."

Eight weeks!

I leave the hospital, thinking of Jon's hands, my white apartment, my calm, clean adult life, my gridded streets.

I leave, thinking: For the first time, I am free.

OVER THE NEXT few weeks I wafted around, sated with the notion that I'd realized a lifelong dream. I could hardly believe it: someone was taking care of Mom.

I'd stayed in Montreal for a few days after the emergency episode, keeping Dad company and visiting Mom twice, averting my eyes from the dirty conditions of the locked psychiatric ward—the gray marks on the walls, the unkempt beds, the toilets strewn with wet paper. My mother didn't even notice. She wanted me to bring her books, pencils, sweaters, socks. *Now.* Then she threw me out.

Facing her anger, her shrill demands, my own cascading guilt, I couldn't take it anymore. I didn't have to. I'd given her care over to a specialized authority who knew so much more than me. I breathed, and walked away.

Relieved that Mom was being watched, excited for the potential results of her therapies, even letting myself fantasize, in tiny glimpses, the happy version of her that might emerge, I began work on my own home. Jon and I had recently achieved another lifelong dream and purchased our first apartment—a completely open loft space with

large windows. I now went about decorating as if under a spell, enthralled by the prospect of designing a permanent place—all white.
Tiles, carpets, walls, blinds, linens—even sofas. I ripped out intri-
cately ruffled moldings and put in open shelving, graphic white built-
ins. It was my childhood dream suburban mini-mansion, but better
because it was a loft smack in the middle of New York. I wanted to
buy the smallest number of furniture pieces possible (An ottoman?
Really?) and keep our shelves half-empty. Or completely empty!
"Militant minimalism," I joked. Clean lines, clean boundaries.

Jon, however, picked out red and orange tiles for the kitchen.

I freaked out when I opened the box. "We. Said. Only. White."

"Don't have a backlash with your backsplash," he said. "Calm
down."

I realized I was going too far, to the opposite extreme of my childhood home, being selfish about our shared sphere. "We can add some
hue," I reluctantly conceded.

The backsplash stayed white, but we got bright orange British-
designed light fixtures.

Jon and I developed a domestic system of stuff. We only purchased major items that we *both* loved, creating an aesthetic from the
overlaps in our tastes. I did not go through or criticize his drawers
but placed any floor-standing junk into his "man cave" closet, for
which he called me "the hoarding police." Introducing new things
into our household meant old ones were jettisoned, including plastic
bags. The curtains on our large living room windows always remained undrawn—we had nothing to hide.

OR DID I?

Two weeks after the commitment, Eli called. "She's out."

I sat on my new windowsill and stared at the daytime traffic that
built up with each red light and then let go. Muffled swooshes of
movement. I tried to breathe along.

From confinement, Mom had asked for a copy of the Quebec
Civil Code, read it, and learned that you can contest being held
against your will. She went to the hospital's legal department, offi-

cially requested a trial knowing it was her right, was taken by taxi to the court, fought her case, and won.

"Dad was there. He says it was a beautiful defense," Eli said. "She charmed the wigs off them."

"She turned off the crazy for them," I said, shaking my head. All my efforts—poof—vanished.

My eyes welled. I stomped my foot. I felt so helpless, fighting this lost cause. Somewhere in Mom, she must have known better, known she needed help; she just refused to get it. But she was sick, I reminded myself. She was traumatized.

Could the ill mind ever be culpable? What about when it affected us all?

Was I allowed to be angry or not?

"So she's back home now," I said, to believe it. "How's Dad?"

"Fine." Eli sighed. "Actually, I think he supported her release."

"What?" I actually pulled my hair from its roots. Why was he foiling our plan?

"He said she was driving him crazy, calling him at all hours from the ward."

Then again, what could I do? I didn't live there, he did. He'd never run away. He had chosen to keep caring for her. My freedom was, to a large degree, at his expense. I'd always felt like the mother of my family, but really, I'd shirked the daily duties and passed them to him. My father, I surmised, preferred not to be alone. He liked being needed. He missed her—insanity and all. I always felt he saw her as the twenty-four-year-old she was when they first met, beautiful and odd, filled with peccadilloes, as he put it, but not yet so twisted.

"Did they give her antipsychotic medication? Is she taking it?"

"They did. Who knows?"

Who knows? swirled through my mind. My whole life I'd assumed this was the solution. The system. Medical help. The hospital. The court. I'd assumed that at some point, someone would step in and take care of it, take care of us. But there was no grand caretaker.

No answer. Not even a clear equation.

My mother was big, too big, bigger than me, uncontainable. How could I fight a force that was so smart, so passionate, so determined, so desperately against helping itself?

I could never save my mother.

"What do we do?" I asked, just to say something. I had the horrible thought that if this was cancer, I'd be telling everyone. I'd get sympathy. And Mom would want help, maybe even appreciate it.

Maybe I just had to let her be, in her house, with her files, just as she wanted. Maybe that was the best way to love her. *I do not know how to love her,* I realized, wondering if it was this confusion that had guided my whole life. Did I see her as a person? An illness? A victim or a perpetrator? I did not know what I owed her.

I hung up and stayed on the white windowsill, my body stretching out as if becoming part of the wall itself. Then I called Melissa. "Remember when I canceled lunch and headed to Montreal? It's time I finally told you what's really going on."

LATER THAT SAME week, I found myself sitting across from my gynecologist in a cramped office space, his various diplomas hung like a Victorian gallery, stacked on top of one another along the entire wall. "You're thirty-three," he began. "Your blood work is, well, off."

"Oh," I stammered, surprised. I'd recently been having unusual cycles, and with a family history of early-onset menopause, I'd decided to have my hormone levels checked. But I hadn't actually anticipated a problem.

"It's possible that long-term use of the pill is causing some of this," he said. "But considering your genetics, and your history of abdominal surgeries, which generally result in a fifty percent infertility rate, I really would look into this now."

Infertility. It was a word I'd heard, of course, but never imagined in relation to myself. Then again, neither was the word "fertility." Children? Lord. I'd barely dealt with my parents. I still wanted time for me. I still wanted to *be* a child. Could I stand to get lost in another person's emotional landscape yet again? The idea of not having kids seemed sad, but in an abstract way.

On the other hand, I did not like the idea that my hormones were out of whack, which I knew could cause other medical problems, and the idea of menopause troubled me with images of facial hair and sweaty temper tantrums.

"Realistically, for someone with your history, I estimate it will take two years to become pregnant."

No problem; I needed two years just to think about that word. This was good news to me. There was medical intervention. There was time to get pregnant. That is, if I even wanted to.

"I recommend you go off the pill now," Doc continued. "If you don't get your period within four weeks, go straight to the fertility clinic."

I sighed. Another medical project.

That night I told Jon the news. "Two years?" He held back from saying anything more. He was about to turn forty, and I knew he didn't want to pressure me. But "Dad or Grandad?" was the game he'd been playing lately as we walked through town and saw a man with a stroller. We both knew he'd be a terrific father, dedicated, involved, loving.

"Don't worry," I said. "I'll go off the pill and we'll start the process." But I was relieved, really, by my time buffer.

I went off the pill. I didn't get my period. I called the fertility clinic. I made an appointment. They told me to repeat my blood work. And so, one morning, I went to see my enthusiastic Israeli GP.

THE TWO PARALLEL LINES.

· NINETEEN ·

38 WEEKS: SURVIVAL OF THE WITTIEST
New York City, 2011

"I need to ask you a favor," Mom said faintly over the phone. "Please."

I sighed. "What is it?" I sat down on my white sofa, wondering for how long it would remain crisp, colorless. And for how long I'd fit on it. I was nine months pregnant, and so many organs sat on my sciatic nerve that for three weeks I'd barely been able to walk without shards of pain running down my leg. The third trimester had been a downer, the hormones less buzzy, the appearance less glowish, the sense of passing time, limited possibilities, and loss of common ground with childless friends heightened. I'd had enough of people accidentally telling me stories of how they went into labor during rush hour, enough internal kicking (or what I was now calling domestic abuse), enough browsing stores that sold only cashmere onesies, enough answering why I wasn't having a baby shower (baby shower? I'm too scared to even take a regular shower), enough of the insomnia, sciatica, and panicka. I was eyeing knives in the desire to self-C-section. Despite my cascade of anxieties, even I was bloody ready for this thing to come out.

"I need Dad and Eli to stay here. At least one of them."

I locked my lips. Hard.

All three of them were supposed to come to New York two days before my elaborately scheduled C-section (to take place on a Tuesday at four p.m.—the only time of the entire week when both colorectal and obstetric surgeons were available) and to stay for a couple more. Mom, however, had called me the week earlier, profusely apologetic, certainly upset, saying that she just didn't see how she'd be able to leave the house. I wasn't surprised, but still, disappointed. Considering that she was more excited about this than about, well, anything, part of me had expected her to rally, as she did for my wedding, sliding in at the last minute like a ballplayer capturing home plate. My immediate ping of anger—it was so unfair not to have a mother when I *had* a mother—dissipated quickly into guilt that I wasn't birthing closer to Montreal for her sake, and finally to calm reason. Our umbilical cord was the telephone line, and that's how she would experience this event too. Besides, I told myself, what I wanted at my side was the image of her—smiling, nurturing—not the anxious reality, making me scared and late.

But at least Dad and Eli were still supposed to come.

"I can't be alone in this house. I know you want them to support Jon, but really, Judy, I need more support than he does."

I removed the phone from my ear, leaving it hanging limply in the air a few inches from my brain. Since when was this about *Jon?* Sure, we both needed them to help out while I'd be in the hospital, which I knew would be at least five days. But mostly, I just wanted them to be here. For me. Not for Jon.

I put the phone back to my head. "Please, Judy," she was begging. I closed my eyes, my lids heavy like the rest of me. "Please." Of course, she was right. She did need help, she needed support, more than Jon, more than me, even if I was about to have major surgery to give birth.

"OK," I said quietly, "I'll ask them."

I never asked them.

"Dad." I shook him awake. "My water broke. I'm going to the hospital."

"What?" he mumbled. Then he opened his eyes wide. "OK, go!"

He and Eli had arrived the evening before, and finally, everything had been going according to plan. I'd worried for weeks that I'd go into labor early, before the highly planned surgery; while other people ate spicy foods to get things going, I clutched and prayed. But at last the day-before arrived and I was still intact and undilated, so I finally relaxed. Me and my three guys, my labor team (who were engaged in intense conversation about the politics of insurance companies while I debated whether or not to pack the nursing pillow) went out for artisanal pizza and a walk. I wasn't allowed to eat or drink after midnight, and complained about this as I downed water and slurped up delicious cheesecake. It was impossible to believe that the next time I ate, I would be a *mother. Don't think, Judy. Don't. Think.* It was all happening exactly right, or at least, as right as I could get it. I licked the final bite from my fork.

Then, bed.

Then, three a.m. A fierce urge to push. I heard a snap.

I'd been worried that I wouldn't notice if my water broke, but this rupture was torrential. I woke Jon ("you won't fucking believe this"), then Dad, and then began frantically looking for what I needed to take to the hospital as I held a bath mat between my legs. "Bring more towels!" I shouted as we ran out to the elevator, the street. An empty cab was right there. "I can't believe I'm going into labor twelve hours before the scheduled time."

"At least there's no traffic at three a.m.," Jon said as I stuffed another two towels under me. Fucking optimist.

At the hospital, the nurses took their time. It was a slow night, and my water had only just broken. But sitting at check-in, the first wave of a contraction came on. Ha—I'd also been worried that I wouldn't know what a contraction was.

They put me in triage, and I met the doctor on call. None of the specialist surgeons were in, nor the anesthesiologist that had been recommended. The ward was calm, my dilation was minimal, so no one rushed, and they planned to do the C-section around seven a.m. "At least she's ready to come out," Jon and I reassured ourselves.

Nurses and doctors came and went, Jon cracked jokes, I signed a slew of forms and they eventually brought Jon his surgical smock. I read aloud from a humor book about baby panic and Jon did a photo shoot of us feigning terror in blue hairnets. My contractions came every fifteen minutes or so. "Shit, I didn't take the class for this!" I semijoked, but really, they were short and relatively bearable; I closed my eyes and squeezed Jon's fists until they passed. Then I swore a little.

Until a tidal wave of nausea, an unusual body-wide vibration, hit me.

It felt like my whole insides had turned to Jell-O, like I was quickly losing clarity, control. Like something was wrong. "Jon, I don't feel good."

"It'll pass," he said, now used to our improvised Lamaze.

"No, really," I said, my eyes closed. "Get a doctor."

I felt dizzy and woozy and turned to face the wall, my arms tingling. Echoing in the distance, I heard him Britishly, politely, tell a nurse that I wasn't feeling well and asking if they wouldn't mind coming in for a second to check on me.

The nurse entered nonchalantly and I tried to explain how I felt. But my mouth was like rubber, my lips like gummy bands. She looked at the readout from the monitor, she banged the machine, she looked again. The next thing I knew she pushed a blue button on the wall and within split seconds I was living a scene from *Grey's Anatomy*: dozens of doctors pounced on top of me, Jon was being thrown out of the room, I was being pricked, prodded, whisked down a hall. What's going on? What's going on? I kept screaming, or at least, trying to scream, as words like shots were flying around me. *Dropping heartbeat, falling heartbeat.* But no one, no one, was talking to me. Please, what's going on? *Low heartbeat. No heartbeat.*

Oh my God. I was losing her.

I was losing my baby. It hit me like a ton of hoarded videos: *I want this baby.* More than anything. I. Want. My. Baby. What was with all my stupid selfish self-absorbed anxiety, my whining ambivalence? Was I crazy? Who would I be without her? I accepted losing control of my body, my sanctified office, my brain synapses, but not this. How would I ever survive if I lost my daughter? My daughter.

Then a mask was being lowered on my face, *how much does she weigh?* the doctor screamed, and no one knew, and I called out, *one fifty*, or at least I tried, and then

Black.

"JUDALEH," BUBBIE SAYS, leaning over me into her cottage cheese, which shmears along the side of her forearm. She's gotten older, more tired, her back fully humped into a parabola of experience, but she seems wiser too, her words coming out more slowly, her wrinkles deepening with every lip movement, making me wonder how far down the cracks ran. Skin is thick, I'd recently learned in sixth grade through diagrams that looked like cartoon sandwiches. Not simply a surface or a contour, but a dimensional volume, filled with organelles, activities, processes. Layers within itself. Entire worlds, complex routines. What I'd thought was transparent and flimsy had a whole inner life. "I'll tell you when I knew."

Her eyes light up, her cheekbones gather at their tops, little round earths that protect her visage on each end. "Me, I have long legs, skinny. Not like your other grandmother. Feh." She cackles. "Me, I not look Jewish so they put me in the ration lines. When the Germans come, *I*, Zelda, wait for bread with the Polacks. And Judaleh, that's when the Nazis come over."

I've never heard this story before. My heart skips like a scratched record. Its beats are louder than her blaring TV, *A Different World*, Dwayne Wayne, louder than Bill Cosby's Thursday night gyrations.

"They ask where the Jews are hiding. And you know what I hear?"

"What, Bubbie? Did they tell on you? Did they find your sisters?"

"I hear the Poles tell them. She's in a basement; she's in an attic; he's at Piotrek's apartment." She pauses. "That, Judaleh," she says, leaning over as if she's about to fall into her piles of bargain textiles, "is when I knew I had to leave. To run. Nothing was safe. Even my beloved Warsaw was not safe."

The TV booms. *Energizer Bunnies. Kool-Aid. Cool Whip. The Colgate Pump.*

"Safety is a *pushkeh* in you," she tells me, staring me straight in the eyes, transmitting to me that very *pushkeh*, that pouch—not of money, but of confidence. She puts her hand on her heart. *Don't fool yourself. Acknowledge the truth and you'll survive. Home is not a building, a city, a relationship, a story.* She puts her hand on my heart. "My only safety was in me."

4TH TRIMESTER:

The Nursery

————

· TWENTY ·

NO FORMULA FOR MOTHERHOOD
New York City, 2011

"Where is she?" I gasp. I want to say, "Is she alive?"

My baby is dead, I am sure. How will I tell people? How will I live?

The world is gray, the walls, the blankets. I smell astringent, bleached linen. Tubes attack my every side. I cannot move.

"The baby is OK," I hear a distant voice say. "K" echoes in the metallic room. She's OK!

"She is? Where is she?"

Then black.

"Judy, are you OK?" It's Jon.

"Is she OK?" Is this real? A dream? "Did she make it?"

He chuckles. "I explained this to you five minutes ago. She's fine. She's with the nurses. The doctor said that the anesthesia would cause you to forget."

"Go to her," I say. "She needs you more than I do."

Then black.

"Is she alive?"

"Yes." I don't know whose voice it is.

"What happened to her? What happened to me? Did I have a baby?"

"You're in recovery. They had to staple your stomach. The baby is fine. We're taking you to a room now."

"OK, a room now." Things start to make sense. The gray is turning yellow in parts. She's fine! I'm fine. Where is she? Where is she?

"Where is she?"

Jon is holding a wrapped blanket. Is that her? Her?! I am in my bed, in a hospital room. Needles prod every part of me. "Hold her," he says, handing her over.

I cannot move.

"Skin-to-skin contact," I say, try to say with thick lips, remembering the rules from my prenatal classes. Must do skin to skin. Or else. Attachment problems forever.

"Don't worry. I did that," Jon says. He moves a web of tubes, places her along my torso. I feel warm, I feel skin, this thing that was of me and not me, weighing on me again, but in a different place, a new way, a companion to the air, the light, others. My body is confused. My limbs feel foreign; the baby, still me.

"There was no brain damage?" I ask. "Are you sure?"

"We've been through this ten times."

Now I'm waking up. I have a clear view of the East River, the November sky pert and blue, the water dark and moving quickly. Jon is talking. Six pounds, eight ounces. Six eighteen a.m. So many eights, so many sixes. He didn't know if I'd make it.

"What happened?" I ask, now with the weight of my child—my child!—on my chest, touching me, being with me. Her skin, her breath, her life. "What happened?"

"The doctor took her out in one minute," Jon says, looking at us, his head cocked to the side, his arms reaching out to embrace us both.

"Makes sense," I reply. "That's about as long as it took to put her in."

"Touché," Jon says. "You're waking up."

I fall asleep.

. . .

I AWOKE WITH a start.

A pang across my stomach, streaking through my shoulders. I've been sliced open. "Holy shit, I need drugs."

Jon showed me my morphine button. I pressed until it wouldn't let me press anymore and then tried to sit up.

"I'll move you," Jon said, using a remote to slide my bed upright until I felt a searing pain and shouted for him to stop. Fortunately, from that position I could see my baby sleeping, resting in the rolling plastic bin that was her first bed. Her first home outside of me. *My baby.*

"Roll her closer to me." I stared at her perfect chubby face, the button nose I recognized from the ultrasounds. "She looks like her," I said. Was it my genetic prejudice or was she particularly beautiful? She had round rosy cheeks, a dusting of light blond hair. Fine features like a porcelain doll. Perfect and delicious like an apple you wanted to bite right into. She fluttered her eyes open: sky gray, mysterious, arresting. She was tall and thin, apparently. It was incomprehensible that this magnificent creature emerged from my stomach, that it had fit.

Jon lifted her and brought her to me once again, and this time I pulled her in tightly, marveling at her silence, her calm. Feeling her warmth emanate onto me, heating my neck, I began to sense how different she was. There was a boundary between us—her temperature was not mine, her demeanor not mine, several layers of thick skin lived between us. I watched her breathe, in and out, felt her heart beat on my chest, her systems faster than mine, clockwork, perfect. I laid out her tiny toes on my pinkie, each one a marvel, lovely and so defined, her minuscule toenails crowned with slender moons of white. She smelled of sugar powder. I breathed her in. An impeccable white page.

"Hey, hey." I suddenly heard the familiar sound of Dad's jangling keys as he stepped into the room, Eli close behind. They took turns holding the newest member of their family. They too were implicated—her birth changed their identities, changed us all. Dad, amazed at how she opened her eyes and looked around, at how eerily alert she was ("I can't believe this is a newborn"), had joy crinkled into the sides of his face. Eli held her out flatly, carefully, with two hands, as if she was a fragile glass tray. "Dear Uncle Eli," I said, recalling a childhood game of ours where I would write him pretend letters from my future children. *Dear Uncle Eli, Mom is crazy, come save me, Mom is nuts . . .* Now I had become Mom, for real.

I watched my baby look around, take in the room, her first sights, first smells, sounds, colors. The world. She was alert—like me. Was she already nervous? Waiting for an attack? Was anxiety inherited, or had I done something to her already?!

"She's incredibly observant," Dad said. Or maybe just that. Maybe she was perfectly fine.

"She looks like Jon," Dad added, but as my baby smiled, her first full one, my whole body chilled. It was a smile I'd recognize anywhere, the smile I'd sought for so many years.

"She looks exactly like Mom," I said, and Eli nodded fiercely in agreement.

She looked nothing like me and Dad, but everything like Mom's side. The genes were in me, dormant but just under the surface, waiting to be expressed. *What else had she inherited?*

A nurse came in. "Do you want to breast-feed now? It's time."

I knew it was—you were supposed to breast-feed within two hours of the birth. "Can I do it, with my emergency C-section and all these contraptions?"

"Of course," the nurse said.

"Everyone leave, please," I said, nervous, as the nurse took my baby and draped her across my chest. Suddenly, myriad theories about football holds and sandwich wraps, head support and neck massage, swirled through my mind but I couldn't recall which way was best. I did not want to make a mistake, harm her forever. *Calm down, Judy.* I didn't want to pass on *my* crazy genes either. How could I shield her from, well, from me? "Please," I said to the nurse, as I opened my gown to reveal my comically enormous breast, "stay here and help me."

But before I could get the words out, my daughter—my daughter—sidled up to me, shimmied her way straight to my nipple, and firmly, confidently latched on. I felt the snip of suction, and let out a gleeful yelp. "Is it working?" I asked, and the nurse nodded. We did it! I was feeding my baby, thanks to her. My tiny little girl was a person who would teach me a thing or two. Motherhood, I understood, was something we'd figure out together.

THE NEXT MORNING, when I was finally mobile, the nurse showed me the security alarm on my baby's leg and warned: "Take her with you *everywhere*."

So there I was, going to the bathroom with my child. No longer in my belly, but as her own entity, wheeled into the fluorescently lit room, watching me. Then she began to cry, little whimpers of discomfort. "Mommy is going to the bathroom," I explained, instinctively. "Then, I'll wash my hands."

I turned on the faucet, and she fell silent, opening her eyes wide. "That's water," I taught her, watching her experience what was for her a pleasant sound. She had her own sensations, feelings. It blew my mind. We were two separate entities now, which made our bonding all the more real, exciting.

I rinsed, she listened. Up to now, my worries had been so much about me, about how I feared being tied to yet another human being, a new identity, squashed, lost, suffocated, no longer in control of the mechanisms that had saved me, made me. But somehow, in all that, I'd forgotten about *her*. I'd been so anxious about what becoming a mother would do to me, but the real concern is what I would do to her. I had to be a *competent* mother. A good mother. I was responsible for another being's emotional development, her psychic welfare, her ability to form meaningful relationships over a lifetime. Not to mention, her basic breaths. My own mother had had so much power over me, catalyzing my life direction, and now I had that degree of influence over someone else. What a colossal responsibility it was to scribble on the beautiful blank slate.

I picked her up, held her tight as she breathed in molecules that were no longer me. I needed to own my role, even if I had no role model. I had influence. I could not be afraid of it.

FOR SEVERAL DAYS at the hospital, my baby ate, slept, and expelled waste. When she cried, Jon and I held her, moved her, or fed her, and she stopped. There were answers. Sucking a finger. A burp. Drying her off. I'd been so worried about the unmanageable screams of the newborn, but so far, at least, they weren't. I could satisfy her needs, sate her unlike I could ever do for my mother, whose needs seemed bottomless. I was exhausted, but swimming, floating even, and not drowning in her being.

"Judy!" Mom's voice boomed through my phone several times a day. "How are you? How's she doing? What's she doing? Is she eating? Sleeping? Sucking her thumb? Cooing? Smiling? Opening her eyes?" Mom may not have made it to New York, but she was certainly excited.

At night, when I heard my daughter's particular little cry coming down the hallway toward my room, a cry I couldn't believe I recognized, I awoke with a jolt. After placing her on the pillow and making sure that she latched on, that I could see her tiny cheeks puff in and out with activity, my mind scurried. I imagined Mom after my birth—how thrilled she must have been, present and loving. Red and elated, shining and hugging. The image was bright, energized. Then I imagined the spark that had slowly leaked out of her, the one I'd craved reigniting my whole life.

I squeezed my baby tight.

We made it through the danger. *We survived.*

My sciatica had not fully healed, my thigh pelted in pain, my horrific red scar—two dozen staples punched right into my abdomen—looked like dirty, twisted stitches on a baggy old boxing glove (and to think I'd been concerned about stretch marks). But I knew these traces were tattoos of transition, blemishes of birth and rebirth. I had survived the making of a new generation.

I had also survived the Survivors. Jon and I talked about her open eyes, her awareness. "She has a feisty, fighter, colostrum-seeking spirit," Jon said the day before I was due to be discharged, making the strong decision that—with its massive implications—was hard for me. "Let's name her Zelda."

"Zelda," I repeated, my cheek brushing her ear. I thought back to my parents' indecision about my name, the three-month period in which they each fought for their own relatives to be immortalized, my identity changing on a daily basis. I grabbed Jon's fingers, warm, giving. "My little Zelda."

Then I prayed that like her namesake, my baby would grow up with the confidence to save herself when she needed saving.

· TWENTY-ONE ·

CODE BLUE
New York City, 2011

It takes four generations for trauma to pass through a family. I thought of this again. I imagined a diagram like the evolutionary monkey-to-man but instead with bespectacled Jews showing increasingly good postures and golden tans. Then again, how could it be linear? The generations react to and against one another, compensating and overcompensating, sometimes instituting more trauma in their attempts to avoid it. The first generation survives, I figured, the second suffers survivor's guilt, the third becomes hyperaware, sensing both the dark past and the light at the end of the trenches. And now, the fourth.

"It's strapped in," Jon said. "You don't need to hold it."

I nodded, and gripped the car seat even more tightly.

Holy shit, I thought. I was doing it. I was *a mother*. I was sitting next to *a car seat*. There was a person in it. I made it. It was OK. I was OK. This thing that had been in my stomach was now in a cab listening to Jimmy Kimmel, stuck in traffic on Fifth Avenue.

Nothing made sense.

"Take Seventh!" my husband called to the driver, as if we were in a huge rush to get home—to begin the rest of our lives.

But I smiled gratefully as the taxi approached our building, my haven. It had been a hectic week in the hospital following our near-loss and emergency surgery. Now I clutched my warm, healthy daughter—my double miracle—as Jon pushed open the door to our apartment. The white walls, white carpets, and white counters, smooth geometric lighting and large windows made me feel grounded and calm. Lord, I'd been aching for this serenity.

"Welcome home, *Mom*," I whispered to myself. "And daughter." Then I proudly added to my new roommate: "Welcome to your peaceful palace."

But mere seconds later, entering Zelda's nursery, my former home office, my mental sanctuary, I grew faint. Next to a half-assembled crib and changing table, there was a stroller, brightly colored hats and snowsuits, a laboratory of breast pumps and sterilizers. My breath quickened as I scanned hospital-grade first-aid kits, towels with fuzzy lion tails. At the baby humidifier shaped like a frog, I felt sweat drop from my hairline. I stared at the unruly piles and touched my bandaged-up stomach. The doctor had explained that to save my daughter, she'd needed to reopen an old surgical wound. Now, I thought, here was my interior really becoming unraveled.

I hugged Zelda closer into my chest and thought about our Montreal house strewn with my mother's used Kleenex, the cobwebbed credenzas, the unopened bargain board games, the closet doors that were blocked from shutting so that the automatic lights stayed permanently on like an eternal flame, the chaos in which bank statements were lost forever, buried by the full stable of My Little Ponies, the descendants of Bubbie's cheap dresses and purses. All the junk that formed physical and emotional barriers between us. What festered in my daughter's genetic code? What colors and moods would it express?

I took a deep breath into Zelda's clean white snowsuit (yes, on my registry I'd listed not the traditional pink, antitraditional blue, or even yellow, but ridiculously impractical white infant clothes), placing her tiny hand around my finger so its teensy nails lined up along my knuckle. I forced myself to remember that I'd combated it all, engineered another life, a new lineage. I'd run away, become a professional neat freak working in galleries, found a husband who understood that our baggage affected those around us and allowed me to adorn this open-plan apartment with a clear backsplash, uncluttered shelves, room to breathe and clear jettisoning rules. Until now.

"Look what I bought at the Chelsea Crafts Fair." Jon excitedly displayed a hemp bag from which he pulled out an elephant made of recycled sweaters, a turtle in a Pac-Man sweatshirt, and a Korean sock puppet. With a mini-iPod.

"How could you do this to me?" I cried. "It's taken me years to accumulate all this nothing."

"Shopping for her is fun," he said, tickling Zelda's feet.

I sat in the enormous new glider (four times my size, even postpartum) and tried to breathe. *Calm down,* I scolded myself. He's a great dad, wants to be involved, has the right attitude. And here you are, your knee jerking madly. Besides. You're a mother. *A mother.* Hum a lullaby, for God's sake.

"Schlaf, mein kind," came out instinctively. "Sleep, my child" were lyrics from an old Yiddish tune Bubbie had sung to me. Now it felt right, all of it, Zelda's warm body, our nuzzling, rocking. *"In Dachau iz dein tateh . . ."* Wait. Dachau? I was singing a song about *Dachau* to a six-day-old? Man alive, I was going to have to work harder to escape my past. Every time I thought I'd made it through, I hit a new wall.

I slowly stood up and walked over to the room's large windows. While Kildare was hidden in a cul-de-sac, my adult home was in the middle of Manhattan, on the seventh floor, offering views of the clear perpendicular streets, of the world outside. I'd survived this foreigner who'd invaded my interior. I'd taken care of things my whole life. I could do this.

I would not be a mother blocked from her baby. I would not let her report cards disappear in domestic maelstrom, nor fill her shelves with useless bargains. I would love her and see her and touch her. By being organized.

I handed Zelda to Jon. Despite doctor's orders not to lift anything, I collected all my strength to do what was most important: clean up.

BUT STUFF KEPT coming. Cousins I hadn't seen since my bat mitzvah arrived with "gifts." I stood speechless as they wheeled in their used goods: two travel cribs, a Jumperoo the size of my bedroom, a six-by-six-foot gray play pen(itentiary), and an Elmo collective. A colleague passed on a tote filled with old nursing bras. My neighbor popped by with several pairs of her niece's baby UGGs. A friend from Ithaca called me before visiting: "I know you're sensitive about clutter, so I just wanted to make sure it was OK to bring you two garbage bags full of summer dresses and an electronic swing?"

"Thanks very much for your kind gesture," I said, "but if you bring plastic bags into my house I'll use them to suffocate myself."

Then there was Zelda's own growing social set. I was keen to host baby playdates and invited my mommy group over. But while I scurried around providing lactation tea and diapers, I caught glimpses of horror scenes: drool puddling on the edge of my sofa cushion, a used wipe tossed into a corner. My apartment was becoming a lost-and-found for teethers, a repository of overflowing formula powder. Stuff, mess, *and dirt*. "That's the last time Jackson comes over," I whispered to myself, wiping mango streaks off a giant Stitch, recalling the hundreds of Barbies that had attracted a kindergarten crowd who used me for my toys.

After cordially waving good-bye and softly tucking Zelda into her crib for a rest, I collapsed on her tainted carpet. Sheer exhaustion didn't help my anxiety. Having to get up every two hours, even for a dedicated insomniac like myself, felt like a whole new layer of torture. And even when she didn't cry, I awoke in a sweat, convinced I was suffocating her in my blankets, even though she was in another bed. Not to mention that Zelda would settle only when I held her while standing and dancing to baby calypso (punishment for my sins). My body felt like it had been through a nineteenth-century war.

Fortunately, however, my expectations for motherhood had been so low, that I wasn't disappointed. For nine months I'd completely forgotten that to balance all the stress was the fact that I'd have an adorable baby, a mini-human to ogle and cuddle, soft like the velvet of my bright pink robe that Jon had bought as a joke, with the word "fabulous" spelled across the back in rhinestones—if you're going to provide the boob buffet, no need to do it blandly. I'd forgotten about the amazing creature I'd be creating, this thing that went from blob to person, each day literally seeing more of the world and expressing her sentiments with more ferocity. (And passing more solid bowels. Who would have thought that so much of my existence would be run by someone else's gas?)

And so, buoyed by each new movement and form of eye contact, each reach for the giraffe teether (I'd become one of those parents), I pushed on, at times a collapsing sack of bones and flesh, at others, hyped from the physical and emotional shifts of my round-the-clock existence. I tried to relax, to go with flows, but every time a new round of shopping was done—now we needed teethers, and ice teethers, and vibrating teethers—I blanched. How could six pounds of person come with six tons of equipment? The proliferation seemed endless. I needed to get ahead of it.

Between frantic doctor visits (was Zelda's labored breathing emphysema, asthma, tuberculosis, asphyxiation, anaphylaxis, suffocation, lung collapse, respiratory arrest? No, just excess snot), I installed open shelving units so all objects could be stacked and seen. I purchased cream-colored bins for stuffed animals, and marked off an area of my sink for the PBA-free bottles, giving Zelda's feeding its own section of the kitchen. When my daughter napped, I tucked items into their place: short-sleeve onesies on one side, long-sleeve on the other. I made sure that there were clear vistas across the apartment, and clean, straight lines always in view.

I managed. Until one afternoon. I sat down to nurse and felt something wet slithering down my side. Milk had seeped through my shirt, staining a new chair. Then the pump leaked across my kitchen counter, wasting precious ounces, traces of blood appeared on my arm (where from?), and I found suspect curdled matter tucked under one of Zelda's many chins. For how long had the crusty schmutz been embedded in there? For how long would I have to stand in the hot shower scrubbing my milk-strewn corpus? I flashed to what was to come—years of cereal in crevices, yogurt congealed around chair frames, wafting smells of rotting pulverized broccoli emanating from undisclosed, indiscernible sources. Spinach stuffed up nostrils, mash flung with abandon, sweet potato chunks lodged in my sweaty bra. Unruly mixes of saliva, seafood, milk. Cheese-and-fish concoctions running down table legs, rice crackers crumbling in crevices, graham crumbs rotting under chair legs, in cupboard crannies. Sticky residues of unidentifiable liquids gracing my previously pristine surfaces. Mini-straws in the bath, banana-shaped toothbrushes in my purse. How would I handle it all?

My phone buzzed: a text from Melissa. "Are we on for tomorrow at seven?" I hadn't seen her since before Zelda's birth. I'd left the house alone only a handful of times, usually to buy more breast supplies. I'd been enchanted by the thought of meeting a friend uptown for coffee, but now I didn't know how I'd do it. I'd have to arrange child care from six to nine if I included travel time, then pump enough milk just in case, which could take hours. There was no longer such a thing as just "meeting for coffee." I had a child, and every minute of *her* life had to be accounted for.

"Sorry. Can't," I texted back, for the first time sensing the rift, the shift from not-parent to parent, the feeling that nonparents did not understand. Of course they didn't. A few weeks earlier, I hadn't either. It was just as I'd feared: I no longer controlled my space, or my time. My fingers shook as I typed.

That night, I asked Jon to put Zelda to bed. He sat on the glider, gave her a bottle, changed her, burped her, and rocked her, while I scrubbed the floors—by hand.

. . .

FOR THE NEXT few weeks, I spent every night frantically dousing the floors with disinfectant wipes and putting each bottle part in its place. I needed to go to sleep knowing that I could create calm. As my cleaning became more intense—every room, and with a new Dustbuster to boot—so did my admin, as I created triple layers of to-do lists and daily schedules for both Zelda and me.

Until one evening when I was using wet wipes and an old toothbrush to loosen some hardened yellow substance that had caked between the wooden floorboards outside Zelda's room. Her light was dimmed and through the partly open door I heard her daddy sing and shush her, the model of intimacy and warmth.

I knew so many special songs, Yiddish ones Bubbie sang to me, folk tunes Mom had hummed, Canadian children's classics she'd been sending me, copied from CDs from her local library and her own decades-old collection. The lyrics came back to me as if thirty years hadn't passed at all. Motherhood meant a loss of control over my time, but also, time warping in weird ways, my past bloated in my mind. At every tired instant, memories of Raffi and giant puppets, clapping games and Chinese jump rope, inundated my synapses. Archived recollections of lyrics to lullabies about various Polish ghettos, the soundtrack of my own babyhood, seeped into my everyday mental terrain.

Singing, soothing, connecting—that's what I should have been doing, what I *wanted* to be doing. I'd been so busy removing obstacles to seeing my daughter that I barely had time to look at her. In my desperate attempt to not-be my mother, I ended up only repeating her behavior. She'd tried to make up for her childhood by filling her home with objects; I tried to make up for my childhood by ridding them. But both of us could be blind when it came to our children. I looked at the rag in my hand. "Jon, can I have a turn tonight?" I asked, getting up from the floor.

He handed Zelda to me, and my warm daughter melted into my arms where she fit perfectly, the most natural embrace. I couldn't believe I'd ever been ambivalent. I began to sing *"Oyfn Pripetshik"* and "Tumbalalaika." There were *good* things I could pass down from the women of my family, like Bubbie's and Mom's love of music, art, singing. *"A shteyn ken vaksn an regn,"* I sang. *"Libeh ken brenen oon nit aufhern, a hartz ken vaynen an trern."* (A stone can grow without water, love can burn without being extinguished, a heart can cry without tears.)

I rocked and she cooed, sucking her fingers. Then I noted a turquoise blanket on the floor. It bothered me, that splash of blue in her white room, but I told myself not to fixate, that I would put it away tomorrow. I could manage domestic mayhem through a mix of toy bins, organic cleaning sprays, and chilling out. But, no matter how much I tidied, I could not control the disorder of motherhood. I could never clean up for good.

Which was OK. A bit of clutter was a small price to pay for closeness.

· TWENTY-TWO ·

LOOKING AFTER YOU
New York City, 2012

We traipsed up the stairs of the Park Slope subway station, Zelda's three-month-old body snug against Jon's hairy chest in a carrier, me drenched in diaper bags filled with fifteen changes of outfits just in case (and that was just for me). We were headed to Saul's first birthday party; Zelda's first any party. On the tree-and-row-house-lined Brooklyn street, we passed couples with strollers and toddlers bouncing on saucerlike apparatuses running into intersections with flustered dads chasing behind them. People whose lives revolved around ketchup stains and preballet classes, bruises and calamine lotion. "We're one of them now," I said as a mother and daughter dressed in matching retro parkas passed by.

"You're gonna be even worse."

"I know." I imagined Zelda and me, holding hands in vintage red tailored coats, fluffy beige scarves, oversize handbags, but I had to block the thought because it was too good. Dreaming still made me scared it would never happen. Zelda's newborn stage, the fourth trimester, was officially coming to an end. Soon this being would no longer be attached to my boob, but would connect to me in a more complicated, less concrete way, and I wasn't sure I knew how to do it properly. At three months, I'd been told, babies can *learn*—to sleep, creep, act. Would I know how to teach?

"Much worse," he said.

It was hard to believe that a year ago we'd made this same walk on the way to Saul's bris. I'd drunk decaf because I'd gone off the pill a few days earlier, but it was just a token gesture, a getting-used-to the idea of sacrifice rather than actually anticipating conception. I didn't know—despite my bursting into tears during the otherwise uneventful ceremony—that I'd just been impregnated. Now Jon and I were reentering this same apartment as parents. As people who assessed the availability of stroller-parking.

Zelda made her entrance. At the front door, Jon unsaddled her from the carrier, and we were met with adoring fans. "How old?"

"Fourteen weeks," I said proudly, feeling like I'd been doing this forever. I propped her up in the way I'd already grown accustomed to, so her purple polka-dot dress draped over my forearm and she was able to look out at the world behind me.

"Can I hold her?" the mom of the birthday boy asked. Zelda was the youngest child by several months; a desirable cuddle. It must be an amazing thing, I thought, to be the center of so much attention and physical affection. I badly wanted time to freeze—I wanted to be the one with the cutest, docilest, adorablest daughter forever. How could she, this warm calm ball, turn into one of those running, sticky, bodily-fluid-drenched, sonically deranged explosions? *Sunrise, sunset.*

"I want to hold her first!" a tall, silver-haired professor father-in-law declared.

"All right, but I get in after," the mom agreed.

I wasn't sure I wanted to give her up to a semistranger. Nor that she wanted to go. But there he was, checked sleeves outstretched, a massive smile, telling me how much he missed newborns.

"Well, we're starting to think about hiring a nanny," I joked, hesitantly handing over my daughter. "Let's see this as your 'trial.'"

He grabbed her up, hoisted her into his large forearms, and walked to the other side of the kitchen.

I stayed outwardly calm, smiled even, and poured myself a droplet of champagne, but I kept my eyes on my daughter. Zelda's body was slinked in those giant arms, her chin resting on a broad shoulder. She looked at me and I nodded. It's OK, I ESPed, I am here, watching you, noting you, registering your desires and feelings so one day you can see them yourself. I sipped my bubbly, trying to use my eyes to create a haven, thinking that I would teach her to find calm in herself by being calm for her. *I* was her first home, the background against which her identity would be formed, the grounding that would enable her to launch into the world and let herself go. I could help make this girl—who'd grown in my interior—comfortable in her own skin.

She dug her nose into the man's neck, listening to his stream of grandfatherly affections, seemingly content. I chitchatted with another guest about babysitter Web sites—a caregiver still seemed foreign, a distant desire—until I noted Zelda begin to squirm. Then she looked at me. I looked right back. *I know, I see you, I'm aware of your needs, and you are safe.* I said it to her. I said it to me.

Then I went to fetch her. "Let's go, dude," I said, and hugged her to my heart.

"That's sunshine. The whoosh is wind. And there's the Hudson River," I explained to Zelda a week later as I pushed the stroller all the way to the end of the Chelsea pier to give her the best view. "Water." I pointed. "Like the womb!" I stood in the soft air, drinking my obscenely priced coffee as the spring wind blew through my hair, the sun shining brightly on shoulders, summer tapping me from behind, reminding me that soon, soon, I'd be able to leave the house without having to bundle either of us up; in other words, in less than two hours.

Zelda's blue-gray eyes were open wide, and she drank in the view, literally flicking her tongue to taste the wind. Every second with Zelda felt alive, filled with wonder, learning, impressions, memories, emotions.

Today was an exclusive Z-and-me day. That morning, I'd gotten her dressed, packed the diaper bag, and taken her to a baby music group, couching her in my lap while the other children—all older, seemingly adult at their six months—sucked wooden drumsticks. I'd held her while lacing up my shoes and schlepping supplies; I'd sung her to sleep. I smiled at her while I stopped at Chelsea Market to peruse eco-knit stuffed endangered animal toys on sale at the organic store that also carried seventeen varieties of imported shortbread. I even considered shopping—I'd been maintaining my ease with stuff with large owl-print storage bags and the awareness that objects could be wonderful, as long as they were useful and respected, and didn't serve as blockades or substitutes. And were machine washable.

After that, I'd made my way here to the edge of town, staring into the maritime distance, not lonely like in South Africa but feeling heroic in the breeze, accomplished. I was doing it. I was managing motherhood. Zelda's calm was, of course, limited—hunger, gas, hysterical crying, hysterical gas could start at any second—but for that moment I was in my element, showing my daughter water and sky, air and land, trees and loud homeless drunks.

Having a child, I'd found, did not mean that I'd lost myself but that there was more of me, new pockets and layers I'd never even known existed. A tendency to teach, an ability to browse. I was at the center of my own experience, fitting into my stretched skin. The fact that I'd had no preconceived image of myself as a mother, nor a strong role model to imitate, turned out to be helpful—I had no standard to live up to! I could develop into a parent in my own way. What better thing could a person do on a Monday morning?

Then, on cue, Zelda began to wail. My breath stopped. This blemishless blond baby had instantly transformed into a howling mammal and looked . . . exactly like my mother. I grabbed the stroller and bolted down the pier, across the West Side Highway, sweating all the way to my sofa without even taking off my jacket. One breast exposed; Zelda having her snack. I tried to put my legs up on our one coffee table (vintage; provenance: Carlton basement) but it was slightly out of foot's reach. Annoyed, I gently moved Zelda and crossed my legs under me, but I felt an ache in my lower back. I turned on the TV and quickly noted that I'd already watched this same episode of *Extreme RV*—more than once.

I sighed, then reached for my iPad and opened my e-mail, bracing myself for the overly cluttered in-box I knew I'd encounter. Instead, I saw a surprising message from a magazine editor. She wanted to buy a story I'd sent in about Mom's hoarding. I'd never published anything about Mom before; I'd wanted to break into this magazine, but could I really do it? *Yes.* I grinned, pleased with the opportunity, with my growing career that had been on pause. *It's still in me,* I thought, *my mind, intellect, interior.*

But as I looked down at Zelda, tasting and sucking, ensconced in her own soothing world, I wondered what I'd be giving up. I'd been nursed for only a few weeks. How tired Mom had always been, working full-time, falling asleep on sofas, distracted, removed. I remembered how I left her notes taped to her door, how she left the house in the mornings before I even woke up, her only trace the awkward sandwiches she'd packed for me in used paper bags.

Mom had been calling to check up on us daily, and the other day, clearly trying to empathize, asked if I didn't just want to run away from it all. *No!* I'd said. I did not want to fall into work, whose stresses were familiar, rather than face the motherhood challenges that I did not know. But. I also really wanted to write this article.

"Hello? Anyone there?" Jon was knocking on my head.

"Oh!" I jumped. "I didn't realize you were back."

"What's going on?"

"I was just thinking about, you know, retreating into the life of the mind."

Jon shook his head, let out an exaggerated sigh. "Zelda's completely asleep." He gestured to her. She'd come off the latch, turned away, spittle dripping from her lip. I hadn't even noticed.

I didn't want to be absent. But what counted for presence was not so clear-cut.

Creating comfortable boundaries was a complicated little project.

. . .

FROM THE CORNER of my eye, I saw Denise showing Zelda the few photographs—all of architectural structures—displayed on our walls. I was at my desk, but her hushed voice pressing into Zelda's fruit-soft head sounded like it ran at a thousand decibels. I found it harder to work, to do anything, when I could see them: Denise caring for my baby, whispering in her ear, Denise and Zelda BFFs. I reminded myself that I'd hired her to help develop my baby so I could also develop as a person, for a few hours a week. Besides, as the literature said, time off would leave me refreshed for the repetitive play. And: it's not just about the baby's needs, it's about the family's needs.

I'd chosen Denise after *twenty* babysitter interviews and trials— I'd neurotically assessed each one, unsure what the perfect caregiver looked like, testing each with the deal-breaking "front to back" wipe. But Denise had stuck—not only had she rubbed the right way, but she was funny and not too earnest. (Her first words to us were "Eight p.m. is a late meeting. I was worried you guys were gonna kill me.") Plus, Zelda loved her, spilling over with giggles whenever she walked in. Maybe that's what I found most troubling.

I couldn't resist butting in. I got up and headed to where Denise was gesturing to a photograph we'd received as a wedding present. "Who is that man?" she asked, pointing at a collage of pictures of Sigmund Freud.

Zelda's face was nestled in her breast, which was bigger than mine, despite my current stint as a cow.

"*Who* is that man?" Denise goaded again in a childlike voice.

The photographer, whom I'd worked for during college, created bright representations of abandoned homes, broken walls, peeling wallpaper, doors on their last hinges, making pictorial order out of actual chaos. When I became her assistant, her project was photographing psychoanalysts' offices, exploring how the space of therapy affected the therapy. Did the architecture and design of the consulting room influence the insights and self-knowledge that were produced?

I wrote papers about her photos, even interviewing analytic-couch designers about what made for a good shrinkage bed (comfortable, but not too soft). We schlepped around Boston as she shot Jungian and Adlerian consulting rooms, the therapists excited and anxious about how she was analyzing their offices. Metasessions.

Now with Denise pointing to the work, cooing in goo-goo speak, I saw how all those years of displacing my emotional anxieties about control and comfort onto intellectual endeavors and romantic possibilities had, well, paid off. I looked around me at Italian modernist couches and not much else. Just days away from turning thirty-five, an indisputable adult, I *loved* my home.

"I don't know who the man is," Denise said, "but I do like the sofa."

"That's Freud," I explained. "At different times of his life." I caressed my daughter's rosy cheek, wanting to take her into my arms instead.

"Who?" Denise asked.

"Freud." I enunciated it, louder than Zelda's gurgling.

"Huh?"

"Freud," I repeated slowly. "The psychoanalyst."

"Nope. Don't know who that is."

I was putting my child's upbringing, ten hours a week of her life, in the hands of someone who didn't even know who Freud was?

"Freud," Denise repeated as if it was a funny sound. Zelda giggled.

She was snug in Denise's strong biceps. I flashed to Bubbie—her chicken flesh arms, her firm fingers—the caregiver who saved me. How awesome, I suddenly thought. Imagine having a daughter who does not know who Freud is! Who might not need a therapist or spend her life searching to make sense out of mess. Who might not blame me!

"Freud. Freud. Freed," I sang, giggling along, knowing my daughter was in good hands. Which, of course, had nicer nails than mine.

· · ·

DAYS LATER, I found myself in an actual gallery, a white-walled space I happened to walk into, drawn in by a photo I saw from the street, which transformed as I walked by it. The image was of a crowded road where each cyclist, pedestrian, and driver was using mobile devices. They were together yet alone, connected, but not to their immediate surroundings. As I passed, the photo morphed, so that eventually someone riding a scooter fell down. Bystanders turned to look, but none moved to help.

It had been years since I'd been to an art gallery by myself; months since I'd done much by myself at all. Such a luxury, the afternoon quiet, my liberty. I walked farther into the exhibition, enjoying the next piece: a family sitting on a couch, watching a fake fire on a TV, each on their own electronic devices. Then, an image of a woman on the toilet using her cell, which she drops into the bowl; a couple on a date while the man checks his BlackBerry; a couple having sex, after which the woman sends a text; a girl on a doctor's examining table, talking on her phone. The disconnectedness of connected modern life. People were together but apart, bonded and blocked by stuff. I loved them.

As art. As an experience that I recognized but no longer lived.

I'd spent years researching precious objects, but only now could I appreciate them for their beauty, not as treatises about home or myself. I was *enjoying* the art because I felt like doing so on a sunny afternoon, indulging while Jon watched the baby, experiencing pleasure and sensation without theorization. *How I've changed!* I marveled, giddy with confidence and freedom.

The perfect time for my mother to interrupt.

I got the first call from Mark, the son-in-law of my mother's late friend. "What's your mother's exact address?" he asked right away.

"Why?"

"She sounds unstable. She called me to say good-bye."

Not again. My stomach churned. I gave him the address, relieved he was going over to check up on her. Then I realized I had two missed calls from her. Uncharacteristically, she hadn't left a voice mail.

I dialed her number. No answer.

I called Eli. No answer.

Dad's work number. Eli again. Mom again. Texted Eli. Mom—not picking up.

Nothing.

Please don't kill yourself.

Oh God. Why this, again, now? What could I do to help her? To stop her?

I took deep breaths and walked outside. I knew, I had to go.

I WAS NEARLY running when my brother phoned. "I'm here with her."

He put her on the line. "What's going on? Please, just calm down," I pleaded.

"It's nothing, Judy. I'm just being dramatic. Oh, wait—the doorbell."

"It's Mark," I said between breaths. It was actually the police.

"Shit, this again," Eli now said. "I'll call you back from the ambulance."

I galloped through the Chelsea streets, panting. I had to go. I had to go.

Cell reception was waving in and out. Eli and I finally reconnected.

"She let me into the house," he explained. "She seemed upset. I saw a belt hanging from the light fixture in the kitchen. Out of the junk, I noticed a stool under it. She admitted she was acting out. She said it was a dramatization."

My head was spinning. I'd been used to the suicide threats, but a physical plan to hang herself? Right in the kitchen? The tuna kitchen.

"She said she was too fat. The belt would have given way. She would have fallen."

I imagined her body bringing down the light, the whole ceiling, turning the room inside out. The hoard that made her heavy would have blocked her fall. Hoarding—its layers, its comfort, the small sense of power and control it enabled—had in so many ways saved her.

"Thank you so much for being there, Eli," I said. And I meant it. "I have to go," I said. And I did, I had to go.

FINALLY, AFTER MANY more trotting blocks, I made it to my destination. Sweating, panting, I opened the door, ran in and found them. Jon and Zelda playing on the floor of her room. I lay down on the white carpet beside them, as if we were all three making adjacent snow angels, imprints of our beings on the space. Even Mones the cat came over to sniff our toes.

"You won't believe this," I said. I was about to relay the latest when I caught sight of the light fixture hanging over our heads. It was pink and embroidered mesh, yet modern—exactly the kind of lamp I would have wanted as a child. Zelda might hate it, but we'd deal with that later. I had picked it, created a space, stamped my design on it, airy and light. I finally had a place to which to run from the harshness of the world and from which I could launch into its wonderful possibilities. A safe center to dip in and out of, for me and I hoped for Zelda too. One she could return to with funny anecdotes as well as tales of disappointment, one that would take her in, recharge her, always heed her.

My mom cared for her mom, shoveling affection and attention in that direction, at the expense of so much. And though half my heart was already on the Voyageur bus, tuna wrap in hand, rushing to Montreal, I knew I needed to break that cycle. I had my own family to protect. And, they, in turn, protected me too.

Then Zelda let out a mighty burp. "Oy mate, you belch like a truck driver," Jon said, matching it with one of his own.

I understood: I was, finally, home.

· TWENTY-THREE ·

THE WALLS HAVE LAYERS
Montreal, 2012

"Here's Zaidy! Where's Zaidy? Here's Zaidy!" my mother cooed while lifting and dropping a pillowcase over my father's outrageously grinning face. She was propped with Zelda—my Zelda—on my childhood bed, which she had cleared for our visit, Zelda's first to Montreal. Mom had also cleaned part of the kitchen, and when we arrived for lunch, she'd ordered us sushi, remembering it was something Jon and I liked.

Even Eli was in the kitchen—plugged into his laptop, his savior—but still. Zelda brought everyone together, I thought amid the wailing giggles. Just look at my parents next to each other on the bed. My daughter united them in the way I'd always wished I could.

I put my hand on my waist and was surprised to graze a hard hip bone. I was thin, I thought, *finally*. Why hadn't my mother remarked on my hard-won post-pregnancy weight loss? "Mom," I said, as I pulled my shirt tightly around me.

"Where's Zaidy?" she shrieked and smiled. "Here's Zaidy!"

My skinniness was silly compared to her happiness, to Zelda's chuckles. I knew that. I sighed and took a photo of them with my iPhone.

Six-month-old Zelda was overwhelmed at first by the mad attentions of her grandparents and uncle. But by the second day, she loved it, smiling, her eyes darting to make eye contact with each one, her head naturally posing coyly for all their cameras (as if modeling was genetically coded—that would be her father's confidence genes). Today was the third day and she was unabashedly enjoying playing with her Bubbie, natural best friends.

I stood in the doorframe, on the threshold of this room that loomed large and loud in my mind, but was small and standard in reality. A few years earlier my mother had had my one pink wall— the single quirky element of the room that felt like *me*—painted white. I was livid. *You are erasing me!* I'd yelled on the phone. *You haven't lived here for a decade,* my mother had answered coolly, as if accusing me of erasing myself. Staring at it now, I noted that fuchsia was still visible underneath the cream.

The walls had layers.

My parents looked old. My father's hair sprouted all over his face, between the cracks of his wrinkles. My mother's hair was tied in a white spongy poof on top of her head, her black sweat suit draped over her beanbag body.

"Where's Zaidy? Here's Zaidy!" The three of them exploded in fits of even more delighted giggles as they played this game of seeing and being seen. "Your grandparents used to play on the floor with you," my mother called to me. "I can see why!"

I took another photo.

Her normalcy, her sheer happiness, was a dream come true, and totally confusing. How could it be that only three weeks earlier, she'd attached that belt to the kitchen light fixture and threatened to hang herself? Even just this morning she'd beckoned me into a corner of the hallway to slip me a five-hundred-dollar cash birthday gift, whispering that cameras installed in pens all over the house were recording this transfer. How could a person be boiling over with love, so engaged in the moment, yet entirely untethered? How could she see Zelda's toes, but not the dust on the sheet that they touched? She would play with Zelda only in my old bedroom, because it was safe, unlike the den. To access her, to interact, to have her see me at all, I had to meet her in her smallest comfort zone, a tiny slice of experience, of space. Literally, a room. One I could choose to enter, and exit, I reminded myself. Staring at her now, tickling my daughter, I knew I would never understand her layered essence, but I would have to accept it.

I ran my hand along the painted wall, feeling the sharp, hidden prickles that speckled the apparently smooth surface.

For several years when I'd come to Montreal I stayed at a hotel, but this was the first time that it felt *right*. Montreal was no longer my home. I was a visitor to this place, to this life. My parents had struggled for decades to detach from their parents and their parents' houses, traumatized by even the thought of selling them. But I could. I had immersed myself in my new family. I could sell Kildare when the time came. I could sell these thick walls.

"Let's go," Jon said, approaching me from behind. "We need to go to your bank."

"Coming," I replied. Closing old childhood accounts seemed like exactly what I needed to do. To Jon, this was for tax purposes, but for me, it was a symbol. The final severance.

My parents barely noticed me leaving. But seeing them enjoying my daughter, and her them, I didn't mind. In fact, I was relieved I could leave them to take care of Zelda for an hour.

"It's fine," Jon whispered as I lingered in the doorway. "Your parents will be fine looking after her."

"I know," I said. But as we were leaving, I asked Eli to be on call. Just in case.

LATER THAT EVENING, before we headed back to our hotel, my mother sat down at the kitchen table with me as I nursed Zelda. Though the counter still hosted heaps of stale food and vitamins, Mom had cleared the table. The kitchen chairs were the only surfaces available for sitting on, especially with a nursing pillow. I tried hard not to think about the crumbs cemented into the chair's fabric borders, not to look at the light from which she tried to hang herself. Instead I focused on feeding my daughter beside the Great Wall of Tuna.

"Want some tuna?" Mom offered, as if reading my mind, genuinely excited to whip some up with pasta or cheese or vitamins or Diet Coke. Vunderfoods die hard.

"I'm good," I said, wondering if perhaps now was my chance to bring up the loss of my baby weight.

Then, "Judy," she whispered, shifting tones in an instant.

My stomach clenched. This was her serious voice, the one that signaled the entrance to the dark side of her mind. I massaged Zelda, rubbing my thumb across her forehead, calming her.

"I need to talk to you about something," Mom continued. I cringed. I was about to tell her to stop, that I couldn't handle it right then, that I was breast-feeding, for crying out loud, that I—

"I read your article."

My cheeks froze.

I knew right away she meant my article about her hoarding and how it had affected me. How had she even seen it? Did she Google me?! Of course she Googled me. What had I done? Why had I told the world about my mother? I knew she was going to tell me how wrong I was. How horrible I'd been to her. How treacherous.

"Judy."

"Yes?" I looked down, as if I could evade the attack.

"I loved it."

She did?

"It explained everything to me. I saw my behavior. For the first time, I really understood why you had to run away from here." She looked me in the eye. "Thank you for being honest."

"I'm so relieved." I almost laughed. My mother had read my work, and enjoyed it. And, it was about her. As always, we connected through literature. "I'm so happy you liked it."

"How could I have lived like this for all these years," she began, gesturing around her, "without it ever dawning on me that it affected you? I must have a real problem dealing with reality. I think it started a long time ago."

"Yes," I answered, writing this admission down in my mind, etching it into my gray matter with a steel-point pen so I could come back to it all the time. My reality check on the tragic reality that my mother could never really experience reality. "It started a long time ago."

I looked down at Zelda, at her blond hair, her blue eyes. She was so different from me. As I was so different from my mom.

My mother put her hand on my hand, which was on Zelda's head, so our fingers formed a shape like a team handshake.

The pen, I imagined, was hot like a horseshoe and hissed as it sizzled on the bold characters. But I also noted the curved lines between the cursive letters, their connective tissue.

THE NEXT MORNING, it was time to drive back to New York. We were running late, Zelda would get cranky, I hadn't slept in days (the hotel room bed, the intensity of family visits, the travel crib suffocation risk, the dermatological dehydration) and Jon had to take some work calls that afternoon.

"But we didn't say good-bye to my mother," I blurted out, surprising myself.

"Don't worry. I'll call her and explain that we can't come over now." He had become used to making excuses. I was invariably trying to avoid her anxious depression. It had almost been a relief when she stopped leaving the house, since it meant I could easily box my time with her.

But not today. Today, I knew it as I said it. "I want to see my mother. I want to say good-bye."

"OK," Jon agreed right away.

At her house, I watched my mom change Zelda's diaper on my old bed, her arm loving with each wipe, confident with experience. Even showing me a new technique, suggesting how confident I could be too. I took photos, trying to solidify this tenderness, make it permanent. When would I visit again? Would it be the last time they would see each other? The last time my daughter would feel that kind of crazy consuming mad impassioned grand-maternal love? I feared my mother's prognosis was dementia like Bubbie. I wanted to hang on to whatever existed of her mind while it was still there.

"Wow!" Eli said, opening the bedroom door, gesturing at the bed. "You're right, Judy. They're still *identical*."

My mother and daughter, both giggling now, facing each other, were locked in a mirror image. My mom's smooth youthful cheeks, her toothy smile, reflected back at her, reinforcing the eerie similarity I'd seen a few months ago. One was now Bubbie, one was now Zelda. "Identical," I agreed.

But as I pressed the little camera icon on my iPhone, I for the first time saw something else: how much *I* was *like* my mother. In this moment, taking all these photos like she used to do, wanting to store happy memories, easily slipping into living life through a lens. But it was even more than that. Our love of literature, our passion for classic British sitcoms, our endless lists, the anxiety, the perfectionism, the desire to control, the black sweat suit, the same varicose veins webbing the backs of our knees. Me and her, me and Bubbie, Zelda and Zelda, we were all of us eternal reflected images.

When it came time to leave, I packed the diaper bag and put on my coat. I handed Zelda to Jon. "It's time to go," I said to my mom, holding back the tears that began to form in the outer corners of my eyes, the toddler terrified of being left alone at kindergarten.

"I know, honey," she said, approaching me, taking me in her warm, soft arms.

I knew that she understood why I always had to go. I reminded myself that she was the one who convinced Dad to pay for Harvard, to let me run away in the first place. She knew, somewhere inside her, in one layer of her internal palimpsest of realities, that she needed to release me in order for me to thrive—and to give her this granddaughter to love, another charm on the umbilical bracelet.

"Please . . ." I tried to block my tears by nuzzling my face into her shoulder, now so much lower than mine. "Please take care of yourself."

And then I was bawling.

And then my mother was squeezing me hard, swaddling my arms with hers. *This is my mother.* This weighty embrace. This person who could—sometimes—hug me. A real hug—the kind I'd spent a lifetime seeking. I couldn't believe this hugger was the subject of so many emergency phone calls. "Don't do anything stupid," I could barely get out.

"I'm so sorry I hurt you so much," she said, her own tears now flowing down my neck. "You are my whole world. Every single thing that is good in my life is you."

"I know," was all I could say.

Jon and Zelda stood by us and watched, silent. There was nothing to hide. I wanted my daughter to see me and my mother—our love. Under my mother's layers of skin and their frantic cells was one strong pillar, one unmovable beam, that had led to all three of us here, today.

"You are my world too, Mom."

Then she whispered in my ear: "Please don't forget me."

As if I could.

· TWENTY-FOUR ·

BREAKING THE FAST
New York City, 2012

"Ba'shana haba'a neshev al hamirpeset . . ." (In the coming year, we'll be sitting on the porch . . .) I clapped along giddily as I crooned the Hebrew song about peace and hope, wishing that Jon and ten-month-old Zelda would join in. Neither uttered a lyric, nor even a babble. They didn't know the words. My daughter's usual Manhattan sing-alongs focused on bath time and taxis; Jon played indie rock in a midlife-crisis man-band. I, however, belted out the song, wildly waving a plastic Star of David flag.

We were here to check out this synagogue, which I'd heard had a good preschool (never too early in Manhattan . . .). Jon had happily agreed to come. He was also interested in building a Jewish community for Zelda, especially as she had no local grandparents' house to host Shabbats or holidays. I'd never been a synagogue member and this was definitely the most verve I'd ever shown in a shul, but the music touched me. It was a song I'd always loved singing at my antireligious Zionist socialist school that taught—instead of prayer—1960s Israeli poetry about kibbutz romance and army medics. I'd loved this bouncy song. Mom, I remembered, loved it too.

I looked over to Jon who was smiling at me as if I was mildly insane; Zelda was in his lap and was watching the older children. "One of your favorites?" he asked, jokingly.

"Actually, yes."

Zelda, however, had less interest in the music than in kicking the chair in front of her and Jon looked only slightly less bored. Knowing his background—his all-boys Christian school, his training in saints and not *tsimes*—not to mention his desire for Zelda to have a global upbringing and education, I became overwhelmed by a realization that had never struck me before. Zelda, my daughter, might never know Hebrew, and even less likely Yiddish, Bubbie's mother tongue, and Mom's, and mine.

Just when I'd thought everything had been going well—motherhood made sense, daughterhood even made sense—here was a new complication. Zelda was becoming an independent person who needed bringing up. And Jon and I were independent people who emerged from different backgrounds and had different ideas for how to do that.

"*Bashana bashana haba-a-a-ah*," I lilted the vocal chorus, getting louder with each syllable. Jon fixed Zelda's shoe.

At least he'd agreed to come, I thought, as I waved the flag in Zelda's face. She ignored it. Its corners, I noticed, drooped down, sullen, cheap.

Jon and I shared most values, I reminded myself. Like me, he was neither self-hating nor God-fearing. We enjoyed Jewish things, but not exclusively. We married at an Orthodox synagogue for the architecture, but sans kosher caterer. We were "lobster Jews." We hosted Passover seders because we both loved the Haggadah's celebration of our five senses (and I loved any excuse to sing *"ma-l'cha ha'yam"* in both soprano and tenor). And then came baby.

"Dada!" Zelda commanded, pointing to the stage. Jon dutifully took her to the bimah and chased her as she waddled after boys twice her age. I watched, wondering if my child would ever feel connected to the grandmother who had so firmly shaped me.

Zelda, with her chubby cheeks and veiny forehead, was a mix of

Jon and me. She would have so many influences on her over which I'd have no control. My daughter will be Jewish, but not Jewish like me, I thought, just like she won't be shy like me. It was hard to imagine that the things that so define us might not define our children.

I waved across the sanctuary, but no one saw me.

Just then, the band launched into Naomi Shemer's *"Od Lo Ahavti Dai"* (I Haven't Loved Enough). I was thrown back to my childhood den, the then-bright red carpet, the Shemer records that Mom and Dad used to play on winter Sunday mornings, on the good mornings, when we all lounged around the house eating French toast that Mom had made from that week's challah. Mom always wished her parents could have afforded to send her to Jewish school alongside her brother. I remembered that she used to be an avid Israeli folk dancer, spending her summer evenings at Beaver Lake on top of Mount Royal, swaying and bouncing through the hora-inspired steps. I wondered now for the first time how she must have felt when I gave up choir, when I became a math nerd—when I turned away from her artistic interests and passions. How did Dad feel when I gave up plans for medical school and he no longer saw himself in me? I'd never before understood how difficult it might have been for them to recognize such otherness in their own child. Didn't it feel like rejection? Like not-love?

"A-A-A-I, Od Lo Ahavti Dai," I sang, suppressing very unexpected tears.

Jon picked Zelda up and, for some reason, they bolted out of the sanctuary. *Now? During this incredible song?*

I'd already had to replace several Bundist bedtime ballads with "Frogs on a Log" so we could both put Zelda down together. I'd sacrificed Polish songs for barnyard ditties. This too?

I wished Jon got it. I wished Jon had a passion for the things that made my childhood rich, defined. I remembered Dad's advice: marriage was hard enough when you were from the same religion. But I thought Jon and I were beyond these kinds of negotiations. Now I saw we weren't. Should I force Jon to be more Jewish? Could I, even? What would that do to our relationship?

I sighed.

I thought about my Jewish parents' differences. Dad was self-disciplined, an early bird who exercised every day, kept a strict no-meat diet, attended shul on holidays and Shabbat. My mother was perennially late, never kept to any regimen, and her Jewishness was entirely cultural. I thought of how one of my art historian friends, a staunch English secularist, was butting heads with her Spanish Catholic partner over their son's affiliation with a church. I knew a married couple whose careers took them to different continents; they were shipping their toddlers between them. Even Maya was struggling. She craved a cosmopolitan existence filled with travel and fine food, while her husband desperately wanted to move back to his parents' small town and preferred to spend their money on home renovations. I suddenly saw how aggravating it must have been for all of them. *Why don't you get it? My way makes sense.*

"Where were you?" I asked as Jon sauntered back to the pew. I could hear the annoyance in my voice.

"Zelda wanted to climb the stairs," he said.

"The stairs?" *But this is Naomi Shemer, the first lady of Israeli song!*

ON THE WAY home, with Zelda in his arms as I pushed the empty stroller, Jon asked: "What's with the sudden zealotry? You spent thirty years running away from your provincial community, trying to be global. All you've done your whole life is rebel."

"Exactly," I barked. "I could."

It was true, but that was my point: I had a firm cultural identity that was suffocating at times, but also gave me something to rebel against. Negotiating this identity drove my ambitions, my explorations. I wanted that for Zelda. I wanted to send her to Jewish school, not for dogma and religion, but to learn songs for Hanukkah, for *Tu b'Shvat*—the anthems of her roots.

"I want Zelda to have a firm cultural identity, a Jewish sense of self," I said, trying to sound open to discussion. Aware that I might be insulting his sense of self.

"I do too," Jon said, "but I can't educate my child to believe in a

God that I don't. I don't do indoctrination. Besides, Jewish schools are so homogenous. I worry they're substandard, focusing on which prayer to say over oatmeal rather than the development of math skills."

I didn't bother arguing that figuring out what prayer to say over porridge (Is it bread? Is it milk?) actually might enhance patterns of logical thinking. Plus, to be honest, I'd always wanted to go to an all-girls academy with uniforms, athletics, and an English curriculum not centered on Elie Wiesel. I, who spent years criticizing my "parochial" training, understood. And yet.

I let Jon's words lie between us in the warm air, wondering how all my years of travel had led me, in many ways, back home. I'd come from Somewhere, even if it was a curious and cracked place. My crazy upbringing had perhaps had more benefits than I'd ever imagined, pushing me onto the world stage for a rich, interesting ride, even if it was a journey of escape.

"I'M GETTING HER," Jon said above Zelda's shrieks. "That's it."

"No, leave her," I pleaded, putting my hand on his shoulder as if to stop him.

We were standing outside Zelda's room. It was two a.m. Again.

Jon clung to the monitor, watching her every movement. I tried to grab it but he clutched it and turned away. "We need to discuss it before we just leave her," he said.

"We've discussed it a hundred times," I said. "For five months, sleep training is all we've been discussing."

"But we never got anywhere."

"Because," I snapped, "you wouldn't go anywhere."

Jon opened the door, ran into the room and picked Zelda up, kissing her.

The other night I'd asked Jon how he'd feel about keeping a kosher home. He'd stared at me quizzically, especially because at that moment we were eating chicken-and-cheese burritos. "Um, bad." I got it. Marriage meant growing with each other, but Jon hadn't envisioned my disturbing his forty-year-old meal habits. My latent lineage was leaking out and making a mess. Having a child meant values I didn't even know I held festered up like my maelstrom of hormones. But of all our hidden ideas, sleep discipline was the worst.

"You won't even try to cry it out," I hissed. "You won't even *try* it."

"*You* tried it," he scolded quietly, "when I wasn't here." He was right. When else could I? "And she puked everywhere. You yourself said you were terrified that she would aspirate on her own vomit."

He was right again. That's why I needed him to help. "That was a few weeks ago. And maybe it would be easier if we did it together." It was horrific for me to hear Zelda cry, to imagine her feeling abandoned or ignored. But I believed that for the sake of everyone—mainly her—she had to learn to self-soothe. And of course, I needed order too. And sleep.

My exhaustion was taking over my entire physical existence. I felt semipresent throughout most of my day's activities, too lethargic to put effort even into yoga classes; I was eating an all-carb-and-caffeine diet to survive. My emotions struck with increased intensity, and I was sure this wasn't helping my relationship with Jon, who was himself wiped out. Every other night was miserable, with Zelda's relentless wake-ups and oxen resistance to going to bed. She didn't want to let go, she didn't want to miss out—both feelings I entirely understood, both feelings I worried I'd passed on, naturally or nurturally. That's precisely why I wanted to help her learn how to sleep, to help all of us rest. But I didn't want to do it alone or seem like the bad cop. I couldn't.

I watched Jon cuddling Zelda, shushing her as he paced up and down her room, no concern in the world except her immediate comfort and pleasure. *You're a pushover,* I steamed, wanting to make gagging noises. I'd teased him about being a sucker when we'd found out we were having a girl, but he was even worse than I imagined. *That's why you like me*, he always countered when I (not) jokingly mentioned it, which I thought was irrelevant. He wasn't *raising* me.

While I hated conflict and my daughter's screams, I also had trouble managing the anarchy that seemed to have taken over our house. At first, I tolerated it (managed by my extreme cleaning). I knew we were supposed to let newborns reign freely, that you could never spoil a young infant. For a while, the lack of schedule was fine—life felt like an extended flu where you were out of sync with the normal world, felt horrible and watched reruns, but you had a beautiful baby. But with time, and enough Lifetime Channel, I began to crave order and discipline. For myself, and for Zelda.

You're a terrible sleeper, Jon often accused me, as if to excuse Zelda's sleeping.

Exactly, is what I always said. *That's why I want to stop this now.*

Like religion and culture, this disagreement reflected our childhoods.

My family had enforced little discipline. There were no meal times, no bedtimes. No one believed in lunch. I grew up eating alone and watching *Three's Company* around the clock. As soon as I could, I created deadlines and schedules for myself, and I needed that for my daughter too. I liked it when the pediatrician suggested that children should be in their rooms from seven p.m. to seven a.m. It wasn't the specific hours that I cared about, but the concrete scheme. But I needed support. I couldn't create law if it would be undermined, or if Jon thought I was a monster.

Jon, on the other hand, grew up with an über-regimented, highly involved English colonial mother who had had him in bed at seven p.m. every night until he was a teenager. He'd felt constricted— his schooling, homework, TV time, his every bite controlled. As a parent he wanted to be just the opposite: chill. He wanted to have fun. He adored Zelda, and was dedicated to her—always on, engaged, affectionate. I'd been so grateful for these things—he actually enjoyed the challenge of changing diapers—but I was starting to lose patience. We were both reacting counter to our upbringings, which meant counter to each other.

In the dark I imagined that it wasn't just frazzled Jon and me, but all our parents, all four grandparents, perched around the crib. Our child was being raised by generations of ancestors, everyone's actions and reactions repeating or opposing one another.

I wondered if my own parents' discord had been in reaction to their parents. I was dizzy with the complexity of forces that went into creating any one of us.

"She's too aware and too physical for cry it out," Jon whispered. "She's too stubborn."

This was all true. Zelda was a highly active and engaged child. At three months, she slithered over to her playdate neighbor and grabbed for her hand. She was social, had long ago dropped her pacifier, stopped sucking her thumb; she'd started walking early.

But still. We needed to do *something*. We were so tired, so lost. How would all these reactions and counterreactions ever intersect?

"I'll put her down," he now said gently. "Go back to bed."

"Fine," I sighed, but I knew his generosity here wasn't an answer. I kicked my white sofa as I headed back to our room—or rather my room, as Jon was sleeping in the den these days so as not to diminish my already minimal slumber with his snoring. *Separate beds, just like my parents.* I was exhausted, but didn't sleep.

EVENTUALLY, THE JEWISH high holidays brought us back to the same synagogue, though with said hyper offspring, we managed only the first few minutes of Kol Nidre. Which had been a fine degree of observance with me, until the next afternoon.

"I need to end the fast at six," Jon said as he pushed the stroller along the East Side River promenade. He was wan. His voice was quiet. "We'll have dinner with Zelda, then put her to bed."

Here we go again, I thought, still exhausted. Yom Kippur, the Jewish fast day, the incredible day on which, six years earlier, I'd first found out about Jon's hoarded past, ended at sundown, which was 7:55, not six o'clock. The thought of eating when it was still light out felt illicit. Wrong.

Of course, I did not fear God's wrath, but I fasted diligently every year because I wanted to maintain a link to my community, to my past. I liked ritual. "Six?" I asked. "Are you sure?"

"My migraine's kicking in," Jon said. "I need to. But you should do whatever feels comfortable for you."

I cringed. Not that I didn't appreciate his gesture but it reminded me unpleasantly of my parents' relationship and how I always felt caught between them: having to choose whether to accompany my father to shul or stay home with Mom to the background of public radio. I could eat kosher like Dad, or nibble on chicken McNuggets with my mother. On Friday nights, we lit the candles and said blessings, but then everyone retired to their own rooms and we each ate dinner when we felt like it, taking turns on the crumb-lined seats, the juice-stained paper towel place mats. Just like every night.

And then I recalled one particularly painful episode.

"Who do you want to go with?" my mother had asked, the final "th" sound hissing through the station wagon.

I was sitting in the back, barred from my parents by the bench seat. On this rainy night, the car smelled of gasoline and damp; drops oozed inside through the rusted openings in the faux-wooden sideboard. Sunday nights always felt the coldest. I could sense the wet atmosphere creep up through the back of my jacket, mingle with my sweatpants, swirling in through the cotton's pores that you couldn't even see.

Both Mom and Dad had had their hands on the door, waiting to get out. Dad was going to get low-fat Edam cheese at the bakery, one of the three my parents visited every single day for provisions. Mom, on the other hand, was headed to Cumberland's drugstore, the yellow-and-red neon logo running vertically down the front of the building. She was armed with coupons, flyers, attitude. She bought what was on sale, fighting with cashiers who didn't understand her complex couponing logic. I knew she would come out with boxes of store-brand Q-tips, bottles of shampoo, free magazines from the check-out area, all the stuff she needed to fill her cracked core.

"Who, Judy?" she pushed. It was always like this. Whenever we walked on the street, Mom, heavyset and fatigued, dawdled while Dad marched ahead, and I spent my time dashing between them, trying to point out things to each, as if I was a tour guide. "Who?"

We all knew the answer. "Dad," I mumbled. "I'll go with Dad."

Dad had opened his door, pulling his hat over his ears, preparing for the cold. Mom huffed, hefted herself out of the car and slammed the door behind her. She walked to the drugstore, lugging her heavy purse which pulled down on her right side, taking the collar of her coat with it.

I knew I'd hurt her feelings.

Dad stood outside my door, waiting for me. I opened it a crack.

"I'm going to wait here."

"But it's freezing."

"I know." I shut the door. I waited. The rain beat down on the windows and I used my finger to draw condensation graffiti. Judy, Judy, in cursive, like a sitcom opener, like a package, like pretty.

"Mama," Zelda called from her stroller, waking me from my reverie. "Is windy."

"It is windy," I agreed. "How does she know 'wind'?" I asked Jon, and together, like most smitten parents, we marveled over our offspring's extreme specialness. Had my parents co-marveled like that? Or even talked about my weaknesses? It was hard to believe.

My parents' lack of unison had made me realize from an early age that there was no one way, no singular correct paradigm for religion or behavior. This lesson had its benefits, had made me more flexible and open-minded, productively critical. And, I thought in my dizzying hunger, perhaps there was a way to give my daughter options, to show her that Daddy and I were different people who—in a respectful and loving way—had certain divergent opinions.

Zelda would choose her own path; I just didn't want her to feel that choosing meant accepting one of us and rejecting the other. I understood my parents' anger at each other, but I did not want to repeat it. I did not want to reiterate their fights about baby names and food, shopping and praying. I wanted Jon and me to forge a united front.

"Mama, Daddy, holdy hands," Zelda called from her stroller seat, as if she'd read my mind, reaching her arms out to the side. I knew she wanted each of us to take one and sing "Ring Around the Rosie" as we walked down the New York street.

Jon and I both sang while pushing the stroller, and Zelda cracked up. All of us did. This was perhaps not the right sentiment for a somber holiday when we are supposed to ruminate on our sins and weaknesses, but it did remind me of how important that circle was. And it reminded me of my Judaism—tradition and religion were not about laws, but community and relationships.

Really, our differences were minimal compared to our similarities. Sure, I was a yoga nut and only had success schlepping Jon to the gym on pizza night, and we may have had conflicting approaches to shul and slumber, but we were both pragmatists, neither of us too caught up in extreme rules, like many of the no-white-flour-or-TV parents we knew. Besides, it was our differences that made us a stronger couple. I thought of our trip to Poland and how his attitude had supported my personal journey. I thought of how he dealt with his mother's hoarding, which had taught me to distance myself from what wasn't mine. His different tone had brought out my brashness and made our love, our life, possible.

So at six p.m., while the crisp sun cast shadows of water towers along the building across the street, I drank orange juice and ate whole-wheat challah with my husband and daughter, despite the fact that I could have managed two more hours of fasting, despite the fact that it was light outside. It still felt odd and wrong, but also right. I was having dinner with my family.

· TWENTY-FIVE ·

I DON'T LOVE YOU
New York City, 2013

"I don't love you, Mommy," Zelda said matter-of-factly, literally pushing my hands off her. "I love Daddy." She continued to pile plastic spoons into one of the many toddler handbags that she kept on her doll stroller.

I was silent, my eyes wide.

For a while now, Zelda had shown strong preferences: for her stuffed cow, *Itsy Bitsy Spider* videos, string cheese, and now Daddy, who carried her through the city, flipped her upside down, played Legos with her for hours, fed her Popsicles on demand. When the three of us were together, she wanted to hold only Daddy's hand when we crossed the street, preferred Daddy's lap and sat only *next* to me, and refused my help stepping down stairs even if it meant falling on her face. For a while, I'd tried to take solace in the advice of the child psychologist who assured me her reaction to me was normal, that she was defining herself against me, that this meant she felt extremely stable, that it was just a phase.

For a while, she'd been making me feel like chopped liver (or pâté, as I preferred).

But she'd never articulated it so explicitly. Extremely. Abruptly. Hurtfully.

"Here's another bag for your stickers," I offered, my voice quaking, not sure what else to say but sure that I could not show that she affected me at all. Sure that I had to keep my cool, could never explode in the ways my mother had.

"No. Stickers don't go in bags." She shook her head, disgusted by my suggestion.

She's two. Breathe.

I habitually reminded myself that I was the one who did bedtime and nighttime, who was literally there for her in the dark, that the "triangle strain" occurred only when Jon was around, that it was fine when it was just the two of us. Until now.

"I love Daddy," she chanted. "Not Mommy."

I paused, still off guard. "What do you love about Daddy?" I tried to stay positive, unaffected. Her glue. Her rock. *Just a phase.*

"Daddy carries me," she said.

That was true. "He'll be back any minute."

"Yay."

I pulled my hair back, digging into my scalp along the way. It was one thing to renegotiate my post-child relationship with Jon; now I had to do it with my child? I was confused about what role to play in this triangular equation, but I didn't want to be the short side.

"Hello?" Jon called as he came in.

"Daddy!" Zelda dropped everything and went running. I froze in the new stillness around me, the silence a reminder of how alone I was.

Suddenly, I empathized with Mom. Hadn't I run out for walks with Dad with the same gusto? It was painful, and confusing, being left on the floor surrounded by Zelda's unruly bags.

(As for Zelda's bags, I reminded myself that she was a *toddler*, not a *hoarder*. Sometimes I did worry about having passed on collector genes; I remained vigilant, knowing I'd get help if I ever noticed even the inkling of any real problem.)

"How are you?" Jon asked, coming into Zelda's room with her on his shoulders.

"I'm OK," I lied.

"Daddy, Madison!" Zelda exclaimed. She meant: put on the British band Madness so they could run around the dining room table to its bopping beats.

"All right," I called after them, "but we have to start bedtime in ten minutes."

She giggled wildly as Jon lifted her, turned on the music (particularly grating in its hundredth playing this week) and kissed her belly. He pirouetted around the dining room table, the two of them, a waltzing partnership. I began the nightly routine of arranging Zelda's room, a task I still did meticulously, putting every single toy and plastic utensil away in its place while Jon did bath time, and then I did rocking and Yiddish lullabies.

"Come, Mommy," Jon called over Zelda's hysterical laughter.

"That's OK," I said quietly. *It's OK if she just likes him better,* I told myself. *At least she has a great father.*

But then I saw myself: cleaning, organizing, instead of having fun. I was actually being like my mom, withdrawing, stuck inside my head, cerebral, working too much. Jon was hands-on, the bather, the chef. A better mom than me.

Jon and Zelda appeared in the doorway. "Bedtime," I said, at least looking forward to my Yiddish cuddle time. Jon had happily agreed to try a moderate sleep-training method I'd read about, and we'd been having mild success.

"I want Daddy to do rocking tonight," Zelda said.

"What? But I do rocking." Rocking was my chance to croon, to connect, to bridge my two Zeldas. Rocking was *my* thing.

"No, Daddy tonight," Zelda demanded.

"Sure," Jon said. "I'll do it. You go relax." Damn accommodating husband.

"Please," Zelda cried.

Don't be like Mom. Do. Not. Sulk. Don't get mad. Don't force yourself on her.

Mood Control.

"OK," I eked out.

As Jon bathed her, I adjusted Zelda's toddler alarm clock, drew the blinds and created the calm room that I'd been creating for over two years, trying to leave my stamp on the space. Then, when the rocking started, I went over to the glider to give Zelda a kiss good night on her cheek. "Too wet, Mommy," she said, wiping her face where my lips had grazed her.

I tried to think the maturest thoughts possible.

I never liked wetness either.

She was teasing me, testing me, because she felt so comfortable. This was just a phase.

I focused on the time the two of us had shared a bed on a trip to London, and she woke up in the middle of the night excited to see me right next to her. "Mama!" she'd exclaimed, scooched over and put her head on my pillow next to me. We fell asleep cheek to cheek. *It would happen again.*

Then I crossed the threshold and burst into tears. Other kids adored their mothers, were obsessed with them, overly attached. What if I just wasn't lovable? Clearly, I had no idea how to do this.

I ran into the bathroom, shut the door, made sure Zelda could not hear me. My brain whirred: I felt hurt like my mother, I acted like my mother, I nearly reacted like my mother. I knew I could not show Zelda my visceral response. Foul moods made no friends. I wanted to consider Zelda's feelings first, not scar her by being self-involved or unempathetic.

But what about me?

I looked in my minimalist wall mirror. I'd spent years cleaning up my house. Was there room for *my* emotions?

I recalled a time when I was six or seven. I was huddled into my mother's side, on my bed. My bony elbow pressed into her soft stomach, two unlikely puzzle pieces that, in that particular angle, in that moment, fit together. Her torso was warm, propped up against my pillows, nestled in my unmade bed among the factory-second blankets.

I'd had a particularly uncomfortable hangnail that day, and I rubbed it with my neighboring fingers until I enjoyed the smarting pain. Mom took my hand in her slender, soft fingers. She was hiding in my room, from my father. Dad was sitting in the den, on his chair, seething over their latest altercation while he pretended to read the newspaper.

"Judy," she said, "should I get divorced like—?"

"No!" I screamed before she finished. This was the dreaded topic of any child in the suburban 1980s, the issue at the center of all our paperbacks. Who would I live with? Who would I lose?

"You're right," she said quickly. "I won't. For you, I won't. I promise."

We were quiet, and after a pause, I thought she might be reconsidering.

"I hurt myself," I blurted out. I showed my mother the long edge of skin, hardened yet raw. My bodily abject, dangling between us. "Don't tell Dad," I said.

"I won't," she said. "I promise." Then she added: "Wash it with soap."

I imagined the soap on my skin, not sliding off but instead seeping through its different layers, cleaning everything from the surface to its bottom, the side that touched my blood. Mom and I had a special secret, and all that, on my little thumb.

Later, Mom went to the den.

"Judy," Dad hollered, "what the hell happened to your finger?"

For years, I'd remembered this as a story of betrayal, but suddenly I saw it from a different angle. Now I understood how my pain, my failings, caused Dad so much anxiety and sadness that he couldn't bear it, and so expressed his feelings as anger, which was easier, less subtle. Perhaps just as Mom had done on those Sundays when I used to walk with Dad, turning her complicated gratitude and guilt that my father had taken over elements of parenting that she couldn't manage, into rage. But there needed to be space for pain and rejection, for dread and discord—mine, Zelda's, Jon's.

I turned away from the mirror. I just had to figure out how to stop hiding, and where to put it all.

. . .

A FEW DAYS later, Zelda showed a new preference. "I don't like blue anymore," she said when I asked her why she was stripping her sheets. Up until now, blue had been her chosen hue, a color that had to appear in at least two items of clothing at every outfit change. Blue spoons were prized, blue crayons, exalted. But now, watching Zelda ripping the navy dinosaur linens off her toddler bed after having separated out and then placed all her blue colored pencils on Jon's desk, I was confused.

"But I thought it's your favorite."

"Pink!" she shrieked. "I only like pink."

"Pink?" I asked. "How do you even know about pink?"

"I love pink!" she declared, and trotted to her closet where she pulled out the pink ballerina sheets I'd bought a few weeks earlier (because she loved dance, like me)—which she had, until right now, shown no interest in. I didn't know she knew those sheets were in there. I didn't even know she could get into the cupboard. "Pink, pink, pink," she sang as she worked hard at pulling out linens.

"Why this sudden change? Why pink?"

"Because girls like pink!"

"Blue is beautiful," I said, trying to sound positive. "Some girls like blue, some boys like pink."

"No, only pink. Princesses love pink and I'm a princess and I love pink."

What had I done to create a princess monster? "But blue is so cool."

"Pink!"

It's so much more interesting to have unusual tastes, I wanted to say. *So much more artistic.* Besides, look at me: glasses, sweatpants, my PhD on feminist art and subjectivity and domestic theory, my work as a nebbishy stand-up comic, my flats.

She pulled out the sheets and fell backward. I went over to help her up. She gracefully gave me her hand, and then got up onto her tippy toes.

She'd always had girly tendencies, I thought. From an early age she adored wearing my high heels (more than I ever did) and organizing my panties in color-matched piles (I threw them in a drawer). She cared diligently for her stuffed cow Moofie, gently changing his diaper as I changed hers, putting bracelets on his arms and feeding him at every meal. She'd always been dainty, "a little lady" people called her as she ate grapes with two fingers while her friends scarfed up chicken nuggets. Even when she could barely speak, she was insistent about donning matching outfits. She loved makeup, begging me to put tiny drops of Cinderella-branded cosmetics on her face and hands.

I agreed to tiny drops, more concerned about the fact that I didn't know how. My own forays into cosmetic education consisted mainly of a trip to the Bobbi Brown counter when I was twenty-seven where the saleslady announced that I had the skin of a forty-year-old who smoked, tanned in bursts, and lived in a pollution corridor. I still felt uneasy with eyeliner, convinced my lines weren't neat and I looked like a football player.

I recalled how I'd seen Zelda that day at the synagogue, recognized that she was different from me in so many ways. I felt like my parents never really accepted my differences from them. To meet either of them, I had to slip carefully into *their* architectures. With my mother and her complex inner worlds—an Escher staircase with levels that never connected, a Magritte landscape with all the wrong shadows—it was like sliding into a soupy, disorienting mess. With my father and his narrow build, rigid and tight, constrained by blinders, not noticing much beyond Yiddish jokes and medical conversation, I had to creep in sideways, hunch my back and hold my breath. He formed a structure for me but it bent me out of shape. I had to try to avoid forcing Zelda into crevices just so she could fit within my limits.

"Girls love pink, boys love blue. Daddy loves blue. I love pink. Mommy, you're a lady-girl so you like red-pink."

There was that. The truth was that I did like red, and even some pink. I'd loved dolls growing up. I loved getting my nails done (someone else was doing it) and loved doing Zelda's nails too (up until then, in sparkling blue, a nontoxic children's brand). I'd always wished for shaving tips, for the lipstick chat. I didn't want to force my daughter to become the pedicure-partner I'd longed for, but I didn't want to deny her self-expression either. Why was I resisting giving her what she wanted?

"I love pink now, only pink," Zelda reiterated as she stretched across her toddler bed, trying to peel off her old set of linens.

"Well, then, you should enjoy it," I said. "If that's what you really like."

"Yes, I really, really do." Sheets were strewn around her. "Mama! Help, please."

"Of course." I was the one who'd bought her the sheets in the first place, I reminded myself. She loved the cartoon about the mouse ballerina, which I also enjoyed. The story lines were good, the characters funny, and the show taught children about dance. Plus, I liked the idea of young characters with creative passions.

I helped Zelda change her little nest from triceratops to ballerinas, clumsily tucking in corners (bedclothes were Jon's domain), hoping that I was enabling her to enjoy her taste, allowing her to go through necessary phases, letting her figure out who she was and what she wanted, and mostly, how to be honest with herself.

AN HOUR LATER, as I put away the morning crafts supplies, I heard torrents of screams from the kitchen. "That's it," Jon said, walking to the bedroom. "I can't take it anymore."

I tried, from the two of them, to deduce what had transpired. Something about Zelda wanting Daddy to make her pink strawberry milk but only with a pink spoon in a particular pink cup all while Jon was holding her. Fulfilling the needs of a toddler was a whole different story from a newborn.

"I need space," Jon huffed, and ran off.

I didn't say anything, made sure Zelda had plenty of room around her so she wouldn't injure herself if her tantrum got more physical, then knelt down to be at her level. I was there, but not too there. If there was one thing I'd learnt from my upbringing, it was patience with emotional breakdowns. I understood what it was like to live with someone who existed in an exaggerated version of the present, id-driven, frustrated. Only Zelda's tantrums didn't try me nearly as much. I didn't need her to be grown up for me. That wasn't her job.

Mom had, inadvertently, taught me a lot about keeping my cool. And, about the power of distraction.

"Zel," I said, when I saw she was starting to calm down. "I'm going to get you some milk. Why don't we go to your room and look at pictures of dollhouses and figure out which one we're going to buy for you?"

"Yeah!" She suddenly perked up, even though I wasn't sure she even knew what a dollhouse was.

And here I was, stuffing one down her throat. A book would have distracted her too, but I was genuinely excited about a dollhouse, recalling the positive elements of my childhood Barbie games, where I ordered my own world, created my domestic narratives. Played goddess.

Mom, who had bought me those dollhouses, adored dolls, dressing them, creating worlds with them. Bubbie, a seamstress, loved dresses and spent hours on the floor with me acting out imaginary wedding ceremonies with left-over buttons. These games, emerging from and blending with their hoards, had helped endow me with imagination, a love of making up stories, a capacity for escapism that could be useful.

Raising a strong girl, I decided, was not about what I gave Zelda to play with, but how she saw me live: working, enjoying myself, not having shame about my body or my house, not putting myself down. Following my passions and desires, even if they happened to be feminine.

"Mommy, you're shtinky, so I don't love you."

This again? "Oh, and Daddy smells great?" I asked, gently but firmly.

"Yup," she said, walking over to the other side of the room to play with Massive Bear, her giant stuffed grizzly.

I crawled over to it, lay down on its paw.

"No!" she screamed. "Massive Bear is for children, not for people. Buy your own."

Again, I felt the urge to crawl away. I also felt the urge to crack up, but I tried to conceal it. Where did she pick up these idioms?

"All right, I understand you want your own space," I said, and calmly backed off.

Then Jon came in. "Daddy can play," she said. "It's for children and men boys."

Jon, unaware of what had transpired, sat near the bear. "I love you, Daddy," Zelda said, giving him a massive bear hug.

"I love you too." He nuzzled her neck, and she climbed right on top of him, glaring back at me once.

All right. This was enough. I dealt expertly with Zelda's tantrums, but for once, I wanted to have my own. I was always promoting household honesty—I got upset when Denise lured Zelda to eat with false promises, I refused to lie to Zelda about Mones' cancer—but I faked my own feelings.

"Can I get a hug too?" I asked. "I'd really like one."

"No," Zelda said. "I don't love you."

"Zelda, that really hurts my feelings," I asserted.

"Please apologize to Mommy," Jon joined in, breaking his hug with her. Taking my side. "That was not a nice way to talk to her. Mommy loves you very much."

She was silent for a minute as she stepped around Massive Bear's contour.

"When you say things like that it makes me feel sad."

She looked at me. "Sorry, Mommy," she said, when she was ready. "I'm really sorry."

And that was it.

"Thank you." I felt like a lifelong weight had lifted. "I appreciate that."

My clean, de-cluttered apartment did have room for feelings, of all kinds. I got up and gave Jon a big kiss.

"Me too!" Zelda said, running over to join our embrace.

WEEKS LATER, I stared at the clock on my phone as I sprinted, kicking myself (metaphorically and physically). I'd been caught up in my work, and was going to be late. Damn. After several more episodes of having to tell Zelda "You're hurting my feelings," I had decided to think about ways that I might have been hurting *her* feelings, or at least, ways I could have been more present for her. Instead of withdrawing or becoming angry, I was determined to be active, to make special time for the two of us. Sometimes being present was just that—being present. I took her out for frozen yogurt. I took her to free concerts in the park. I enrolled Zelda in a new ballet class and made sure I was the one who accompanied her each week. Now, I dashed down the street, grateful that Denise was already there to get her dressed. I arrived at the dance studio just in time, sweating, and Zelda jumped from her stretch circle.

"Mommy!" She squeezed my legs, reminding me of the excitement I'd felt back in kindergarten when my mom's glowing buck-toothed smile appeared in the crowd at assemblies and class Shabbats, the events that, in those early years, she always tried to come to.

"So sorry I'm late. I'll sit right here," I said, perching on the bench, ready to make eye contact, to see her, to smile when she looked at me for approval. Eyes might not be hands, I reminded myself, but they too reassured. I couldn't pretend to be a master chef or have any knowledge of ironing. All I could do as a parent was just be me, but hopefully, with a bit more self-consciousness and flexibility.

THAT NIGHT, INSTEAD of rocking to Yiddish songs, I told Zelda stories about Princess Zelda and her best friend, Princess Zoe, who lived in adjoining pink and purple castles and ate pink and purple ice cream and dreamed pink and purple dreams. Zelda was enthralled. "And pink mac and cheese!" she added to the menu.

It struck me again how my mother's yarns and dolls left me with a passion for characters and surreal worlds. These were the fictions that Eli and I had relied on for years to communicate, to create bonds. To make fun in our family.

"Mom," Zelda asked, sitting up. "Does Princess Zelda have a baby sister?"

"What?" Had she read my mind?

"Princess Zoe has baby Anabelle. Can we go to the baby store and buy one?"

"Babies are really expensive." But also fun, I thought. And incredible. I could do it again. I could. Yes, I could! Eli and I hadn't lived in the same country in nearly two decades and were still in touch almost every day. I wanted Zelda to have a sibling, to experience that fundamental friendship. "We'll talk about it."

"Hug, Mommy!" Zelda now asked, startling me. "And another one." She grabbed me around the neck and pulled me into her.

"I love you, Mommy," Zelda said.

"Me too. I love you so much."

"So much."

"Smuch."

"Smuch."

And even though I wanted to stay in that headlock forever, I pulled away after a minute. "Good night, sweetie," I said, and kissed her madly on the cheek.

"Ooh, still too wet," she said, wiping her face with her hand.

At least she knew what she liked. I hoped that feisty decisiveness was not just a phase, but a positive segment of the survivor gene that ran in my family.

· TWENTY-SIX ·

ECTOPIC
New York City, 2013

"I'm pregnant," I whispered to Jon across the speckled diner table as I tried to engage Zelda in place mat activities. I smiled. "I can totally feel it in my uterus."

"We started trying two days ago," Jon said. "Literally."

"Just like last time . . ." Now that I knew how this whole impregnation thing worked and how insanely fertile we were, I was convinced. Jon and I had recently—very recently—decided to start trying after several doctors had freaked me out about being thirty-six. *If you want another child, I wouldn't wait even a month,* my very reasonable new GP advised a few days earlier, handing me a thirty-page document showing the latest fertility research and the rapidly declining quality of my eggs. I pictured yolks turning gray.

Here we are again, I thought a few days after the diner when I had implantation spotting. I knew it! Only this time, I was in control. I still hadn't thought through how I'd manage two children, but I was relieved to have succeeded, excited by my continued fecundity. I started calculating due dates, making appointments, planning a new life.

Which is why I was surprised to find a negative result on my pregnancy test. The single line that now resembled a stern frown, a solo I. And then, my period. An extra-long, unusual period. "Probably a very early miscarriage," GP advised, cocking his head in sympathy. "Very common. Just try again next month."

A miscarriage? Me? I felt like I'd failed. It didn't *make sense*. But I also felt unsettled. I called my OB. It was Friday afternoon. He asked me to rush in for a blood test. I did, then we set off for a road trip. But the bleeding worsened over the weekend. And on Monday morning the office called. "You *are* pregnant," the nurse said, remarkably less chipper than during my first foray into conception. "You'd better come back for more tests today." Scared, we turned the car around on the highway and headed straight to the maternal-fetal ward.

And so began six more weeks of confusion, hemorrhaging, fainting, and daylong visits to the emergency room. My blood tests kept indicating a growing pregnancy, but neither the invasive exams (performed by the entire gynecological student population of New York) nor the ultrasounds could locate where this pregnancy might be. My increasing symptoms—heavier bleeding, weakness, paleness—endowed me with a bad feeling. I could be experiencing an odd miscarriage, a loss of one twin, or, worst-case scenario, an ectopic pregnancy, a life-threatening condition where the baby implanted in the wrong spot, risking a rupture of whatever organ it was in. But my case wasn't presenting as any of the above. My work and my daughter were pushed to the side as I was either absent from home, or absent from reality, my anxiety full-blown. They couldn't find my embryo. A million tests and yet no one knew what was going on inside me.

Until one night when a whole new pain, like a shard of glass splicing through my thigh, took hold. "Jon, we have to bring Zelda to the neighbors." Ten hours, ten doctors, and ten tests later, I was on the phone with Mom, my tone militaristic. "They're still not sure, but they think it is ectopic, lodged on the very edge of my fallopian tube. In any case, they can't take a risk anymore. They're admitting me for an emergency abortion to be done with chemotherapy drugs."

"Oh my God, sweetie," she said. "I'll call Dad. We're coming."

I'm coming, I remembered myself saying, a reverse Voyageur.

"Why did this happen?" I drilled my OB, in shock. Ectopics occurred in less than two percent of pregnancies. I'd been hyper-anxious, which was supposed to stave off bad fate, my shitstorm prophylactic. It was never supposed to actually *be* the worst-case scenario.

"It could be due to scar tissue from your colitis surgery," he said. "Or, it could just be completely random." I didn't know what upset me more. That the operation that had saved me was now, twenty years later, killing me? That the ways we heal come back to haunt us? Or that there was no explanation at all?

My light-headed mind whirred. I couldn't believe it. Any of it. Chemotherapy. My bad luck. My failed pregnancy. My loss of control.

AND THAT SHE was here, in New York. This was the first time she'd left her house in two years, the first time she'd visited me since my wedding. I'd been lying on my den sofa exhausted, my limbs on strike, my eyelids heavy from the weeks of emergency rooms, dizziness, blood loss, the stress of being constantly on watch (your fallopian, they said, could erupt at any second), the risk of death, of internal explosion, implosion, and finally the chemotherapy treatment to abort the misplaced fetus. After all that, I thought the sound of her voice in the vestibule might have been a fevered delusion. "We came up with the deliveryman," she said, walking into the den with Dad.

"Special delivery," I said, pulling myself upright, heading to hug them. "Thank you for coming," I whispered into my mother's black sweatshirt. *She had come to help. Despite everything, she had come.*

I was so happy to have them there, with me, in my space. Mom and Dad went on laughing about the coincidence of them arriving at the same time as the food, but suddenly I thought of the dwindling life in my stomach that would never get delivered. *I lost my baby. Eyes, ears, nose. I might never be able to have another baby.* I sat down, shaking. "Can I get you a drink?" I tried to sound fine.

Mom stood in the doorway, behind her the teak dining room table—her table, which we'd had refurbished. She didn't look around, didn't ask for a tour, as I would have. As always, I wondered what she saw when she saw me. "Sure, some water would be nice."

Motherhood and daughterhood kept me on my toes.

THE NEXT MORNING, Zelda awoke at six a.m. "She's up, Mom." I nudged her. Mom was sharing my bed and had planned to wake up with me and help me take care of Zelda, especially since I still wasn't allowed to lift things. Mom was being like a regular mom!

"Coming, coming," she said, but she didn't move.

Attuned to Zelda's cries, the most extreme of alarm clocks (no snooze button once you have a baby), I rolled to my side and out of bed as gingerly as possible, darting to her room. I'd wanted Jon, who'd been taking care of the two of us for weeks, to sleep in.

"Mama," Zelda said when she saw me, and I hugged her in the crib. I'd been trying so hard to keep my normal routine going these past two months, to be there for Zelda as much as possible between hospital visits. To at least be physically present, even if mentally I was panicking. "Out!" Zelda instructed.

I stared at the door. No Mom. I sighed. "OK, sweetie." I lifted her as carefully as possible, trying to concentrate all my effort into my arms. I placed Zelda down on the floor and she ran out of her room to an approaching Bubbie.

"Judy, why did you lift her? Why didn't you wait for me?" Mom asked, finally appearing.

"You weren't here," I mumbled. "It's fine. I'm fine. Just help me feed her."

Zelda was already at the kitchen table, her arms reaching up to her high chair. I knelt down. "Bubbie's going to put you in your chair this morning."

Mom held her arms out at a distance. Zelda looked at her awkward pose. "No!"

"It's OK, sweetie. Bubbie is going to help me carry you today."

"No!"

I watched my mother's face crumble. She backed away.

"Mom, just do it," I said.

"But she doesn't want me to," Mom whispered.

"She's just a toddler," I whispered back, annoyed. She'd been so good with Zelda as a baby, but it was different now that Zelda had opinions. Or was it Mom's increasing age? Her condition? Regardless, I saw in my mother's eyes the hurt of rejection that I now understood too, a primal insecurity, a horrid sense of failure. I saw the disappointment of her life: how she'd wanted nothing more than to be a mother but could never play the role as she dreamed.

I recalled a few months earlier, during our last trip to Montreal, when Mom had pulled me aside, told me she'd found a letter I'd sent her from camp when I was eleven. I wrote that I saw how stressed and tired she was; I promised that when I got home I would cook my own dinners and take care of myself so she would not have to take care of me. *How could I not recognize how horrible that was?* she'd asked me, twenty-five years later, tearing up. *If I read it in a book, I would have found it an awful, heartbreaking scene, but in my own life, I just didn't see the problem.*

Despite this revelation, she had not changed. She'd been hospitalized several more times, but each time had been so useless, so traumatizing for her, I began to wonder who was crazier, her or her psychiatrists. And here she was. Our connection might have been dysfunctional, but it was fierce. My family was both more pathological and more loving than I ever remembered.

"Just pick her up," I said softly.

Mom halfheartedly put her arms out again. Zelda cried "No!" even more loudly, and I couldn't bear it. I couldn't bear the hurt my mother was experiencing, all the hurt I'd put her through, admitting her to hospitals, yelling at her—I wanted only the best, but still, I caused her so much pain. She was so vulnerable, her emotions like a toddler's.

"Don't worry," I said, and quickly picked Zelda up and put her in the chair.

. . .

AN HOUR LATER, I saw that Dad wasn't all that different. After he awoke at seven, complaining he was still tired from his night on the couch, he came into Zelda's room where we'd been playing. "Zaidy!" Zelda shrieked excitedly, which delighted him. For about a minute. Then he got up.

"But Zelda's so excited to see you," I said quietly as he left.

"Boy, she has energy." He shook his head in pleasure as he waddled to the den to watch his new favorite cable channel (There's a Jewish Channel?—who knew?) which he'd discovered the night before.

Zelda was hyper, a handful, and he was older and exhausted, but still I felt upset. I remembered him playing with Eli and me all the time, though mainly games like "crazy hospital" where he was the patient and lay on the sofa reading newspapers as we operated on him. Were my parents always this removed from me and Eli, or was it their age? The nature of grandparenthood? I was noticing different things about them now that I was a parent too, which was both elucidating and unsettling.

Denise arrived and we got Zelda ready for a concert in the park a few blocks away. I'd suggested that we all go, but as soon as I corralled the Batalions, trouble ensued. Mom insisted on bringing her wheeled suitcase filled with documents. It was too heavy for me to roll even without my recent fallopian drama, and Dad didn't want to help either. Mom hollered that we were walking too fast, and she couldn't make it to the park. Like my childhood self I dashed between Mom and Dad and then even Zelda and Denise too, trying to negotiate everyone's wishes, everyone's paces, a frantic mouse scurrying along the sidewalk. "I can't go on," Mom said, after one block. Dad, though he refused to walk next to her, also refused to go on without her. I waved Denise and Zelda away along with my own sadness about the lost bonding opportunity. There were so few chances for us all to be together. I didn't understand how my parents couldn't see that.

"Let's just get something to eat," Dad said.

"I don't care," Mom said, in a huff.

"There are lots of breakfast options," I began, eager at least to show them Chelsea dining. I ran through the list of bagelerias, Italian bakeries, Israeli and French diners, breakfast taco joints, high-end sit-down.

"What's that?" Dad interrupted, pointing across the street.

"Oh, it's just a deli."

"That's as far as I can go," Mom said.

To the deli? There was nothing for me to eat at the deli. It took every bit of strength left in my overworked dying cells not to scream that if she didn't drag around her bags, she might be able to go a bit farther. In every way.

"Fine." I sulked like a teenager, still playing pinball between them, knowing it was easier to be angry than sad.

An hour later, Mom walked home with us, but didn't enter the apartment. "I have things I'd like to attend to," she said. Was she getting Zelda a gift from buybuy Baby? A breakfast I'd like? I wondered why she could suddenly walk. I knew she moved literal mountains of junk to be here; I knew leaving her house for another country was an enormous emotional challenge; I knew she wanted the best for me. But still, I felt rejected. "Where's she going?" I asked Dad to break the new silence.

Dad deliberated. "Probably banks," he said as we got in the elevator.

We rode up in the rickety car, and I waited for Dad to explode, but he was silent.

"What can you do?" He shrugged his sagging shoulders. "I used to get angry, so angry. But she's sick. She's really sick. It's pathetic that such a brilliant person lives in a state of constant internal terror, as if she's the victim of a massive impending threat."

His resignation seemed noble, his sad acceptance honest. In his way, he loved her; he really, really loved her. Just as he loved delis and didn't need fancy croissant hybrids. His needs were different

from mine, his happiness achieved in ways that I might deem code-
pendent or false, but who was I to say? I reminded myself how terrifically lucky I was that he'd stayed with her, cared for her, been so
utterly dedicated, allowing me to have all the freedom in the world,
to run away and have my life.

"Are you still hungry? Do you want anything else?" I offered, as
if that would make up for my leaving him.

"No, no, I'm stuffed. Delicious eggs."

It was strange to me, how hard it was to make peace with my
own parents' happiness. Or at least, their comforts.

As soon as we entered the apartment, I plopped down on the
sofa, convinced I couldn't have walked another step. My uterus was
contracting, the abortion at work. I did anything not to imagine my
baby being squished, suffocated, my fallopian tube like a noose. It
took all my strength to turn on the TV to *The New Adventures of Old
Christine*. I lay on one side of the couch. Dad sat with the *New York
Times* and the remote on the other. For nearly forty years, I thought,
these were our positions. I'd be sick, he'd be there, mirroring me,
watching reruns alongside me.

"Hey, you think we can change it?" he asked this time. "I can't
even hear what they're saying."

My eyelids at half-mast, I looked over to Dad, his crouched back,
his deepening web of wrinkles, his sinking features. He was nearly
eighty. He had recently sold his parents' house on Carlton. I could
barely believe it, but he had, ridding himself of almost all the con-
tents, letting go. Kildare remained a disaster, but my parents had sold
their parents' homes, overcome their attachments. I wondered, what
was left?

And then, as I dozed off, the fear and anxiety of the past ten
weeks, the past two years, crashed through my mind. Birth was so
much about death. Zelda's dangerous delivery, the incredible fragility of newborn life, the way that having a child made me realize that
I was next in line, a cog in a very simple generational scheme, your-
job-on-this-earth-is-done-thanks. We are all replaceable, the life
cycle cackled, just as I'd begun to realize how important my exis-

tence was to someone else, how utterly damaging my end would be to Zelda. Reaching thirty-five, middle age. And then, this. The pregnancy that nearly imploded me, my fetus that had to be aborted.

I touched my stomach that was contracting in more toxin-fueled cramps, and held back tears. I would have to wait at least three months for the chemo to leave my system before trying to conceive again. But I knew with a ferocious certainty that I wanted to have another child, to make more life. And pronto. I wanted to be able to spend as many days with my future as possible.

I *wanted* to mother.

"Are you coming out to the diner tonight?" Dad asked when I awoke from what must have been an hours-long nap.

I wanted to hang out with Dad. I wanted him to enjoy himself. He never traveled anymore: this could be his last vacation. Then again, I could barely move. "Not sure."

"Come on," Dad said. Though he'd taken a backseat in this diagnosis, he'd still been dissuading me from even Motrin. "I want you to come."

My whole life had been trained by Dad's bravado, his refusal to surrender to the elements and facts, but even he'd finally given in to the reality of my mother's illness. Some things were unchangeable. Death was everywhere, bigger than me, poking into my every organ, obvious.

I could have done it, could have taken on his challenge, beat the body, asked Jon to babysit. But I was sick. I was really sick. "Not tonight," I said softly. "I don't feel up to it. But you and Mom can go." That's what was left. Them. Mom would go with him. And they'd be fine. Even happy, in their way.

"OH, HONEY," MY mother said, sitting on my side of the bed late that night, her weight pressing down so that my head popped up. My bed. My king-size marriage bed, in my white-walled bedroom, with white carpets, white fixtures, a white light, and nothing more. Her presence, heavy, dark, ungeometric, was in every way out of place. Talk about ectopic.

"Sweetheart," she said, shaking her head. She took my hand in hers, and I felt her fingers, still so skinny, so elegant and smooth, anachronistic. The lock of our grip recalled a yoga gesture, the kind when the instructor tells you to intertwine your fingers with the awkward hand on top, the unfamiliar feeling like you are holding hands with a stranger instead of yourself. Only now we were bonding two different bodies, strangers and selves. The blue light of the baby monitor cast a shadow over us, and I looked to the screen to see Zelda, sprawled out like a sunbathing angel, dreaming in her own head that somehow came out of me. What did I know of my daughter's inner life? What did Mom know of mine? As if in response, my stomach jolted with a pang, and I was reminded of the "fetus reabsorbing into my abdomen" as they put it, its juices merging with mine, its tiny cells becoming one with my own, squeezing in between my organelles, forever a part of me. We are not just made up of our dead ancestors, I thought. We are also our dead children.

"It's so unfair," she whispered. "It's so unfair that this happened to you."

"Thank you," I said. Things had been going so well, calm, settled, happy, forward. And then this. God's little trick. As if he was saying, you did it. You learned to have a positive attitude, to dream, to want. Learned to feel good about your life. So now: life.

Or not.

"It's so, so unfair," Mom repeated, her hips sinking farther into my mattress, her fingers squeezing tightly. I recalled once again how she was the one who was there after my colitis surgery, in the recovery room, holding my hand. That very surgery that was, twenty years later, possibly responsible for this disaster. She was right. It was so unfair. That our cures created their own problems. That I'd spent so many years in hospitals. That she was how she was.

That now that I wanted to be pregnant, I couldn't be, and might never be again.

Tears welled up in my eyes. "Thank you," I repeated. In all the weeks of hospitalizations, I hadn't had a chance to think. To feel. *It was so unfair.* "Thank you."

"It's horrible, Judy, just horrible, horrible."

"Thank you."

"No, really horrible. Really, truly, horribly, horrible."

"Th—" But I stopped. I turned on my back, and out of the corner of my eye, glimpsed my current bedfellow: Mom's one hundred–pound suitcase of files that she'd hid under Jon's pillow. I'd always made room for her in each and every one of my beds, and yet hers had always been full, covered in clothes and papers, no room for me. I couldn't watch TV with her. I couldn't crawl in when I had a nightmare.

"Horrible," my mother repeated, her voice growing thin, distant. Internal.

"No," I said, seeing the clean life around me and the successes I'd created. I'd been so lucky to survive this ectopic pregnancy intact. "It's really not that horrible. But you're right, it is very, very unfair." There it was, the word I'd never felt comfortable with. "Unfair" meant random, it meant it wasn't my fault, or anyone's fault, no excuses, no blame; it meant it was out of my control. So much was out of my control. The bad—I touched my stomach; then glanced at Zelda's grainy image on the monitor—the good too.

I clutched my mother's fingers, still slender, still firm against their underlying bone. Still alive. Still there.

· TWENTY-SEVEN ·

EMOTIONAL EDUCATION
New York City, 2014

"We're leaving in ten minutes," I called out, giddy. Sure, it was seven forty-five a.m. and school started at nine o'clock, but that was just it. School was starting! In the previous week, I'd reread all the parent handbooks and notices, labeled Zelda's clothes, and pored over calendars. I barely slept the night before and that morning, I'd been up with her since six, preparing her backpack with a small favorite oinking pig toy, two outfit changes, and snacks for the road. I'd gotten Zelda dressed (only an all-pink ensemble would do), fed her breakfast, put her hair in a ponytail for maximum visual clarity, and hummed tunes about teddy bears touching their toes and going off to the academy.

Any more gusto, and Zelda, though only two and a half, would likely have murdered me.

Fortunately, she remained as excited as I was. "I'm going to school today," she said to Denise, "like a big girl." Well, maybe not *as* excited, but still.

Denise now corralled my daughter into a sweatshirt and prepared the stroller. She still helped care for Zelda, but I'd decided that

I was going to be the one to take my daughter to preschool—not just today, but for the entire "separation" process, if not forever. This was the beginning of my daughter's independent existence. I wanted to be the entity against which she divided, and unlike my mom, who worked full-time, I had the flexibility to be the bow that had to bend for Zelda's launching into the world to occur.

I was also worried. Was I a solid enough presence for her to separate from?

"Take a photo, Daddy," I requested, putting a cup of cold coffee in Zelda's hand. "The beginning of education." Jon, still in his bathrobe, nabbed a shot.

Zelda was not impressed. "Let's go, Mama," she said, a little bit rolling her eyes.

I cruised down the street, my feet bouncing as I pushed the Bugaboo. I checked the time repeatedly. At the parents' meeting a few nights earlier, they'd warned that bringing children to school late might make them feel like the last one to enter a cocktail party, insecure about where to go or who to mingle with. Preaching to the overly converted, I'd thought. But that flame of warning only got my early tendencies warmed up. It was eight a.m. The preschool was twenty minutes away, max.

"Mama, snack," Zelda said. I reached into my specially prepared snack pocket and whipped out several Cheerio-based options. I double-checked that I'd brought along everything, including Zelda's summer "homework." Back in July, each preschooler had been sent a beautiful, pristine white notebook that they were to fill with specific information about themselves: my favorite books, songs, foods. My imagination had gone wild, planning meticulously arranged collages, sticker work, and a sparkling pink "Zelda" scrawled minimalistically across the blank canvaslike cover. "Um, *her* homework," Jon had reminded me.

"But with *our* guidance," I had argued. (The legacy conflict struck again, generations perched on those white pages: Jon's mother had supervised all his homework; my parents never even knew what homework was.) Then, I braced myself, and let her explore "the marker" by making red streaks across the entire middle page range.

Though the creative collaboration was successfully adorned with a shimmering "Zelda" on the front, inside, the blank slate was filled with shades and doodles, bright yellows and purples, prints and finger traces. It also resulted in a lot of leftovers: spare photos of Zelda, bits of drawings, tracings of her hands. It was terrifically difficult for me to throw out these scraps of her creativity and growth, these markers of our togetherness and happiness, even though I knew there would be thousands more. For the first time, pausing over the recycling bin, I understood how hoarding could be a form of love and connection: even more than photos, a way to capture the good times.

"Mommy, will you come to school with me or will you wait outside?" Zelda asked between mouthfuls. I'd been explaining the separation process over the past few weeks.

"I'll probably come in for a bit, and then I'll wait right outside when the teacher tells me to," I said. "But I'll be right there in case you need me." I brushed her cheek with the side of my hand.

"Don't worry, Mama," she said, her new favorite expression. "I'll be OK."

Heart. Broken. "I know you will, sweetie."

This preschool, like most in our neighborhood, had its own "separation philosophy," though unlike other schools, this school did not publish booklets about their ethos. Selecting a preschool for Zelda had been a high-end Manhattan nightmare, taking up the better part of the preceding year. Rounds of tours, open houses (if you could even get in), cross-fire interviews ("What's your parenting philosophy?" *Um, Stoicism? Pragmatism? Absurdism!*), elevator pitches ("Quick: describe your child in one word"), essay applications ("She aced the APGARs"), reference letters, schmoozing at Zelda's movement classes so I could collect names to drop, two-hour PowerPoint sessions on the ideology behind the running of a crafts corner, and serious parents armed with lists of prepared questions who seemed like they'd just come from Mommy-and-Me physics. At some schools you had to apply in order to be put into a lottery in order to apply. It was both ridiculous and fascinating, insane and interesting in how conscious it made Jon and me about selecting a pedagogical approach for our particular child. We had to really think about what was important to us, and for her (even though she was still one).

I didn't take it lightly. School—albeit less fancy school—had been my savior. There I had ownership, control over my little gray desk, which I kept meticulously neat. I'd needed the rigor of schedules and bells, clean tiles and grades, clear systems with straightforward rewards and punishments. I felt in control of my achievements, and had gotten attention for them.

As such, I'd been somewhat shocked by the alternative, deskless, Continental-influenced philosophies of many New York schools that prided themselves on teaching fruit cultivation, yogic collaboration, and emotional buoyancy. (More taboo than feeding your child juice was asking about literacy or numeracy.) But of course, as I saw Zelda convulse with joy in the large doll corners during the "playdate" assessments, I reminded myself that she did not come from the same house I had. She did not have the same need for order, and I wanted her ambition to emerge, not from pathology, but from internal curiosities, as these schools claimed to develop. Plus, couldn't I have done with some emotional buoyancy classes myself? ("Do you offer courses for thirtysomethings?" I asked on one tour. "How can an insecure parent raise a secure child?" I'd wanted to ask on all the others.)

To top it off, through this process I'd been through another depressing one: secondary infertility. After the chemo treatment, I suffered from shortness of breath, which led to CAT scans, which led to severe allergic reactions, then worse shortness of breath—a new cycle of emergency hospitalizations. I'd been treated for odd asthmas, afraid to leave my house by myself for weeks on end, terrified to care for Zelda alone lest I stop breathing. When Jon traveled for work, I had a roster of friends stay over. In the end, a specialist pulmonologist showed me that nothing was wrong but my brain mechanism; I was breathing fine even though I perceived myself not to be. I had to consciously talk myself out of, basically, panic. The unexpectedness and lawlessness of the ectopic pregnancy, the fragility of my life, the way that an implantation that was just a few millimeters off had caused such vast repercussions, had taken its toll. Many months later, I was still exhibiting symptoms and being followed, sometimes daily, at a fertility clinic uptown, taking hormones, trying to rebalance my damaged system that had never returned to normal so I could conceive again. I was frantic to make a family. I'd become desperate to give Zelda a sibling, feeling terrible that my body was failing her and might not provide her with this fundamental companionship, a fellow in the face of her parents with whom she could negotiate love and hate and learn to couple—the longest relationship of her life. Plus, making a choice about Zelda's preschool seemed even more urgent: it was looking increasingly likely that she'd be my only child. My only chance to get it right.

"We're almost at school," I announced to Zelda, slowing down.

"Is it there?" Zelda asked, pointing to the leafy courtyard in the distance.

"Yes, you remembered!"

In the end, we'd chosen the synagogue preschool. Jon had been taken, not by the Israeli classics, but by the down-to-earth tone of the director who'd welcomed us by saying how insane the preschool admission process was, and how she never even told parents when elementary school pretesting was going on so as not to worry them. We'd both been drawn to the small class sizes (especially if Zelda's classmates were going to be her "sibling substitutes") and the community focus. The school did not offer a toddler ceramics atelier, science lab, or organic sustainable rooftop garden like several of the others, but an in-house therapist was available to chat with parents every Friday (only in New York).

I looked at my clock. Eight thirty-five.

The first ones in her class to arrive.

"Let's read a book in the library," I suggested, embarrassed by my overcompensating tendencies. No one wanted to be the *first* guest at a cocktail party either.

"Yay!" Zelda replied, and I felt a bit better. At least my insanity could make her happy, I reasoned, but reminded myself that too-early might be just as pathological as too-late.

I had Zelda get out of her stroller and cross the gate into the yard by herself, as the teachers had instructed, and made sure Zelda walked down the stairs to the school independently. I was still the ambitious student, following all the rules.

Zelda picked a book in the library and we read it as I checked the time and watched to make sure that the door to her class hadn't opened yet. Other children and their moms (it was all moms today) began to arrive. I'd met most of them before at parent events; two of them had even gone to the same school as me in Montreal (talk about a return to the shtetl). I tried to exchange smiles, but couldn't quite make the right eye contact from my seat. "Oh my God," I heard one mom say to another. "Did you get those yoga pants in Southampton?"

Another was carrying a Balenciaga diaper bag. A third wore heels. And she was nine months pregnant!

These women were so put together.

Suddenly, I felt like I was back in time, on the first day of high school, the girl who wore puffy, bright blue polka-dot shorts that the night before had seemed so cool. I thought of Mom, and how she didn't wear Roots aerobics gear. I remembered Bubbie, arriving with her orange and brown headscarves, her plastic bags of produce. Oh God. Was I, in my Gap leggings and tattered sweatshirt, without makeup, *that* person?

Fortunately, the class doors opened and I snapped back into taking Zelda into her new life. Parents had been instructed to sit in the chairs at the edges of the room, and to interact with one another, and their kids, as little as possible. I found a seat alone (unlike some other moms, who knew one another already and pulled their chairs together) and watched, reminding myself not to feel left out, that I was there for Zelda.

Zelda immediately went to the Play-Doh station and began to create a multicolored mountain. I wasn't sure how she would react in class—she was older and more verbal than many of the children, and Jon and I had been worried she would boss them around or act out in frustration. She could be feisty, demanding. But instead, I saw a girl who concentrated on her activities, who was quiet and obedient, who looked up to observe everything that was going on around her. When any of the teachers spoke, she froze and gave them her full attention, doing exactly what they ordered. If they asked her a question, she replied. I saw someone who put her colored pencils away. I saw a real student. I saw—lord almighty—a mini-me.

Sure, Zelda and I shared the same large eyes and lips, even the same current wardrobe—she was wearing Gap leggings, an oversize shirt, and purple sneakers like me. But used to her social confidence, her delight and ease introducing herself to older children in the playground, her tendency to chase and tackle boys, I'd always pegged her as a mini-Jon. I'd never before seen her act so much like I recalled myself acting.

But even more surprising was what I saw next. Zelda moved across the space to pick up another child's doll-accoutrement mess. *My daughter likes to clean up.* Then she put each bottle in its right place. *My daughter is a neat freak!*

She'd always been big on classifications (shouting "dog," "cat," or "girl," "boy" at passersby on the street) and went crazy if her sippy cup rested on the windowsill instead of the side table. I'd put those tendencies down to toddlerhood, but maybe they ran deeper.

For years, I'd blamed my own order obsession on my parents. It was their disarray that pushed me to array, self-consciously, madly. But perhaps my organizational tendencies had not been in reaction to them, but simply ingrained. Instinctive. Perhaps I just wasn't brought up in the ideal context for me (and why Jon was so much less affected by the hoard of his home). As a child—and especially one raised in a psychoanalytic age—I blamed everything on nurture. But as a parent, I was starting to think that a lot was due to nature.

"Adults," the head teacher said. "It's time to say 'bye. You can wait outside for the rest of the session."

I kissed Zelda, assured her I'd be outside in the coffee corner that I'd pointed out to her on our way in, and left. She waved.

"So you're a writer," one mom said as we walked to the sofas. "That's great. What do you work on?" She was interested, talking to me. I breathed in relief.

Conversation turned to career changes, summer camps, and the best places to get rapid strep throat tests. Though these moms did not at first seem like my natural social crowd, and I had no idea what parental demons *they* might be combating, they were warm and welcoming. And, we had our children in common. And, I reminded myself, Jon hadn't even seemed like my social crowd. The truth was, like Mom, like Bubbie, there was no way I would wear mascara in the mornings or carry handbags and designer juices. I'd wear outfits that were comfortable and carry my laptop and triple espressos. I could still be friendly, and be an overinvolved-but-trying-not-to-be school mom in my own particular way. By maintaining my differences, I told myself, I also hoped to teach Zelda a bit of "outsider vision," as my parents had taught me through their odd, critical, humorous perspectives. I wanted to raise a daughter who felt belonging and passion but was still quirky. Let's say, productively off-kilter.

Besides, I may not have looked like a typical school mom, but I looked like the mother *I'd* always fantasized having.

"Judy." The school director approached, grinning. "I was just in the classroom. One of the boys was crying and Zelda went up to him, gave him a hug, and told him that there was no reason to cry because his mommy was sitting outside having coffee."

I laughed, my heart aching from her maturity, her instinctive gentleness.

"She was probably saying it to soothe herself," the director said. "Probably to soothe them both."

"Either way," I said, secretly exploding with *naches* and gratitude.

Then, as if no time had passed at all, it was done. We were being called back to pick up our children. I waited in the line and when it was my turn, the teacher called for Zelda. My baby had been sitting on the floor cross-legged, clutching her backpack. Now she bounced up, sprinted across the room and straight for my arms, laughing, grabbing at my neck, hugging me harder than she'd ever hugged me before, kissing my cheeks and lips. "You came back, Mommy," she exclaimed as other kids started to trample over us.

"Of course I came back." I kissed her forehead and squeezed her back. "I told you I would, and I did."

Then she wiped her nose all over my shoulder.

I breathed, and let the wet lie. I'd passed separation.

"Mama, Mama," she chanted as we walked out.

"Yes," I said. "Yes."

· EPILOGUE ·

MOTHER OF ANOTHER
New York City, 2014

The doctor's office almost never called me, and when they did, it was important. My heart fluttered as I answered. I knew they had the test results.

Everything was normal. "Do you want to know the sex?"

My eyes stung with tears. It had been eleven weeks, and still I could not fathom that I was actually pregnant, holding life inside me. Nearly a year after my ectopic, a year of infertility and continued symptoms, a scan revealed that only one of my tubes worked—if that. My otherwise patient reproductive endocrinologist had advised that at my age, there was no point waiting. I had nightmares about IVF ripping open my stomach, my body once again pulled apart in a fertility attempt, and it was with much hesitation that I agreed to review the forms and contracts, all the while my gut telling me that perhaps my gut wasn't getting pregnant for a reason and I should leave it be. Zelda was enrolled in school; our lives were once again organized, structured. Even my mother's condition seemed to have plateaued, and though she was not leaving her house at all, she was generally in a calmer mood. Perhaps I could move on. Perhaps not. I transferred my files to the IVF ward and made my intro appointments.

Then, the test. This time, it was a home test, digital. I left the bathroom, unable to watch it work. Zelda was asleep. Jon was out of town. I paced. I texted him. Then I went back to the bathroom. No two parallel lines.

Instead, a flashing "YES."

Shaking, I threw the stick in the air.

I texted Jon the picture. MAZEL TOV, I whispered to myself.

(Then I called ten times until he woke up. It was five a.m. in the Midwest.)

A mad week passed until doctors could confirm the pregnancy was in the uterus. I giddily joked: *My Jewterus saw the prices of those fertility treatments and said forget it, I'll do it myself!* My hormone levels skyrocketed. I'd spent the better part of the past six weeks on the sofa, binge eating toast, gaining ludicrous amounts of weight, suffering searing headaches, bitter nausea, faintness, palpitations. An eyebrow fell off. Where the first pregnancy had been a complicated surprise, this one had been badly wanted. Where the first pregnancy had been all emotional turmoil, this one had been all physical turmoil. I'd promised myself I was going to enjoy pregnancy if it ever happened to me again, and instead, I felt horrific and lived in constant fear of a miscarriage, bracing myself for the sight of blood every single time I went to pee (which was twenty times a day).

The difference in symptoms, I was certain, meant it was a boy. Besides, there were so few girls in Jon's and my family—we had loads of uncles, no biological aunts at all. Jon and I had even, against all superstitious wisdom, picked out a boy's name. I envisioned a family like mine, older sister, younger brother.

"Yes," I said. "I want to know the sex."

The nurse was chipper. "Girl."

My hands felt fuzzy. I almost dropped the phone. "Another girl?" A girl. A girl? A girl! No way had I expected this, imagined this, being part of an estrogen team, living in a gaggle of gals. *I'll never have a son*, rang through my head. *I won't re-create my childhood family.* But that thought was quickly replaced with: another daughter. As different a person as my first. A new line, this one lateral. I'd have a clan, a team, a whole nexus of relationships. I'd have another chance to redo the mother-daughter bond.

More love. More dynamics. More family. More work. More healing. Eventually, more sassy teenage daughters. More. More. More.

THAT NIGHT, I dreamt that my pregnant friend Emily and I were looking for shelter, and we entered a building for intellectually handicapped children. The floor was quiet, white. Hushed murmurs peppered the background. I suggested we get into the elevator and go upstairs. The lift moved slowly, carefully, like liquid oozing up a syringe, until it didn't. Suddenly, the elevator completely veered off course, routing us right up through the building as if shooting up a roller coaster and jetting us out into the sky, turning the entire building's roof into a shambles of tiles and shards that crashed around us, my heart in my throat along with my stomach, my lower half tingling in midair.

I woke up, my chest palpitating, drenched. More. More. More. More *mess.*

I went into the den to where Jon had been banished with the child monitor and shook him awake. "Where are we going to put her?" I thought of friends who had two children, of their houses strewn with plastic toys and pasta.

"Hmm," he said this time. "Do you have to keep waking me up for this stuff?"

"Sorry," I said. "But yes." *Strollers. Carriers. Teethers and pacifiers. Stacks of molded tuna cans.*

"Well, at least this time, in our two-bedroom, it is a good point." *Buried alive.* "Shit."

"Don't worry," he said. "You won't lose your makeshift office."

But as I retreated to our room, my stomach bloated and in-between—no kicking yet, but not just-me either—I realized that there were solutions. The girls (the girls!) could share a room. Or the baby could go in the den. Or, I could move my desk to my room, or place it near the bookcase. My brain was with me, transportable, permanent; I would not lose it. The transition to motherhood had been made; this was just an administrative challenge. I knew that there would be moments of calm, and ones of sheer exhausted chaos. I would be on top of some things, and way beneath others. There would be mess and order, progression and regression, panic and peace. Everything would seem slow, easy, even boring, and then take a bender, shoot me through the roof.

Plus, we already owned the equipment. There was nothing new to buy, no need to add to the "hoard." The nursery already had color, even blue pen marks on the white walls where Zelda had once scribbled, and I had survived. It took me thirty years to feel independent, and three years to feel like a mom. I knew already that I'd go through all the anxiety again, relearn lessons; only this time, I hoped, I'd do it a touch more quickly.

Now my mind reeled with a squillion plans. We'd move the changing table to the den, the bassinet to the living room, the soft toys from storage. We'd be at the preschool for six years; Zelda would enter kindergarten as baby would begin. Then again, I reminded myself, touching my tummy, who knew who this new creature would be, what she would be like, how our home would evolve, and what walls we'd have to build—maybe even new partitions?

I'll work it out in time, I thought, carefully getting into bed. Or maybe, I considered, the baby could sleep with me for a while. No walls at all. Zelda had shown me that there was so much space in my cleared home, in my heart. I could fit worlds inside without suffocating or bursting open.

I turned over to find a comfortable position and looked up to see my ceiling hovering high above me. I'd make room for us all.

AUTHOR'S NOTE

The act of writing memoir is an act of cleaning up: one creates, rather than finds, clear narrative strands that run through the messy material that comprises a life. No wonder I've always been drawn to this form that seeks answers, developments, straight lines. In sculpting this narrative—which is, needless to say, told from my singular perspective and one that continues to change as I grow—I've had to make tricky choices. Consciously, I've obscured names, dates, and identifying characteristics of certain people and events portrayed in this book for literary cohesion and to protect privacy. Subconsciously, as I've attempted to convey experiences from decades back, I'm certain I've made changes as well. Memory is fluid, flexible like pregnant ligaments, bending unexpectedly to suit unusual poses. It is difficult for me to recall past scenes without my knowledge of present ones, of current diagnoses, of how the story turned out. I did the best I could to authentically portray my recollections.

ACKNOWLEDGMENTS AND CREDITS

It takes a village to raise a child, but it took an urban megalopolis to nurture this book. Thank you:

To the editors and producers at *New York Times* Motherlode, Salon, *Anderson Live*, *Jerusalem Post Magazine*, Nerve, Babble, Tablet, and Jewish Telegraphic Agency who first enabled me to share bits of my story.

To my most incredible and savvy book team (dare I say, book mothers): Tracy Bernstein, for wisdom, wit and kindness, for diligence down to the detail, and for tremendous patience with this terrible hoarder of words; Lauren Burnstein for ardor and acumen; and Alia Hanna Habib, for believing in my voice, and consistently reminding me to follow it.

To Sarah Mlynowski and Leigh McMullan Abramson, for such generous, gentle care and commentary in the final stages of book labor. To Kimberlee Auerbach Berlin for cheering me on at conception. To Amy Klein, Susan Shapiro, Melissa Johnson, Trey Sager, Nicole Bokat, Abby Sher, Sue's Thursday group, Columbia University workshops, and all the writers and teachers who've helped heal and shape me on the page, and in life. To Erin Edmison, Lisa Brennan-Jobs, and Iris Glaser for auxiliary help along the way.

To friends and family, doctors and therapists, colleagues and ex-boyfriends who did not choose to be memorialized in a published work; I hope I've done your representations justice. You feature in my story only because of the tremendous impact you've had on my journey to love.

And to Jon, for being crazy enough to choose to marry a memoirist, and optimistic enough to have taken a second chance on an obnoxious thirty-year-old (that's thirty).

Parts of chapter nine first appeared in the *Jerusalem Post Magazine*.

Parts of chapter twelve first appeared in *Nerve*.

Parts of chapters thirteen and fourteen first appeared in Salon, a Web site located at http://www.salon.com.

Parts of chapter twenty-four first appeared in Tablet.

Parts of chapter twenty-four first appeared in JTA.

Portions of the article "A Hoarder's Daughter Yields to a (Little) Mess" by Judy Batalion originally appeared in the *New York Times* on 4 January 2013 and are used here by permission. Portions of the series "Preschool Admissions Diary" by Judy Batalion originally appeared in the *New York Times* from 11 February to 29 April 2014 and are used here by permission.

Photo by Sharon Perlman

Judy Batalion has written for the *New York Times*, the *Washington Post*, Salon, the *Forward* and many other publications. She grew up in Montreal, worked as an art curator and comedian in London, and now lives in New York with her husband and two daughters.